THE ULTIMATE QUESTION
AND ANSWER BOOK

5x 6/08 (6-08)

# LATINO HISTORY
# AND CULTURE

HarperCollins books may be purchased for educational, business, or sales
promotional use. For information, please write: Special Markets Department,
HarperCollins Publishers, 10 East 53rd Street, New York, NY 10022.

Produced for HarperCollins by:

HYDRA PUBLISHING
129 MAIN STREET
IRVINGTON, NY 10533
WWW.HYLASPUBLISHING.COM

**FIRST EDITION**


Library of Congress Cataloging-in-Publication Data

Stavans, Ilan.
  Latino history and culture / Ilan Stavans.
    p. cm. – (Collins Q & A : the ultimate question and answer book)
Includes bibliographical references and index.
ISBN: 978-0-06-089123-7
ISBN-10: 0-06-089123-8
  1. Hispanic Americans—History—Miscellanea. 2. Hispanic Americans—
Social life and customs—Miscellanea. 3. Hispanic Americans—Social
conditions—Miscellanea. I. Title.

E184.S75S76 2007
973'.0468--dc22
2006051864

07   08   09   10     QW      10  9  8  7  6  5  4  3  2  1

# Collins
# Q&A

## THE ULTIMATE QUESTION
## AND ANSWER BOOK

# LATINO HISTORY
# AND CULTURE

## Ilan Stavans

### Collins
*An Imprint of HarperCollinsPublishers*

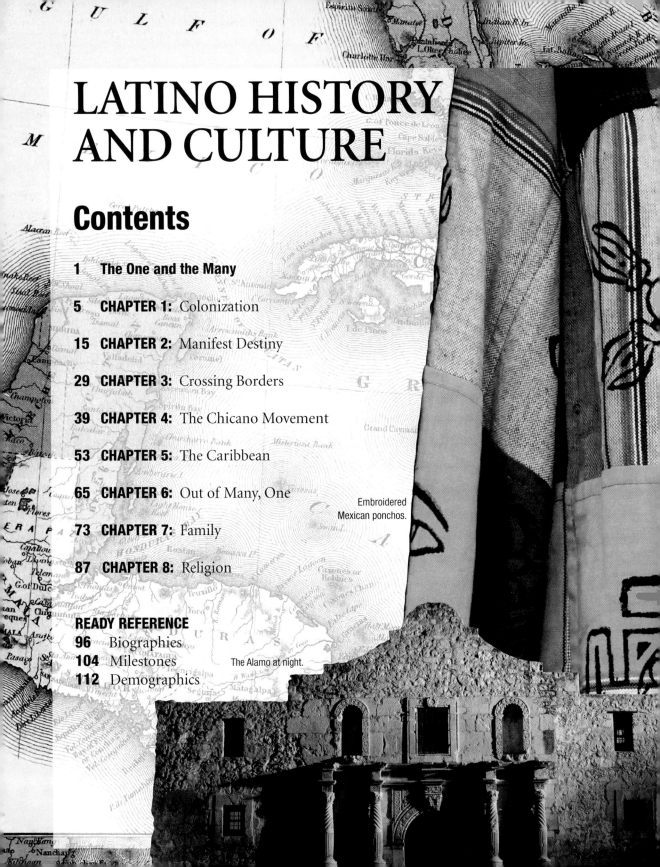

# LATINO HISTORY AND CULTURE

## Contents

**1**    **The One and the Many**

**5**    **CHAPTER 1:** Colonization

**15**    **CHAPTER 2:** Manifest Destiny

**29**    **CHAPTER 3:** Crossing Borders

**39**    **CHAPTER 4:** The Chicano Movement

**53**    **CHAPTER 5:** The Caribbean

**65**    **CHAPTER 6:** Out of Many, One

**73**    **CHAPTER 7:** Family

**87**    **CHAPTER 8:** Religion

**READY REFERENCE**
**96**   Biographies
**104**   Milestones
**112**   Demographics

Embroidered Mexican ponchos.

The Alamo at night.

Little Brazil street sign on Manhattan's 46th Street.

**119 CHAPTER 9:** Education

**129 CHAPTER 10:** Spanglish

**139 CHAPTER 11:** Politics

**153 CHAPTER 12:** *La Música*

**167 CHAPTER 13:** Sports

**179 CHAPTER 14:** *Letras*

**191 CHAPTER 15:** Art and Taste

**204 América, America**

**206** Glossary
**210** Further Reading
**212** Index
**218** Acknowledgments & Picture Credits

*Calaveras* at the Hollywood Forever Cemetery on *Día de los Muertos*.

# THE ONE AND THE MANY

Understanding the essential role of Latinos in America must start with an etymological discussion—an explanation of the ancestry of certain words and categories. Where does the word "Latino" come from? To whom and to what does it refer? What other labels have been used in the past?

The term "Latino" emerged in the late twentieth century to describe the richly heterogeneous minority comprising people from different parts of what had been the Spanish Empire, an area that once spread from Florida and Puerto Rico to the archipelago of the Philippines and from California to the Argentine pampas. Even before the *Mayflower* dropped anchor in what is now Provincetown Harbor on Cape Cod, Hispanic outposts— missions, settlements, encampments—had been established in Florida and different parts of what are

The Rio Grande is part of one of the longest binational borders in the world.

Below: Christopher Columbus kneels with his sword and a flag along with two others after reaching ground in the New World.

COLUMBUS TAKING POSSESSION OF THE NEW COUNTRY

today the states of Arizona, New Mexico, Texas, and California. In the middle of the nineteenth century, after the Mexican-American War, these areas became part of the United States, bringing the Spanish-speaking population into citizenship. Latinos were variously known as *mexicanos*, *tejanos*, and *californios*, depending on where they lived.

Símon Bolívar (1783–1830)

At the same time on the East Coast a handful of Cubans began establishing businesses in Key West. In the closing years of the nineteenth century, the expanding and expansionist United States pulled Puerto Rico into its orbit. As the Americas shaped and reshaped themselves, others who lived south of the Rio Grande made their way to various areas, including the states of Missouri, Oregon, New York, and Rhode Island. These Spanish-speakers were referred to in a number of ways, including words that described their jobs, such as *braceros*, and words denoting origin, such as *jíbaros*.

To further complicate categorization, each national group also has its own naming history. At various times, Mexican Americans have been called Chicanos, People of Aztlán, and Mex Americans; Puerto Ricans in New York are known as Nuyoricans, Boricuas, and so on. As the various national groups established political, social, and artistic alliances, more cohesive categories were sought. "Hispano" and "Spanish" were popular in the 1960s. During the Nixon administration, "Hispanic" was adopted in government documents to refer to Spanish-speakers living in the United States. However, the term carried a heavy historical baggage, signaling the often coercive and violent means Spain had employed in colonizing the Americas. ("Hispania" was the name given the Iberian Peninsula by the Romans.) In 1992, the quincentennial of Christopher Columbus's landing in the Bahamas generated much soul-searching. People felt the need to divorce their identity from that of the conquerors of the New World. Accordingly, a different term—Latino—became preferred. Not that this was necessarily less confusing—the term "Latin America" was coined in the mid-nineteenth century by Chilean exiles in Paris looking to find a common name for the South American nations (all of which spoke a Romance language derived from Latin) that had adopted a republican spirit epitomized by Simón Bolívar. Known as *El Libertador*, Bolívar had fought to create a consortium of republics in South America. The Chileans came up with *l'Amerique latine*. "Latino" or "Latina" also comes from the Spanish *latinoamericano*, meaning simply a citizen of Latin America.

Language is in a state of constant change. Words in current use will be out of fashion in a few years or a decade; meanings are modified according to the need of the users. "Latino" is *la palabra del día*, the "word of the day." Its use also conveys an ideological intent. It attempts to understand this minority—which, according to the U.S. Census Bureau, by the year 2025 will constitute one-fourth of the overall population of the United States—not as disparate national groups but as a whole. Thus, a "real" Latino might not exist anywhere because individuals are more particular in their self-identification: Nicaraguan Americans, Costa Rican Americans, and Venezuelan Americans, for example. Nonetheless, for purposes of politics, education, and

A Mexican girl babysitting another woman's baby.

the media, unity creates a louder, stronger voice. For better or worse, the main political parties, Republican and Democrat, approach Latinos as a single entity, as do school administrators, job agencies, corporations, and radio and TV networks.

For purposes of this volume and to minimize confusion, we use the term "Hispanic" to refer to a person anywhere in the so-called *civilización hispánica*, from Spain to the Spanish-speaking countries of the Caribbean Basin and Central and South America. People from different countries are labeled by their national background: Panamanians, Uruguayans, Chileans, etc. The term "Caribbean" is used for someone living in Cuba, Puerto Rico, the Dominican Republic, Jamaica, Haiti, and the Bahamas. "Latin American" denotes someone living anywhere from the southern side of the U.S.-Mexican border to Tierra del Fuego, the continent's tip near Antarctica, including those in French- or Portuguese-speaking nations—citizens of French Guiana and Brazil, for example. For a Mexican living in the United States, either as a result of immigration or by birth, we use the term "Mexican American." The same goes for other national groups. And Latino is the group name we use for Hispanic people living in the United States: immigrants, native born, or naturalized.

Contrary to what is commonly assumed, not every Latino speaks Spanish. Equally important: The Latino minority cannot be defined by categories like race, class, and religion. In racial terms, Latinos are dark-skinned, *mestizo*, Caucasian, Asian; they belong to every economic strata; and Latinos are of the Christian—both Catholic and Protestant—faith,

Cross in church in Cuzco, Peru.

they are Jewish, Muslim, and Buddhist, or they are members of other religions or no religion at all.

To permit the reader to fully appreciate Latinos' lives, contributions, and collective and individual identities, the following pages delve into history and culture from the perspectives of colonization, language, religion, education, activism, music, media, and domestic and foreign politics. Only through such a multifaceted approach can this group composed of peoples dramatically diverse in background and customs, all living in the United States, be understood.

Mexican maracas.

# CHAPTER 1

# COLONIZATION

I n August of 1492, Christopher Columbus's three caravels, the *Niña*, the *Pinta*, and the *Santa María*, departed
from the port of Palos, Spain. After a near mutiny,
the fleet arrived in the Bahamas on October 12. The date
is officially celebrated in the United States as Columbus
Day and in the Spanish-speaking world—and among some
Latinos—as *Día de la Raza* (Day of Our Race) in honor of
indigenous peoples and their contributions to all aspects of
national and Hispanic cultures. The journey was made at
a time when Spain was expanding its colonial borders and
looking to invigorate a stagnant economy with resources
from unexplored lands. During that same year, Muslims and
Jews were expelled from the Iberian Peninsula or forced to
convert to Catholicism under the Inquisition. Spain saw itself
as a steadfast upholder of the Catholic faith and a force for
the saving of souls through Christian evangelism. Following
Columbus, a series of Spanish explorers and missionaries
surveyed and settled parts of what is today southern and
southwestern America; the missionaries both colonized the
land and converted, often forcibly, the indigenous populations to Christianity. In so doing, they imposed a different
language and worldview on the Americas.

Though Amerigo Vespucci
is the continent's
namesake, Christopher
Columbus is arguably
the more consequential
of the two because he
was the first to claim
land for Spain. This map
shows the Americas as
conceived in the 1600s.

# American History and Latino History

## Q: When does the history of Latinos in the United States begin?

A: If the starting point of the United States's history is its Revolutionary War  from 1775 to 1783, it must be noted that the number of Hispanics in the thirteen colonies that fought for independence was minuscule. If, on the other hand, American history is charted from the first interactions of Europeans with Native Americans on the North American continent, then the presence of Latinos in territories that constitute the current United States precedes the arrival of the Pilgrims on the *Mayflower*. When the Pilgrims anchored in 1620, Spanish settlements, built by conquistadors and missionaries, were already established in Florida and the southwestern regions. The interaction between the Spaniards and the Western Hemisphere's native populations lasted for hundreds of years and has had dramatic influences on the nation's history. Spanish colonization throughout the Americas united many pre-existing cultures and is ultimately represented in the sizable Latino population that the United States contains in the twenty-first century.

## Q: What was Spain's attitude toward colonization in the sixteenth century?

A: At the time Columbus set sail, the Iberian Peninsula was concluding *La Reconquista* (the Reconquest), a centuries-long battle to regain territory from the Islamic Moors and a simultaneous purging of all religions but the strictest of Roman Catholicism—even though the three major Western religions, Christianity, Judaism, and Islam, had coexisted in the region for centuries. The marriage of Ferdinand of Aragón and Isabel of Castile, which had joined those two regions, also combined their governance into a central authority that defined the nation's

The Spanish mission of Saint Augustine was founded fifty-five years before the English settlement at Jamestown, Virginia, and is the oldest permanent European settlement in the United States.

to Europeans, edicts of expulsion were promulgated against the Jewish and Islamic communities. The last Moorish stronghold, Granada, fell in 1492.

Spain's colonies across the Atlantic served many purposes. First, they were lands rich in gold, minerals, and other natural resources. Second, they were populated by "heathens" ripe for receiving the expansionist Christian vision. At first the Crown held tight economic and political control. With time, the colonies grew more independent and developed stronger forms of self-rule, though the model for self-governance continued to be that of the Old World.

"regained" lands in religious and military terms. Concurrent with Columbus's crossing the Atlantic in search of a new route to the Indies and his "discovery" of a gigantic continent previously unknown

This painting depicts the arrival of European explorers and conquistadors in the Americas. Many Native Americans later perished from European diseases such as smallpox, to which they had no immunity.

Italian-born Christopher Columbus petitioned King Ferdinand and Queen Isabel of Spain to finance an expedition for a new trade route to the East Indies. He sailed westward from Europe and "discovered" the Americas when he landed in the Bahamas in 1492.

# Early Explorers

**Q:** Who were some of the most significant Spanish conquistadors and explorers?

**A:** In 1513, the Spanish governor of Puerto Rico landed in Florida, and by 1565 Saint Augustine, the oldest permanent European settlement in what was to become the United States, had been established by Pedro Menéndez de Avilés.

Hernando de Soto explored much of Florida as well, then continued into what are now the states of Georgia, North Carolina, South Carolina, Tennessee, and Alabama. Crossing the Mississippi River in 1541, he ventured farther into Louisiana and Texas.

Among the most significant and ill-fated of Spanish explorers, Alvar Núñez Cabeza de Vaca also began his journey in Florida. A member of the failed expedition of Pánfilo de Narváez, which shipwrecked off the coast of Florida in 1528, he traveled for the better part of a decade, along with other survivors, coming across Indian tribes and passing for a healer in order to save his life. When he returned to Spain he published *La Relación* (1542), known in English as *The Chronicle of the Narváez Expedition*, in which he tells of his incredible journey from Florida to the Southwest and back, passing along the Gulf of Mexico. Because his narrative was written in Spain a long time after the experience, the narrative has been contested as a trustworthy historical document.

Explorers of the southwestern territory, especially New Mexico and Arizona, included Fray (Friar) Marcos de Niza, who set out from Mexico City in 1538. His quest, which ended in disaster when his three hundred men were killed by the Zuni, was to find the fabled Seven Cities of Cibola. Francisco Vásquez de Coronado was inspired by de Niza and, from 1540 through 1542, explored the central and southwestern parts of the present-day United States, reaching as far as Kansas. A third explorer of what is now New Mexico was Captain Juan de Oñate, whose expedition began in 1595 and interacted significantly with the Pueblos. Father Eusebio Francisco Kino, of Italian descent, founded the first mission in Arizona, calling it Nuestra Señora de Dolores.

Juan Bautista de Anza explored the more northerly portions of the continent, preceding Lewis and Clark by crossing the Rocky Mountains in the mid-eighteenth century and exploring as far west as San Francisco. Other explorers included Juan Crespi, Fray Francisco Palou, and Fray Junípero Serra. The last was an evangelist who established almost two dozen missions in California.

By the eighteenth century, Spain was competing with France, England, and Russia for American territory from Louisiana to Alaska. Many Spanish expeditions were deliberate attempts at settlement in order to shield their southwestern lands from other European powers with equal ambitions for conquest and empire.

Captain Juan de Oñate was a notable explorer of New Mexico. Inscription Rock, with an accompanying message in Spanish, was left by him in 1606.

**Q: What accounts survive from these explorations?**

**A:** Journals, diaries, travel writing, poems, and even plays were composed about expeditions and the native populations of Florida, New Mexico, Arizona, Texas, California, and the Pacific Northwest. Hernando de Soto's adventures were described by the Portuguese chronicler Caballero de Elvas, who published *True Relation of the Vicissitudes That Attended the Governor Don Hernando de Soto and Some Nobles of Portugal in the Discovery of the Province of Florida now just Given by a Fidalgo of Elvas* (1551), as well as by el Inca Garcilaso de la Vega, a *mestizo* known for the account *La Florida del Inca* (The Inca's Florida, 1605), and by de Soto's personal secretary, Rodrigo Ranjel, who authored the *Diario de Rodrigo Ranjel* (Diary of Rodrigo Ranjel, 1546).

Alonso Gregorio de Escobedo wrote an epic poem, *La Florida* (in English, it is known as *Pirates, Indians, and Spaniards*) that includes valuable ethnographic information about Florida. Fray Marcos de Niza kept a diary of his experiences in New Mexico in the late 1530s that inspired future adventurers to embark on similar journeys. Francisco Vázquez de Coronado's journey to New Mexico, Texas, and Kansas between 1540 and 1542 was told by Pedro Castañeda de Nájera in *The Narrative of the Expedition of Coronado*.

The expedition led by Juan de Oñate to New Mexico is compellingly related by Gaspar Pérez de Villagrá, a Creole (an American-born person of Spanish descent) who joined the journey, in a poem composed in eight-syllable verses.

Titled *Historia de la Nueva México* (History of New Mexico), it was published in 1610. Juan Bautista Chapa wrote *Historia del Nuevo Reino de León* (History of the New Kingdom of León), which was published between 1630 and 1690; Fray Juan Agustín Morfi authored *Memoirs of the History of Texas*, 1778. Captain Juan Bautista de Anza's travels to Arizona and California were chronicled by Fray Hermenegildo Garcés and Pedro Font.

**Q: Did Native Americans leave any documents?**

**A:** Unfortunately not. Missionaries sometimes related the opinions of their subjects in their narratives, but even if their statements were accurate, readers inevitably approach them with a degree of skepticism: The accounts were filtered through the perspective of the powerful ruling groups, who were coercive in extracting the stories from the population they controlled.

Moctezuma (above; also spelled *Montezuma*) was the Aztec ruler who welcomed Hernán Cortés (below) to his sophisticated and wealthy empire. Soon, though, Cortés, with the support of surrounding Indian civilizations on poor terms with the Aztecs, attacked and controlled most of central Mexico.

A 1555 edition of Alvar Nuñez Cabeza de Vaca's *La Relación* or *The Chronicle of the Narváez Expedition.* The explorer describes in detail his 1528 shipwreck and the subsequent years of often fearsome travel throughout the Gulf of Mexico region and the Southwest.

Bartolomé de las Casas, a historian and Dominican missionary (1474–1566), is known for his benevolent attitude toward Native Americans and his efforts to abolish their enslavement and other forms of ill treatment at the hands of Spanish colonizers.

# Missions

**Q: What was the function of the missions and how did they operate?**

**A:** The missions were influential colonial institutions established—first by Jesuits and then by Franciscans—to convert, educate, and subjugate Native Americans through Catholic instruction and to develop economically self-sustained communities. Missions were established in present-day Virginia, South Carolina, Georgia, Florida, Alabama, Mississippi, New Mexico, Oklahoma, Texas, Utah, Nevada, and California, and in other areas. Designed to be self-sufficient enclaves, they included water systems, schools, jails, ranches, fields for cultivation, and carpentries; initially they were established to serve Spanish military men and settlers, complementing other colonial institutions like presidios (military forts) and pueblos (towns).

Junípero Serra is one of the most famous priests of the Spanish missions. He zealously converted thousands of Native Americans to Catholicism using, as is depicted in this painting, a crucifix in one hand and a stone in the other.

The earliest missions were built by Jesuits along the eastern seaboard. Of particular note is the one constructed in 1570 in the area that later became Jamestown—37 years before the English established a permanent colony. Missions were later built in present-day New Mexico and Arizona, as well as along the Texas-Louisiana border in the early 1770s as protection against French ventures into Spanish territory.

The primary objective of the missions was to convert the Native Americans to Catholicism, but they also had economic and political goals. Colonizers hoped to turn peoples such as the Pueblos in New Mexico and the Chumash in California into a solid labor force. Tasks included the construction of buildings and aqueducts, pottery making, raising cattle and other livestock, and the planting, harvesting, and processing of wheat. The religious instruction was delivered in Spanish, thus turning the missions into instruments of acculturation. Transgressions of different kinds (theft, idolatry, sexual intercourse) were punishable with prison sentences, whippings, humiliation, and torture.

At the same time, compassion and education were professed aims of the Catholic missions. The priests and other ecclesiastical figures believed they were instructing their subjects in the superior teachings of Christ, thus saving their souls and gaining them entry into heaven. Some missionaries not only taught the Indians but learned from them. Fray Junípero Serra, for instance, learned several Native American languages as he set up missions during the 1770s and 1780s. Yet he was also harsh in his treatment of his pupils; to this day he remains a controversial figure. He converted close to five thousand Native Americans to Catholicism. In 1988, Pope John Paul II beatified him.

Over time, through the construction of missions, the Catholic church became the biggest landowner in the Southwest. The church and its priests and missionaries became responsible for pacifying, administrating, and educating (from their perspective) large portions of the native population. Today, several colonial missions have been turned into museums and historical preserves, offering a window into the Spanish colonial past. The California missions are the best known and preserved.

## Q: What rebellions were organized against the missions and their leaders?

A: The colonization of the New World was not achieved without resistance from indigenous peoples. Often Native Americans ran away from missions and Spanish settlements to escape the harsh treatment and labor requirements. Franciscan friars were sometimes assassinated. In a more organized fashion, the Pueblos revolted in New Mexico in 1680,

killing 21 Franciscans and 380 colonists. The Pueblos' independence from Spanish rule lasted until 1692. The Chumash Revolt of 1824 involved less death and destruction than the earlier Pueblo revolt but concentrated on attacking the missions in the Santa Barbara, California, area. During the first part of the nineteenth century, however, after Mexico became independent and a wave of anticlericalism swept the northern territories, the mission system fell into disarray.

Below, top: The Pueblo Indians of the Southwest interacted turbulently with European missionaries and are famous for throwing off the Spanish yoke during their great revolt of 1680. The site below is the Wupatki Pueblo ruins.

Below: Many California Spanish missions, such as this one in Santa Barbara, have been restored as tourist destinations.

“If I had been present at creation, I would have given some practical advice on how to organize better the universe.”
—*Alfonso X "El Sabio"* (1221–84), crowned king of Castile and León in 1252

# The Birth of the *Mestizo*

**Q:** What is a *mestizo*?

**A:** Sexual encounters, both forced and consensual, between European men and indigenous women during the colonial period resulted in children of mixed race called *mestizaje*. Accordingly, in Mexico and Central America, native cultures played a much larger role in shaping the development of countries. Although sometimes considered useful as a way to unite populations, such "racial mixing" did not result in a leveling of social caste. During the colonial period the racial hierarchy in the Americas was quite clear: Spaniards were at the top, Creoles (American-born, pure-blood Spaniards) came second, with *mestizos* in third place, Indians in fourth, and blacks at the bottom. This hierarchy manifested itself in politics, business, education, and every other level of society. This changed when Mexico gained independence from Spain—Creoles rose to the top, and the power of *mestizos* expanded. When the Treaty of Guadalupe Hidalgo and the Gadsden Purchase were concluded, the United States gained the multi-race and -heritage population of the southwestern states. The status of this entire new population fell precipitously, notwithstanding the treaty's provisions for fair and equal treatment of all inhabitants of this new territory. Such was the discrimination that in 1849, California and the New Mexico territory restricted citizenship to whites.

Many Latinos today are *mestizos*. The importation of Africans to what were island territories for use as slaves resulted in a strong African component to the population. Cubans, Dominicans, and Puerto Ricans, as well as Venezuelans, Panamanians, and others from the larger area of Caribbean influence, share this African ancestry. Indigenous heritage is also strong in this region. The

Aztec king Moctezuma receives Cortés and his entourage, which included his Indian interpreter and mistress whose Christian name was Marina. She and Cortés produced a son named Martín in 1522, symbolically the first *mestizo*.

Arawak American Indians populated the islands mentioned above and parts of South America when Columbus arrived. The Taínos were the first inhabitants of Borinquen, as Puerto Rico was called.

**Q:** **How is the past of pre-Columbian civilizations perceived by Latinos today?**

**A:** People of the Americas—and, by extension, Latinos—have always been ambivalent about their indigenous forebears.

Should one look at Europe for inspiration? Or should the Indian past serve as a model? Periodically movements arise to reclaim the aboriginal past. Attempts are also made to turn *mestizaje* into a philosophy. José Vasconcelos, a Mexican educator, politician, and philosopher, wrote a treatise, *The Cosmic Race* (1927), in which he discussed a synthesis of races and suggested that *mestizos* were called to dominate the Earth in the twenty-first century. The volume became a manifesto for many students involved in the Chicano Movement of the 1960s.

Once the Spanish colonies gained independence, the *mestizos* were given a slight boost in the caste system and began to develop their own cultures particular to background and geography. This engraving represents *mestizo* men and women in 1850 California.

# CHAPTER 2

# MANIFEST DESTINY

As the nineteenth century progressed, the Spanish Empire was crumbling and the United States was on the rise as a world force, embracing an expansionist ideology known as Manifest Destiny. Americans were given incentives, such as the Homestead Act of 1862, to settle the "wild" western part of the continent. Through annexations, military conquest, and diplomatic maneuvering, the most notable of which were the Mexican-American War and the Treaty of Guadalupe Hidalgo that ended it, the United States took control of the northern half of Mexico, then of Cuba, Puerto Rico, the Philippines, Hawaii, and Guam. The political relationship between the United States and independent Mexico, with their 2,000-mile common border, has long been defined by what is most advantageous for both nations and has experienced periods of harmony, misunderstanding, and violence. The border itself is a result of push-and-pull policies. The inhabitants of all the U.S.-acquired territories were promised respect, but their land claims and sovereignty were quickly put in jeopardy, their Spanish language was ridiculed, and their labor and educational opportunities were curtailed. Over time, tensions grew between Anglos and these newest citizens of the United States, resulting in violence in some cases and eventually organized activism.

The Mexican-American War dramatically changed the face and character of the Americas. It ended by the Treaty of Guadalupe Hidalgo, which facilitated one of the largest nation-to-nation transfers of land in history. At left is a manuscript map of the war from south of the Rio Grande. The above lithograph depicts General Winfield Scott's important victory at the Battle of Cerro Gordo in April 1847.

# Texas Seeks Independence

**Q:** How did Texas become an independent republic?

**A:** In a drive led by Miguel Hidalgo y Costilla, a priest, Mexico achieved independence from Spanish rule in 1821 and subsequently controlled a large portion of what are today the southwestern states and California. The boundaries, however, were not strictly marked. That same year, Mexico allowed Stephen F. Austin (son of Moses Austin who had secured permission from the Spanish government to colonize 300 families on 200,000 acres) to settle American families in Texas, thus beginning a series of conflicts between Spanish-speaking *tejanos* and Anglo ranchers. Just five years later, on March 2, 1826, Anglo Texans declared the region independent from Mexico, and by April 21, 1836, under the leadership of Samuel Houston, they had defeated Mexican forces under Antonio López de Santa Ana. In later years, during the California Gold Rush and the American Civil War, more Anglos moved to Texas, which was by then a U.S. state.

**Q:** How did Latinos' lives change in an independent Texas?

**A:** The Texas Constitution of 1836 gave citizenship to its Spanish-speaking population—*tejanos*, as Mexicans from the region are known. The state constitution of 1845 also confirmed this status. In reality, their situation was less than equal. *Tejanos* of the political elite more or less retained their status and standard of living, but the majority of former Mexicans and their descendants did not. *Tejanos* had difficulty maintaining ownership of their lands and were segregated from Anglos. Throughout the second half of the nineteenth century racial animosity was open and many times turned violent. The 1857 Cart War was fought over the low pay offered to Mexicans, and the 1879 Salt War was a battle for ownership of natural resources.

Between 1880 and 1920, the Texas Mexican community (reluctantly U.S. citizens) was forced to adapt to Anglo-driven changes. The most significant of these was the farm revolution, in which traditional *tejano* ranching was edged out in favor of larger, Anglo-owned agribusinesses in which *tejanos* became the brush-clearers and farmhands rather than the owners. They also sought menial work in the growing urban areas. Despite the unrewarding nature of available work, Mexicans continued to move into Texas during these years. The large demographic presence of Texas Mexicans slowed their assimilation into the mainstream American culture and reinfused residents with Mexican national pride.

Many Mexican Americans in Texas, however, flowed with the tides of change and were comfortable with their bicultural heritage. A contingent of this

For nearly a decade, Texas was an independent republic and minted its own money.

generation worked within the system of American institutions to effect change, raise standards of living, and increase opportunities for *tejanos* and, gradually, for all Latinos. In 1921, they established the short-lived Orden Hijos de América (Order of Sons of América). Their true grounding, however, came with that organization's successor, the League of Latin American Citizens (LULAC), founded in 1929. Today LULAC continues to be a significant force for change in Latin American communities.

Above: In this 1844 cartoon, the expansionist President Polk hauls Sam Houston and Stephen Austin on a boat called Texas toward the United States. Those being dragged to the bottom of the sea are the anti-Democratic forces, the Whigs, such as Henry Clay. Abolitionist William Lloyd Garrison stands to the side, protesting against keeping company with pro-slavery forces.

Left: In the post-Civil War era, the western lands of the United States were populated mostly by Native Americans and the descendants of Spanish conquistadors. The government urged Anglos to settle these areas. Their arrival in the Southwest, particularly Texas, often provoked hostilities with former Mexican citizens.

# The Battle of the Alamo

**Q:** What happened at the Battle of the Alamo?

**A:** Although the Battle of the Alamo (1836) was not the most significant engagement in Texas's drive for independence, it is the most well known and celebrated. The battle helped invigorate the Anglo and *tejano* forces who, under the leadership of General Sam Houston, were ultimately victorious over the Mexican army at the Battle of San Jacinto.

Originally, the Alamo was a group of buildings in the Mission of San Antonio de Valero, which had been founded in 1691. It was turned into a secular fort in the early nineteenth century. In late 1835, the Texan forces captured the Alamo and stationed some two hundred men there under the leadership of Colonel William Barrett Travis. When Texas declared its independence on March 2, 1836, General Antonio López de Santa Ana ordered between five thousand and ten thousand soldiers (the exact number remains unknown) to fight Sam Houston's separatists. In the days following the Texas declaration of Independence, the Mexicans bombarded the fort with heavy artillery. Aware of certain defeat, Travis gathered his people and asked them if they wanted to leave before the fight started. Lore has it that nobody left, although historians believe one soldier did. A bloody hand-to-hand battle took place on March 6, killing one thousand Mexicans and everyone on the Texan side, including Colonel James (Jim) Bowie and David (Davy) Crockett. A decade later, Mexico would again engage in war, this time with the United States.

General Antonio López de Santa Ana (right) and his Mexican troops defeated the Texan army at the Battle of the Alamo. However, the Mexicans lost the war and Sam Houston (below) became the first president of an independent Texas.

# Q: Why has the Battle of the Alamo become legendary?

**A:** Through media and history books, the battle has acquired mythical proportions infused with ideals of martyrdom. The performance of American soldiers has become the subject of legend while the role *tejanos* played on the Texan side has been largely eclipsed. Ironically, the Mexican army's victory has become irrelevant. For nationalistic reasons, what matters, it seems, is that a small group fought to the death against an aggressive, Spanish-speaking army. Over time, the Alamo has become a popular tourist destination.

# Q: How is the Alamo portrayed in art?

**A:** The representations are plentiful, from John Wayne's *The Alamo* (1960) and John Ford's *Two Rode Together* (1961),

During his lifetime, Davy Crockett was a well-known Tennessee politician who often played up stories about his life on the frontier. His death, along with that of all the other greatly outnumbered American defenders of the Alamo, at the hands of the Mexican army, helps keep the memory of that battle alive in the public imagination.

to novels about the battles and Davy Crockett and Jim Bowie. The battle, the fort, and its artifacts, including diaries, are still subjects of scholarly investigations, posters, postal stamps, books for children and young adults, and comic strips. The material is almost always patriotic. Purportedly the phrase "Remember the Alamo!" originated with one of the volunteers in Sam Houston's army during the later battle of San Jacinto.

# President Polk Goes to War

**Q:** What were the causes of the Mexican-American War?

**A:** In 1823, President James Monroe set forth in his second inaugural address what would become the Monroe Doctrine, a set of policies that profoundly affected geopolitical dynamics in the Americas for the next 150 years. The doctrine declared that European countries could not intervene in the Americas. In return, the United States vowed not to interfere in European colonies elsewhere or in internal European affairs. Defying the political power of the Old World was a bold move by the young United States. Ultimately, the doctrine was reinterpreted into something altogether different: a justification for the United States to insert itself into all affairs on its side of the Atlantic Ocean. The concept of Manifest Destiny grew out of that justification. The Mexican-American War was sparked by the United States's westward expansionist drive to reach "from sea to shining sea."

Soon after Texas achieved independence from Mexico, President Polk pushed for its annexation, which in turn created a border conflict with Mexico. The United States wanted the border to be the Rio Grande, while Mexico believed it should be some thirty-two miles to the north, at the Rio Nueces. Though Americans refer to the present-day border between the United States and Mexico as the Rio Grande (which is some 1,885 miles long and was designated an American Heritage River in 1997), Mexicans refer to it as *el Río Bravo del Norte* (*bravo* means strong, restless). The river became a binational border in 1848 with the signing of the Treaty of Guadalupe Hidalgo, which ended the Mexican-American War. Until that time, a large portion of the river had not been mapped. In 1853–54, the Rio Grande was

The Monroe Doctrine of 1823 was a bold move for a young United States. It declared that European countries could not interfere in affairs on its side of the Atlantic Ocean. Over the next twenty-five years, the spirit of this doctrine evolved into an idealist and expansionist mentality known as Manifest Destiny. President James Polk (right) embodied this ideology in his provocation of the Mexican-American War.

surveyed for a second time as a result of the Gadsden Purchase.

While Texas was being annexed by the United States, Mexico suffered severe political instability. In 1845, when a U.S. envoy was refused entry into Mexico, President Polk requested that General Zachary Taylor send troops to the southern Texas border and that he secure some ports on the Gulf of Mexico. Mexico reacted by militarizing the border. A tense period ensued until Mexico underwent a series of changes in leadership and General Mariano Arista dispatched a battalion across the river. The American army captured the Mexican troops and held them prisoner. Congress declared war in early May 1846.

## Q: What battles and tactics defined the war?

**A:** The Mexican-American War was fought between 1846 and 1848. U.S. troops, under the command of General Zachary Taylor, first advanced toward Matamoros and then took possession of Monterrey. General Santa Ana (recalled from humiliating exile in Havana, Cuba) waited for Taylor's troops in the town of Buena Vista. Santa Ana was unable to defeat Taylor's army though the Mexican general's troops outnumbered Taylor's by nearly four to one. Winning this battle permitted Taylor to take control of the territory north of Mexico City. The U.S. military also attacked Tampico, in the Gulf of Mexico, by sea, which put Mexican ports under U.S. control. Commanded by General Winfield Scott, the Americans soon marched confidently toward Mexico City, defeating Santa Ana once more along the way. They raised the U.S. flag in the capital on September 14, 1847.

## Q: Did Americans support the war?

**A:** The war was perceived as "Mr. Polk's War" and was quite unpopular because it required a tax increase. Much of the public and Congress believed President Polk was interested in expanding territory and the reach of slavery. Abolitionists believed that southern states planned to create more slave states out of the newly acquired Mexican lands. Lack of support for the war eventually forced the administration to strike a deal with the Mexican government and sign the Treaty of Guadalupe Hidalgo.

It was not until the signing of the Treaty of Guadalupe Hidalgo that the Rio Grande became the definitive boundary between the newly shaped nations of Mexico and the United States. Today the border region continues to unite and divide the two countries.

# Buying the Land

**Q:** **What were the terms of the Treaty of Guadalupe Hidalgo?**

**A:** Negotiated by the chief clerk of the State Department and signed on February 2, 1848, the treaty officially brought an end to the war. The Americans had the upper hand—both because they occupied the capital of Mexico and because Mexico was disorganized politically (the country had had ten presidents in the previous thirteen years). The treaty stands as one of the largest transfers of land from one country to another in history.

The treaty, which had twenty-three articles, set the southern U.S. border at the Rio Grande and forced Mexico to sell more than half of its territory to the United States for $15 million and the purported protection of its citizens. The land gained included the present-day states of New Mexico, Arizona, California, Utah, Colorado, Nevada, and parts of Wyoming. Residents of the former Mexican lands were given the choice of moving south of the Rio Grande or becoming U.S. citizens. Most stayed with their homes and lands. After the treaty was signed, but before it was ratified by the U.S. Congress, the document was altered: Article 9 was rewritten, lengthening the time allotted for Mexicans to gain U.S. citizenship; and Article 10, which had guaranteed Mexican land grants, was deleted. The Mexican government asked the United States to reconsider these changes and the Protocol of Querétaro was signed. The U.S. Congress, however, considered this agreement nonbinding, thus putting thousands of land claims in jeopardy and

The Treaty of Guadalupe Hidalgo brought about a radical change in North America. The entire northern half of Mexico (see map far right) was sold to the United States for $15 million; the territory included what are now the states of New Mexico, Arizona, California, Utah, Colorado, Nevada, and parts of Wyoming. The treaty initially promised the continuity of property claims for former Mexican citizens and civil rights equal to Anglos. In actuality, neither of these promises was kept.

at the mercy of the admittedly biased U.S. judicial system. The unfairness of the Treaty of Guadalupe Hidalgo lives on in the minds of Mexican Americans, many of whom regard the southwest region as their ancestral lands.

**Q:** **What was the Gadsden Purchase?**

**A:** Also known as the Tratado de Mesilla (The Treaty of Mesilla), the Gadsden Purchase was signed by James Gadsden, President Franklin Pierce's minister to Mexico, on December 30, 1853, almost six years after the signing of the Treaty of Guadalupe Hidalgo. In it, Mexico officially ceded 30,000 square miles of present-day southern Arizona and New Mexico for $10 million. Originally, the United States was interested in buying Baja California, Sonora, and other parts of the country but Mexico refused. Armies were again mobilized, but in the end Washington got only the mineral-rich region of the Mesilla.

**Q:** **How did Mexico react to these losses of land?**

**A:** While tourism, trade, and immigration have forged unbreakable links between the United States and Mexico, a common view south of the Rio Grande is that Americans are both arrogant and gullible, pretending to be peacekeepers when, in fact, their drive is unquestionably imperialistic. The Mexican-American War is deeply ingrained in collective memory as an embarrassing disaster that solidified the U.S. grip on power. Mexicans talk about Moctezuma's revenge, a time in the future when there will be an opportunity to regain what was taken away by *el coloso del norte* (the colossus of the north). (Moctezuma's revenge is also a reference to the unpleasant digestive effects

Mexico's contaminated water can have on tourists.) For Mexican Americans, the Treaty of Guadalupe Hidalgo in particular is seen as a double betrayal: by Mexico, a weak country incapable of recognizing the value of its northern provinces and citizens, and by the United States, a colonizing force whose interest in Mexican Americans was minimal.

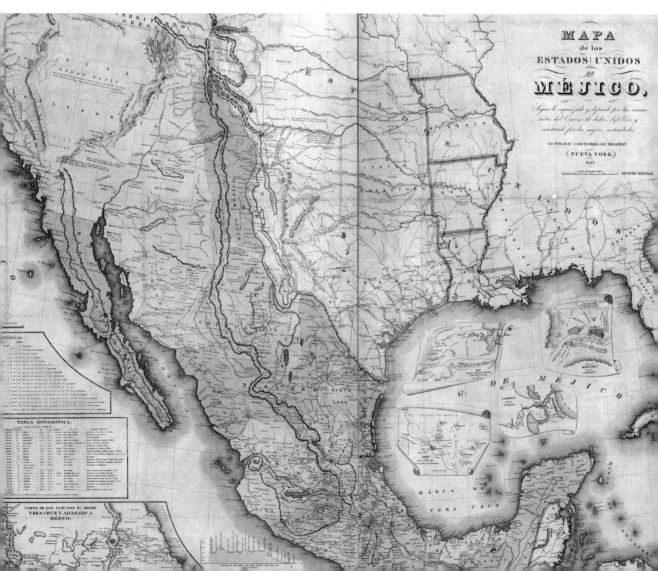

# The War of '98

After being expelled from Harvard College after only two years, William Randolph Hearst (right) became one of the most successful newspapermen in United States history. His papers combined investigative reporting with unabashed sensationalism.

Hearst's New York papers stirred up anti-Spanish sentiment with inflamed rhetoric and political cartoons like the one below, featuring a Spanish brute stepping on the bodies of a victim of the USS *Maine* and a starving Cuban child.

## Q: What factors led to the Spanish-American War?

**A:** Throughout the nineteenth century, the Spanish Empire slowly disintegrated. The Iberian Peninsula was portrayed in William Randolph Hearst's *New York Journal* and Joseph Pulitzer's *New York Sun* as politically awkward and even stagnant, its population uneducated. The media pushed people to see the Spanish-speaking Americas and their inhabitants as primitive. Public opinion in the United States was also sympathetic to Cuba's fight for independence from Spain. These views, along with the ingrained conviction that the United States was called to play a larger role in the Caribbean and Latin America and the ideology of Manifest Destiny, led to the military confrontation with Spain.

"re-concentration." The Spaniards forced Cubans into Spanish-controlled cities, resulting in chaos, hunger, and epidemics of diseases. The cruel military encounters between Spanish forces and rebels were sensationally reported in the American press. The fighting destroyed U.S. and other foreign businesses. In the United States, public opinion turned against Spain for its failure to control the insurgents.

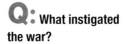

ACE IN CUBA UNDER SPANISH RULE IS WORSE THAN HELL

## Q: What instigated the war?

**A:** Since 1868, at the time of the so-called Ten-Year War, Cuba had struggled for independence from Spain. In 1895 a series of revolutionary leaders, including Antonio Maceo, Máximo Gómez, and José Martí, traveled to Cuba with plans for unconventional warfare to be waged by insurgents. The Spanish army reacted to Cubans' guerrilla-war tactics by removing populations from the countryside—a strategy called

## Q: Who was José Martí?

**A:** José Martí was the most famous of the Cuban rebels and is now a national hero. Born in 1853 in Havana, he became a martyr after he was killed on May 19, 1895, in one of the early battles of the Cuban War for Independence. He was an ideologue who, while living in the United States, wrote extensively. He authored essays and political and travel pieces for newspapers in Latin America and wrote a children's book, *La edad de oro* (The Golden Age, 1889). He is principally known, however, for his poetry, including *Versos sencillos* (Simple Verses, 1891); the Cuban song "Guantanamera" is based on one of his poems. The iconography surrounding him is extensive, both in Cuba and around the world.

### Q: The war seems to have been between Spain and its colonies' revolutionary forces. Why is it called the Spanish-American War?

A: The name is a misnomer. The United States had not yet entered the conflict when the battleship USS *Maine,* anchored in Havana harbor "to protect the lives and property of American citizens," exploded on February 15, 1898. More than 260 sailors on board were killed. What caused the explosion is still unclear, but a naval inquiry indicated that Spain was responsible. U.S. citizens were outraged and cried, "Remember the *Maine!* To hell with Spain!" President William McKinley reacted by organizing a military intervention and blockading some Cuban ports. Spain was furious and declared war on the United States. A more suitable name would be the War of 1898.

### Q: How did the conflict evolve?

A: The first battle took place on May 1, 1898, when U.S. naval forces destroyed the Spanish fleet in the Philippines in a single morning. (A three-year war for Philippine independence ensued.) Troops then set out from the West Coast of the United States to conquer Guam, annexing Hawaii—which until then had been independent—along the way.

In Cuba, the U.S. troops landed on territory controlled by the revolutionary forces. American troops, including the Rough Riders led by Theodore Roosevelt, captured San Juan Hill and the fort of El Caney on July 1, 1898. The battles were fierce, with epidemics of yellow fever breaking out on both sides; the casualties from both war and disease finally forced the surrender of twenty-two thousand Spanish troops on July 17, 1898. In the Treaty of Paris, signed December 10, 1898, Spain ceded Cuba, Puerto Rico, Guam, and the Philippines to the United States. (Cuba became a protectorate, not a territory, of the United States.)

Images and stories of the sinking, wrecked **USS Maine** in Havana Harbor (believed to be the work of Spanish hands) turned United States public opinion toward entering the war against Spain.

The Rough Riders, of which Theodore Roosevelt was second in command, was a volunteer cavalry unit in the Spanish-American War that received extensive publicity for its unorthodox tactics.

# Shifts in Power and Sovereignty

**Q:** What happened to Cuba and Puerto Rico after Spain ceded its Caribbean colonies to the United States?

**A:** The Teller Amendment, approved by Congress, was added to the U.S. declaration of war against Spain; it established that the United States was forbidden "to exercise sovereignty, jurisdiction, and control [over Cuba] except for the pacification thereof." In the end, the peace agreement that ended the War of 1898, known as the Treaty of Paris, was negotiated between Spain and the United States—without Cuba. In addi-

tion, the Platt Amendment of 1901 gave the United States control over Cuban foreign affairs and established an army base in the island's Guantánamo Bay. Cuba was only nominally independent. In 1902, a U.S.-supported president, Tomás Estrada Palma, was inaugurated. The Platt Amendment was annulled by Cuba in 1933 and dropped by President Franklin D. Roosevelt in 1934.

The situation of Puerto Rico was different. After the war, the United States established a military government on the island. The U.S. Congress then passed the Foraker Act, which President McKinley signed into law in 1900; the act established that the president of the United States, with the advice of the Senate, was responsible for selecting the island's governor. The governor's term was for four years, but the U.S. president had the right to replace him at any point.

**Q:** Why was the Jones Act signed?

**A:** The Foraker Act did not extend U.S. citizenship to Puerto Ricans or allow them representation in the U.S. Congress. Puerto Rico existed under total U.S. control until 1917, when the U.S. Congress passed the Jones Act, granting citizenship to Puerto Ricans and allowing them to democratically elect their own legislature, though they were still without representation in Congress. The island was granted full territorial status but remained under the mantle of the United States. Over time the political establishment, the

Tomás Estrada Palma, a U.S.-supported candidate, was inaugurated as president of Cuba in 1902. Palma, at right, is shown with his cabinet.

intellectual elite, and even the population at large divided into three groups: those supporting the status of a commonwealth (*estado libre asociado* in Spanish); those advocating independence from the United States; and those endorsing a change to full-fledged statehood under the U.S. Constitution. Poet, journalist, and politician Luis Muñoz Marín, governor of Puerto Rico from 1948 to 1964, and his Popular Democratic Party worked closely with the United States to create the island's commonwealth constitution, bring about economic reform, and stabilize the island politically. Luis A. Ferré, a businessman, art patron, founder of the New Progressive Party, and governor, defeated Muñoz Marín's Popular Democratic Party in the 1968 elections and established a line of statehood-proponent leaders.

On March 2, 1917, President Woodrow Wilson signed the Jones-Shafroth Act, which gave U.S. citizenship to Puerto Ricans. The mainland government retained control over the island's fiscal, economic, and basic foreign and domestic affairs. At the left is the first administrative cabinet under the Jones Act.

Governor of Puerto Rico Luis Muñoz Marín, left, presents actor José Ferrer, winner of the Academy Award for *Cyrano de Bergerac,* with another "Oscar" at La Fortalena Palace in San Juan, Puerto Rico, on April 15, 1951.

> **In spite of its limitations, capitalism continues to be the most effective system invented to stimulate the production of wealth, and democracy continues to be the sole system of government guaranteeing individual freedom.**

—LUIS A. FERRÉ

# CHAPTER 3

# CROSSING BORDERS

**W**ith the exception of those living in the southwestern territories before the Treaty of
Guadalupe Hidalgo was signed, the majority
of Latino families in the United States are defined by immigration: a parent, a relative, a friend reached the U.S. in search
of a better life, escaping bankrupt economies, repressive
regimes, and armed struggles. Some arrived as refugees, others as temporary workers. The number of newcomers from
the Spanish-speaking Americas was relatively small at the
turn of the twentieth century. One hundred years later, the
U.S. Latino population is large (14 percent of the population)
and its influence tremendous throughout the culture—from
politics to cuisine.

The United States, left,
is separated from Mexico,
right, by the border fence
running through down-
town Nogales, Arizona.

Immigration laws have always been a source of contention
among the American public, and those regulations relating
specifically to Latin Americans, such as the Bracero Program,
have often sought to balance the number of immigrants
with the country's economic needs. Large flows of illegal
immigrants and the attempts by the United States to thwart
them—including floodlights, steel fences, and computerized
tracking technology—have made the land on both sides of
the U.S.-Mexican border into an unrecognizable country
with ever-changing rules. The border region is not just a
vast no-man's-land, however; it has seen factories known
as *maquiladoras*, mostly U.S.-owned and employing young
Mexican women, spring up along the southern side.

# A Land of Immigrants

**Q:** What is the history of immigration laws in the United States?

**A:** The idea of closed borders was not in place at the beginning of the United States; in fact, until the late nineteenth century, the country paid little attention to immigration. The United States had the Alien and Sedition Laws of 1798, three of which aimed to detain pro-French Irish and French immigrants in the face of the threat of war with France, but these did not close the nation's borders and expired or were repealed by 1802. After the American Civil War, the need for labor was so acute that the increasing flow of immigrants was embraced.

Only when fearful and protective notions of nativism began to target the number and ethnic backgrounds of newcomers did the United States establish its first border-tightening law. The Immigration Act of 1875 prohibited criminals, convicts, and prostitutes from immigrating to the United States. This act also forbade "the immigration of any subject from China, Japan, or any Oriental country," because they were deemed undesirable. This approach was modified by the Chinese Exclusion Act of 1882, which excluded from the above law Chinese laborers and their wives already in the United States.

Among the most significant laws passed by Congress was the Immigration Act of 1917, which introduced a literacy test. This test served to filter out many Mexican laborers previously able to enter the United States. This act famously included "All idiots, imbeciles, feeble-minded persons, epileptics, insane persons; persons who have had one or more attacks of insanity at any time previously; persons of constitutional psychopathic inferiority; persons with chronic alcoholism; persons afflicted with tuberculosis of any form or with loathsome or dangerous contagious diseases; persons not comprehended within any of the foregoing excluded classes who are found to be and are certified by the examining surgeon as being mentally or physically defective, such physical defect being of a nature which may affect the ability of such alien to earn a living."

A Mexican emigrant heading from Nuevo Laredo toward the United States in 1912.

The National Origins Act of 1921, a response to post-World War I immigration, was the first to establish national quotas. Congress passed the act three years later. The 1952 Immigration and Nationality Act codified the national origins provisions and, in the wake of Nazism, established a preferential system based not on race but on skill and relatives already living in the United States. Congress allocated the first 50 percent of the quota to skilled immigrants and the second half to relatives of citizens and persons already in the United States. This act also excluded people with psychiatric disorders, among which homosexuality was included.

The 1965 Immigration Reform Act abolished all national origins quota systems and eliminated the restrictions placed on Asian immigrants in the 1952 law. It also established specific numbers:

A limit of 120,000 newcomers from the Western Hemisphere was set, with no country to exceed 20,000. This act also emphasized family connections, giving preference to those with relatives already in the United States.

**Q: Which laws specifically affected Latin American immigrants?**

**A:** In 1924, the Border Patrol was established to police the U.S.-Mexican border. Its purpose was to exclude newcomers perceived to be potential "public charges"—reliant on welfare. This issue has continued to be central to immigration debates specifically about Latin Americans.

Despite the 1965 Immigration Reform Act, Latin Americans entered the United States in growing numbers to fill low-wage positions, largely in agriculture. In 1986, the Immigration Reform and Control Act attempted to stem this tide by requiring employers to vouch for their employees' work eligibility, which resulted in the rapid rise of lucrative businesses that manufactured fake documents.

The Border Patrol was officially established by the U.S. government in 1924, but informal patrols, including government-sponsored and vigilante groups, have been in effect since the Treaty of Guadalupe Hidalgo.

# Immigrants on the Move

**Q:** Have immigrants from Spanish-speaking countries always been coming to the United States in a steady stream?

**A:** Economic insecurity and political repression in Latin America are central reasons for the massive northbound movement of people in the Western Hemisphere. Ever since the nascent republics of Latin America—Mexico, Argentina, Colombia, Venezuela, and Peru, among others—fought Spain to achieve their independence, their stability has been uncertain and their people's desire to self-governance often thwarted. Only in the late twentieth century did democracy become a more consistent, if often threatened, pattern in many Latin American countries. Since the 1920s, Latin Americans have been arriving both legally and illegally in the United States. Different groups have come at different times in response to political and economic situations in their homelands. The largest portion of Spanish-speaking immigrants in the first two decades of the twentieth century came from Puerto Rico. From the 1980s onward the majority of illegal immigrants came from Mexico and Central America. Civil wars in Guatemala, El Salvador, and Nicaragua forced people to seek haven and better opportunities in *El Norte*, as the United States is called by many Latin Americans.

Representative William A. Jones

**Q:** Puerto Ricans are U.S. citizens—should they be considered immigrants?

**A:** Most Americans consider Puerto Ricans who move to the mainland to be immigrants: They have left their native island, which is a commonwealth of the United States. However, Puerto Ricans were granted citizenship in 1917 with the Jones Act—legislation named for Representative William A. Jones of Virginia. The act conferred full territorial status upon the island and addressed the structure of its government. It included a bill of rights and a established a nineteen-member senate. Those who remained in Puerto Rico benefited somewhat from the above changes. The same year, however, President Woodrow Wilson signed a compulsory military service act and 20,000 Puerto Ricans were drafted into World War I. The island did not become a commonwealth until 1950, under the leadership of Luis Muñoz Marín.

**Q:** What brought Puerto Ricans to the mainland?

**A:** In the second half of the nineteenth century, Puerto Rican and Cuban political exiles organizing for independence from

Spain lived in New York, Philadelphia, New Orleans, Tampa, and Key West, in settlements called *colonias*. This group of separatists fighting for the independence of the colonies in the Caribbean and Latin America included José Martí, Ramón Emeterio Betances, Segundo Ruíz Belvis, Eugenio María de Hostos, Sotero Figueroa, Francisco "Pachín" Marín, and Lola Rodríguez de Tió. In addition to political organizing, these immigrants established economic bridges to their homelands—sugar and tobacco soon connected the Caribbean with the United States. When tobacco shops and factories opened in Tampa and New York City, they usually employed Puerto Rican and Cuban workers.

By the late 1910s, Puerto Rican migration to the United States had intensified because the Puerto Rican government had facilitated the hiring of agricultural and industrial workers from the island by mainland companies. A significant number were employed in New York City in the manufacturing and service industries.

# Q: Who were the *jíbaros*?

A: *Jíbaro* is a word used by Puerto Ricans to describe a poor dweller of the island's countryside. After World War II, Puerto Rican communities in cities like New York, Chicago, Newark, and Philadelphia expanded rapidly. This wave is known as the Great Migration.

Between 1940 and 1950 the number of Puerto Ricans on the mainland expanded by 330 percent; between 1950 and 1960 by 194 percent. Most *jíbaros* moved from agricultural jobs on the island to factories in U.S. cities. As Puerto Rico industrialized, its agriculture withered, leaving farm workers and their families destitute. To reduce unemployment, the Puerto Rican government promoted migration to the mainland; this migration began with what

Sugarcane workers resting in Rio Piedras, Puerto Rico.

became known as Operation Bootstrap— in Spanish, *Operación Manos a la Obra*. For decades, Puerto Rican enclaves in the Northeast were a magnet for Latinos. By the 1980s, however, the Census Bureau began to register a stabilization and even diminution of this community and the explosion of other national groups within the Latino minority in the region, especially Mexicans and Central Americans—Salvadorans, Guatemalans, and Nicaraguans being the most numerous.

> " If you want to know what injustice is, let yourself be hunted by injustice. "
>
> —*Eugenio María de Hostos*

# Finding *El Norte*

The 1911 fall of the thirty-year dictatorship of Porfirio Díaz (above) brought about the Mexican Revolution and led to enormous social and economic upheaval. These changes caused many Mexican nationals to look to *El Norte* for opportunities.

The Bracero Program was in effect from 1942 to 1964. During these years, five million Mexicans legally entered the country to fill labor shortages. They primarily labored in agricultural fields and on railroads. Not all workers were fully paid for their work. Here, one former *bracero* (below right) sits in his living room in Irapuato, Mexico, in 1998, wondering what happened to the percentage of his wages that the Mexican government supposedly put into a collective savings fund.

**Q:** When did Mexicans become the largest group within the Latino minority?

**A:** The fall of the thirty-year dictatorship (1881–1911) of Porfirio Díaz in Mexico brought violence, political turmoil, and economic upheaval. When the Mexican Revolution (1910–20) began, large numbers of Mexicans moved to the United States to work in agriculture and industry. These first two decades of the century were a period of economic expansion in the United States, and Mexican seasonal workers filled a labor need. In 1927, for instance, the Midwest had 63,700 Mexican residents, but the number increased during the summer to 80,000.

World War II increased the demand for labor—especially for the manufacture of weapons—at a time when men were being drafted into the military. An emergency labor program was implemented.

**Q:** What was the Bracero Program?

**A:** It was a formal binational agreement that allowed the United States to import labor from Mexico. *Bracero* refers to a legally contracted Mexican worker (*brazo* means

"arm" in Spanish). The program ran from August 4, 1942, to December 31, 1964. In those twenty-two years a total of five million Mexican workers entered, and settled, in twenty-four different states. Many of those workers were employed in the railroad industry.

The provisions of the program were clear: *Braceros* were to be provided free housing, sanitary labor conditions, and meals at reasonable prices; they were to be paid at least the equivalent of what Americans citizens received for the same job and not less than 30 cents an hour; they were to have guaranteed employment for three-fourths of the contract period and a subsistence wage of $3 per day if they were unemployed for more than one-fourth of the contract period; employers were to pay occupational insurance, similar to disability insurance; the employees were guaranteed round-trip transportation from and to Mexico; and *braceros* were exempt from military service. In time, U.S. employers gained the upper hand in labor negotiations and the above stipulations were often ignored, with working conditions and wages deteriorating as a result.

## Q: What were the living conditions of Latinos at the time of the Bracero Program?

**A:** After World War II, even during the Bracero Program, the living and labor conditions of Mexican Americans in the Southwest were poor. Xenophobia, racism, immigrants' lack of knowledge of the legal system, and language barriers all kept Spanish-speaking people in entry-level jobs. The Latino middle class was small and, in general, disconnected from the working classes. The poor lived in ghettos in major urban centers on both coasts—for example, East Los Angeles in California and Spanish Harlem in New York.

## Q: Was the Bracero Program well received nationwide?

**A:** Controversy engulfed this program. The American Federation of Labor joined many others who argued that domestic workers were being badly affected by this influx of cheap labor and that the mistreatment of laborers in general was being willfully ignored. Others believed that illegal workers were taking advantage of the system to infiltrate the country. Operation Wetback was one reaction. Developed in 1954 under the Eisenhower administration and launched by Attorney General Herbert Brownell, Operation Wetback was a deportation program, the second-largest in U.S. history. The first had been called Repatriation and occurred during the Great Depression of the 1930s. According to the Immigration and Naturalization Service, during Operation Wetback an estimated 1.3 million people were sent back to Mexico.

## Q: Did Latinos fight in World War II?

**A:** An estimated 375,000 Latinos served in the U.S. armed forces during World War II, some 65,000 Puerto Ricans among them. Latinos received twelve Medals of Honor. Still, the period was characterized by domestic intolerance. The Sleepy Lagoon Case and the Zoot Suit Riots (see chapter four) in southern California were events in which violence broke out between Anglos and Latinos, thus serving to confirm the former's stereotypes of the latter and dramatically exposing widespread racism. The Bracero Program contributed to America's war effort by placing millions of workers in factories, but Latinos' sense of alienation and Anglo America's accusation that they "took away American jobs" put them in a difficult position. Many of those who had joined the armed forces in World War II ultimately became agents of change. They benefited from the G.I. Bill, enrolling in college and buying new homes. A generation of business and political leaders began to emerge.

Mexican *braceros* picking chile peppers in California.

# *La Frontera*, real and metaphorical

**Q:** How can *La Frontera,* the U.S.-Mexican border, be characterized in the post–"Operation Wetback" era?

**A:** The 2,000-mile border extends from southern California along the southern edge of Arizona, New Mexico, and Texas, and to the northern reach of the Gulf of Mexico. On the Mexican side, the border defines the northern edge of the states of Baja California, Sonora, Chihuahua, Coahuila, Nuevo León, and Tamaulipas. It brings together—or divides, depending on how one sees it—two dramatically different civilizations: the English-speaking Anglo-dominated north, and the Spanish-speaking Hispanic south.

Although the border has always been extraordinarily porous—the United States has gone from welcoming *braceros* and extending amnesty to illegal workers to blocking their passage through a specially trained patrol force—the current era of border patrol has only grown stricter since the end of the Bracero Program. Border patrol has been, and is sometimes still, supported by vigilantes and other civilians. It should be noted that the passage is not always one way: People fleeing the law and financial problems cross from north to south.

Approximately twelve million people live in the border region. Ninety percent of them live in fourteen paired sister cities, one on each side of the border. It is home to sweatshops, known as *maquiladoras,* that employ workers, particularly young women, to manufacture inexpensive items for export. A global economy and specific laws have encouraged Mexican and U.S. companies to create these kinds of factories. Depending on the location, the language spoken along the U.S.-Mexican border ranges from English to Spanish and—more consistently—Spanglish.

Increasingly harsh crackdowns on illegal immigrants and the flow of drugs across the border has resulted in immi-

A Mexican border policeman in 1903. Both sides of the Rio Grande have been consistently guarded and monitored in the twentieth century.

grants employing riskier methods, such as walking dozens of miles through scorching desert or spending days trapped inside large vehicles, in their attempts to enter the United States.

## Q: What prompted the mass immigration protests of 2006?

A: After the Al Qaeda–organized terrorist attacks on the World Trade Center on September 11, 2001, the U.S. government declared a "war on terror." This war materialized first in Afghanistan against the Taliban regime, then in Iraq against the dictatorship of Saddam Hussein.

Simultaneously, the nation's geographic borders attracted much attention and concern. Could another attack take place inside the United States? What measures could be implemented to stop potential terrorists from infiltrating the country?

At the same time, dramatic ethnic changes became evident as the U.S. Census Bureau declared in 2003 that the Latino minority, ahead of all expectations, was already the largest in the country, larger than African Americans, and that Spanish is the second-most frequently used language in the United States. Conservative groups proclaimed that the nation was visibly under threat. Of utmost domestic concern to many, after national security, was the widespread use of Spanish and the seeming lack of assimilation among Latinos. Were Latinos learning English at the same pace as previous immigrants? Was the United States about to split along ethnic, cultural, and linguistic lines?

As Congress and the Senate debated immigration reforms in the first months of 2006, considering another guest-worker program, the extension of amnesty, the strengthening of border patrols, and the building of a wall on the U.S.-Mexican border, large numbers of Latinos, especially Mexicans, and other immigrant groups and immigrant rights activists took to the streets in support of more lenient policies. They marched all over the country, from Los Angeles to Dallas and Washington, D.C., while conservative opponents fought the ideas manifested in the protests through the media and on the floors of Congress.

An anti-immigration protestor broadcasts her views on a corner near the Fort Lauderdale, Florida, courthouse, where immigration rallies were held in April 2006.

In April of 2006, hundreds of thousands of activists rallied on the National Mall in Washington, D.C., for U.S. citizenship for illegal immigrants.

SI·SE·PUEDE ~ IT·CAN·BE·DONE

southport, chicago, illinois 60657

**BOYCOTT LETTUCE & GRAPES**

# CHAPTER 4

# THE CHICANO MOVEMENT

**D**uring the Civil Rights era, Latinos as well as African Americans struggled to make their voices heard and improve their working and living conditions. The fight that came to be known as the Chicano Movement began with efforts to aid migrant workers in the Southwest— who were predominantly Mexican and who had been brought over during the Bracero Program that began during World War II and ended in 1964; the movement's epicenter was California, although Texas, Arizona, Colorado, and New Mexico were important also. Its principal leader was César Chávez, a *mestizo* of humble background who rose to prominence by expounding a philosophy of nonviolence inspired by Mahatma Gandhi and the Reverend Martin Luther King Jr. Chávez and the United Farm Workers Union (UFW) benefited from several committed activists, including Dolores Huerta, Reies López Tijerina, and Rodolfo "Corky" Gonzáles. The vision of *el movimiento,* as the movement is called in Spanish, crystallized in *El plan espiritual de Aztlán* (The Spiritual Plan of Aztlán; see page 46).

Left: César Chávez and the United Farm Workers drew national attention to the poor working and living conditions of migrant workers by encouraging boycotts in key industries, such as the lettuce and grape agribusinesses.

Above: Chávez during a 1990 talk at Boston University, where he stressed the importance of halting toxic pesticide use in agriculture.

# Hostilities Turn to Riots

**Q:** What was the Sleepy Lagoon Case?

**A:** On August 1, 1942, twenty-two-year-old José Díaz, a Mexican American, was stabbed near Sleepy Lagoon, a reservoir in Los Angeles; he died later that day. The circumstances of his death remain unclear but were suggestive of retribution for the beating of a young couple at the reservoir earlier that day. The incident was interpreted by the Los Angeles Police Department as an explosion of juvenile delinquency among Mexican Americans. The LAPD eventually arrested six hundred youngsters of Mexican descent, indicting twenty-two for involvement in the crime.

**Q:** What role did the media play in agitating the public?

**A:** The Los Angeles media, from the *Times* to the *Herald Express* and the *Daily News*, were deeply involved in reporting the case and swayed public opinion against the youths. Stereotypes about rowdy, brawling *pachucos* (young Mexicans) were employed regularly. World War II occupied the minds of mainstream America and fueled fears of "foreigners."

During the trial, the defendants were not allowed to consult with their lawyers. They were forced to wear the same clothes they were wearing on the day of their arrest and were forbidden to shave

Mexican youths beaten by "raging bands of servicemen" during the Zoot Suit Riots.

and cut their hair. Judge Charles Fricke labeled the defendants as gangsters. The prosecution described Mexican Americans as cowards. Even though evidence connecting the defendants to the murder was lacking, the verdict, announced in January 1943, declared seventeen young Mexican American men guilty of second-degree murder, assault, or criminal conspiracy. Ten were sent to San Quentin Prison. Within a year, however, their convictions were overturned on appeal, citing bias, denial of counsel, and insufficient evidence.

## Q: What were the Zoot Suit Riots?

A: On Main Street in East Los Angeles on the night of June 3, 1943, eleven white sailors engaged violently with a group of Spanish-speakers dressed in zoot suits, a distinctive style of clothing popular among many Mexican Americans and African Americans: a suit with broad

shoulders, a narrow waist, and ballooning pants, worn with shiny leather shoes, and a broad-brimmed hat. The LAPD was called to clear the area. A day later, some two hundred navy recruits arrived in the neighborhood in twenty taxicabs; a boy in a zoot suit was soon found and beaten. The violence exploded and continued for four days. Targets included African Americans and Filipinos. Businesses were looted and Mexican Americans were stripped of their clothes and humiliated in public. No one was killed, but the racially based riots sparked similar violence across the country—in San Diego, Detroit, Baltimore, and Philadelphia. The zoot suiters, who included women, or *pachucas*, were viewed as threats to the ideals of wartime masculinity and industry. The Zoot Suit Riots overshadowed the nonviolent relationships among ethnic groups in Los Angeles, evidenced, for example, by the nighttime jazz clubs where young people of all races played music and danced together.

Above: Club-wielding U.S. armed forces personnel patrol the streets of Los Angeles during the Zoot Suit Riots of 1943.

Left: Full-length portrait of a zoot suiter in 1943, wearing a broad hat, long, loose jacket, ballooning pants, and shiny shoes.

# Chicanismo and Activism

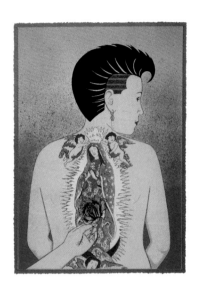

*La Ofrenda II (The Offering II)* by Chicano Movement artist Esther Hernandez. Hernandez celebrates Chicano pride by depicting the Virgin of Guadalupe on the back of a Chicana, inspiring the offering of a rose.

**Q:** What is Chicanismo?

**A:** Chicanismo is an ideology of self-determination built upon the motifs of Mexican American life. These include the origin myths of Aztlán (the name the Aztecs used for their homeland and afterlife) and imagery of the pre-Columbian period, as well as images of the Virgin of Guadalupe, the art of painter Frida Kahlo, and the iconic face and philosophy of Argentine freedom-fighter Ernesto "Ché" Guevara. Chicanismo reached its apex in the 1960s and 1970s, but its roots date back, though loosely, to the signing of the Treaty of Guadalupe Hidalgo, and it remains alive to this day. But even more than an ideology, Chicanismo has become a philosophy that argues in favor of resisting mainstream American culture, emphasizing an alternative approach to public education, and strengthening social and political organizations devoted to improving the status of Mexican Americans in the United States.

Carmen Lomas Garza's 1983 painting *Cakewalk* depicts a block party and fund raising event for the American G.I. Forum, an important Latino organization generally run by and focused on middle- to upper-class populations.

**Q:** How did the Chicano Movement take shape?

**A:** The decade of 1965 to 1975 is generally agreed to be the period of growth, consolidation, and early decline of the Chicano Movement, the era of Mexican American civil rights activism. The movement comprised multiple and diverse activities—strikes, rallies, marches, sit-ins—by organizations in several locations. The time had come for the development of more popular, grassroots groups that represented a wider and more economically diverse constituency. César Chávez, surrounded by a number of loyal activists, eventually arose as the movement's public face and voice as the leader of the United Farm Workers Union. He directed these grassroots groups to put their energies behind demonstrations that would draw attention to the poor working and living conditions of Latino laborers.

**Q:** What kinds of relationships existed between Chicanos and African Americans and other ethnic groups during the Civil Rights era?

**A:** Most important was the dialogue between the Mexican American leader César Chávez and African American activist Martin Luther King Jr. The activities of the Chicano Movement were concurrent with many of those of African Americans fighting Jim Crow laws and segregation in the South.

The UFW itself was formed in 1965 as a result of the merger of the National Farm Workers Union and the Filipino Agricultural Workers Organizing Committee. Filipinos were also an important source of migrant labor in the fields and consequently were involved in marches and strikes and worked closely with Chávez. Their experience is chronicled in Carlos Bulosan's autobiographical novel *America Is in the Heart* (1974).

**Q:** Who were the Puerto Rican Young Lords?

**A:** The Puerto Rican Young Lords (PRYL) were not intimately involved in the Chicano Movement, but they fought for similar advances for Puerto Ricans. The PRYL was a national activist organization seeking the social, economic, and political improvement of Puerto Ricans on the mainland. Their ultimate goal was the liberation of Puerto Rico. Originally led by a Chicago gang member, José "Cha Cha" Jiménez, the Young Lords shifted their

A poster by the Puerto Rican Young Lords, calling for a conference to discuss its foremost priority: the liberation of Puerto Rico from dependence on the United States.

main operations to New York City, primarily because of the high concentration there of Puerto Ricans. Branches were also active in Philadelphia, Boston, Newark, Connecticut, and Puerto Rico itself. The group organized health screenings, offered free food and clothes, presented workshops about Puerto Rican history, and sought to persuade the New York City Board of Education to include Puerto Rican and Latino courses in the public school curriculum. They published a community-based newspaper, *Pa'lante*. They were also involved in "offensives," drives that at times forcibly occupied churches and hospitals.

The organization fell apart in 1972. In 1977, some of its former members hung a Puerto Rican flag over the crown of the Statue of Liberty, both to commemorate the independence of Puerto Rico and to denounce its present status as a dependent of the mainland United States.

# A Leader Is Born

**Q:** Who was César Chávez?

**A:** Chávez was undoubtedly the most important Mexican American labor organizer of all time. His legacy still lives in the efforts of fighting for civil rights and the consolidation of a pan-Latino identity.

Born on March 13, 1927, in Yuma, Arizona, Chávez was the second of five children in a family of modest means. They lived on a 160-acre farm, where they engaged in subsistence agriculture. When the family moved to California in search of better opportunities, they ended up as seasonal laborers, picking cotton and carrots. Chávez's education was defined by his itinerant life. He attended some sixty-five different schools, "for a day, a week, or a few months." At the age of nineteen, Chávez joined the Agricultural Workers' Union. He then served in the navy during World War II, after which he returned to California. Although he again did itinerant work, he had time to read. His personal discovery of the work

of Mahatma Gandhi, the Indian pacifist leader who advocated nonviolence as a strategy of protest and national recognition, was a turning point. He consistently emphasized peaceful demonstrations as the only road to recognition and reconciliation. Chávez himself went on several hunger strikes, also inspired by Gandhi, as a way to bring attention to and denounce abuse and corruption. In 1968, he drank only water for twenty-five days. Another fast in 1974 lasted twenty-four days. In 1988, in the so-called Fast for Life, he lasted thirty-five days. Chávez also modeled himself after his contemporary, the Reverend Martin Luther King Jr., another pacifist ethnic leader.

**Q:** How did Chávez become a union leader?

**A:** In 1952 Chávez met Fred Ross, leader of the Community Service Organization. Along with Chicago-based organizer Saul Alinsky, Ross worked with Chávez to implement new strategies to mobilize workers. By the age of thirty-three, Chávez was organizing working

Below: United Farm Workers President César Chávez leads a 1985 boycott against Jewel supermarkets for its purchase of goods from an agricultural company convicted of workers' rights violations two years earlier.

Right: Martin Luther King Jr.'s practice of nonviolent protest was an inspiration for César Chávez. The two leaders were in contact during the Civil Rights and Chicano movements.

families in vineyards. Soon he was involved in the creation of the National Farm Workers Union, which eventually became the United Farm Workers. He used *la huelga* (the strike) as a strategy to force business owners to respond to their workers' petitions.

## Q: Did religion play a role in Chávez's career?

**A:** Chávez's most enduring inspiration was his Roman Catholic faith, a fixture of his childhood. In speech after speech, Chávez talked of the patience and endurance that came from believing in God. He also established partnerships with religious figures who sympathized with the plight of the poor and oppressed Mexican labor workers. Even though the institutional Catholic Church maintained a neutral stance, local priests in Arizona, New Mexico, and California joined his movement and supported his public demonstrations.

## Q: What is Chávez's legacy?

**A:** Chávez died on April 23, 1993, in San Luis, Arizona. Some 50,000 people marched at his funeral. He was buried in La Paz, California, at the headquarters of the UFW. A foundation in his name was established to keep his legacy alive.

Chávez put his own life on the line to improve the situation of migrant workers. He negotiated tirelessly with owners of agricultural businesses and campaigned against harmful pesticides. He used his fame and reputation to persuade the average American to boycott products from industries with poor labor practices. In an age of civil disobedience, he became a folk hero. Biographies have been written, documentaries made, picture books printed, and *corridos* (Mexican ballads) sung about him; public schools, community centers, and streets, particularly in the Southwest, are named after him, honoring his legacy. The United States Postal Service issued a stamp in his honor in 2002.

Members of César Chávez's family, celebrities, and state and local dignitaries join the commemoration of the tenth anniversary of the leader's death.

> ❝ When we are perfectly honest with ourselves we admit that our life is the only thing that belongs to us. Therefore, how we use our life is what determines the type of people we are. ❞
>
> —*César Chávez*

# Aztlán in the Heart

A sixteenth-century Aztec depiction of the Mexica departing from Aztlán.

their place, like the Canaanite patriarch Abraham, and wander until a sign appeared before them: an eagle devouring a serpent sitting on a cactus emerging from a stone in a lake. The sign would be proof that the land was theirs to settle and civilize. This very image is now portrayed on Mexico's national flag.

**Q: Where is Aztlán "located"?**

**A:** Some believe Aztlán is in the Mexican state of Nayarit, in the town San Felipe de Aztlán. Others locate it in the valley of the lower Colorado River. In Nahuatl, the Aztec tongue, the word Aztlán means "the land of the north" and "the land of white reeds." It could also be understood as a place of whiteness. Increasing the importance of the Aztlán myth during the Chicano Movement is the belief that the Aztec emperor Moctezuma prophesied that his descendants would one day conquer the Earth.

To Chicanos, whose connection to Mexico is often several generations removed, Aztlán is a utopian port of

**Q: How should the concept of Aztlán be understood?**

**A:** Aztlán is a crucial myth for Mexican Americans and was a profound source of inspiration during the Chicano Movement. According to lore, the founding of Mexico came about when the Aztecs, who emerged from the depths of the Earth through seven caves and lived in a place called Aztlán (also spelled *Aztlatlán*), were commanded to abandon

The Mexican flag contains the mythical symbol of the Aztec homeland, Aztlán.

arrival and departure, a place first abandoned by its people then betrayed by the Mexican government in the signing of the Treaty of Guadalupe Hidalgo and in the agreement with the Gadsden Purchase and subsequently colonized by the United States. It is important to keep in mind that the time of the Chicano Movement was also the time of anti-Vietnam demonstrations, and of counterculture anticolonial rhetoric.

## Q: What was *El plan espiritual de Aztlán?*

A: *El plan* was a manifesto drafted at the Chicano Liberation Youth Conference held at the Centro de la Crusada in Denver in March 1969. The conference was attended by some three thousand students from various Mexican American organizations and the Puerto Rican Young Lords. The rhetoric was militant, ethno-centric, civil rights oriented, anticolonial, and nationalistic. Rodolfo "Corky" Gonzáles was instrumental in developing the manifesto. Inspired by the myth of Aztlán, the manifesto called for the development of a working-class Chicano consciousness distinct from other cultures. Despite this proclamation of separateness, the plan sought to develop unity, improve education, achieve economic self-determination, and defend Chicano interests. It also called for restitution for lost property, such as those claims that were voided when the promises of the Treaty of Guadalupe Hidalgo were not upheld.

# The Crusade for Justice

Above: "Indefinite hunger strike" reads the sign posted in Tegucigalpa, Honduras in 2004 by immigrants from several Latin American and other countries protesting their detainment without deportation to their home countries.

Right: A scenic photo of the Carson National Forest, which Reies López Tijerina occupied with members of his *Alianza Federal de las Mercedes* (Federal Land-Grant Alliance) in 1966.

primarily immigrants; working-class Anglos tended to take jobs in factories. Through walking out and halting production, agricultural workers affirmed their essential role in the owners' businesses. In the 1920s and 1930s, agricultural strikes began to be significant in California: In 1933, within a period of eight months, there were thirty-three. Many years later, César Chávez and the UFW successfully used *la huelga* to effect change in laborers' working conditions.

**Q:** Where does the concept of *la huelga* come from?

**A:** *La huelga* (the strike) is a strategy to bring the attention of business owners and people in power to the plight of workers. In the preindustrial age, farmers established alliances with their labor force to protect their mutual interests in a rural economy. In the twentieth century, as capital consolidated and the desire for greater profits achieved by increased worker productivity rose above other concerns, workers sought stronger means to fight for improved working conditions. Organized labor strikes were a significant feature of the developing national economy. In agribusiness, laborers were

**Q:** Who was Reies López Tijerina?

**A:** Tijerina was another significant figure in the Chicano Movement. Born in Falls City, Texas, in 1926, he did much of his work in New Mexico. He was a Pentecostal preacher and a leader of the Alianza Federal de las Mercedes (Federal Land-Grant Alliance), a group committed to reclaiming the land that had been lost at the signing of the Treaty of Guadalupe Hidalgo. Legal claims for lost property had been filed by individuals and groups but had resulted in little action or recom-

pense. So on October 16, 1966, Tijerina led a one-week Alianza takeover of the Echo Amphitheater campground in Kit Carson National Forest in New Mexico, an area that had been part of a Spanish estate in the eighteenth century. When Alianza members returned to the area a second time, they were arrested.

More Alianza meetings and activities led to confrontations with police and elected officials. On one occasion, several Alianza members were arrested and jailed. Two days later, Tijerina and some supporters orchestrated a rescue. They also intended to make a citizen's arrest of the county district attorney, Alfonso Sánchez. In the attack on the courthouse, a deputy sheriff and a state trooper were wounded. Tijerina fled and hid out in the nearby hills, but the National Guard captured him on June 10, 1967. More than a year later, he successfully defended himself in court and was acquitted of all charges.

In subsequent years, while he was still researching and pressing for the reclamation of historic lands, his audacity and militancy led to more jail time. In the mid-1990s he moved to Michoacán, Mexico. In the history of Latinos in the United States, he symbolizes both the legal and armed struggle for land rights dating to the mid-nineteenth century.

## Q: Who was Rodolfo "Corky" Gonzáles?

A: An activist and author born in Denver, Colorado, in 1928, Gonzáles was a leading political figure of the Chicano Movement. Although he lost his run for Denver City Council in 1955, he launched a career coordinating the state's "Viva Kennedy" presidential campaign in 1960. Four years later, after the death of John F. Kennedy, he was named director of the Neighborhood Youth Corps, a social program sponsored by Lyndon B. Johnson's administration. In 1966, frustrated by the lack of a Latino representative on the Equal Employment Opportunity Commission, he walked out of one of its meetings along with fifty others.

Rodolfo "Corky" Gonzáles

Gonzáles is best known as the creator and leader of the Crusade for Justice, an organization promoting Latino empowerment. He published a powerful myth-based poem *Yo Soy Joaquín/I Am Joaquín* in 1967 in which he probed into the Chicano psyche. It became one of the banners of the Chicano Movement. He also established the newspaper *El gallo: La voz de la justicia* (*The Rooster: The voice of justice*) that advocated self-sustaining Chicano communities, and he was a principal organizer of three youth conferences between 1969 and 1971 in which *El plan spiritual de Aztlán* was drafted. Finally, he was Colorado chairman of La Raza Unida Party (The Party of a United People).

# Militant Chicanas

Above: The song "Adelita," about a woman who follows her husband to war, inspired a group of women to join the male troops of the Mexican Revolution; they were called *Las Adelitas*. The term has come to mean a female soldier or warrior.

Right: Betty Friedan, a leader of the feminist movement, was influential in Latina circles.

**Q: What role did women play in the Chicano Movement?**

**A:** In the early decades of the twentieth century, before feminism acquired the momentum of a movement, a group of Mexican women known as *Las Adelitas*, or female soldiers, after a Mexican folk song about a woman who follows her husband into battle, joined the Mexican Revolution; they were united with the male troops, cooking and otherwise providing for the soldiers.

When United States civil rights leaders like Betty Friedan and Gloria Steinem came to the fore in the 1960s and 1970s, their message promoting gender equality reached the wider population. Their impact was evident when Chicana migrant laborers raised their voices during the Chicano Movement. Even though machismo was strong at every level in the Chicano Movement, photographs of marches during the era show many forceful women. The film *Salt of the Earth*, about the 1950 strike of miners in Grant County, New Mexico, and the role of laborers' wives in carrying out the strike, is one example. The movie, which starred Rosaura Revueltas, was directed by Herbert J. Biberman and released in 1958.

Some Chicanas, including Anna Nieto-Gómez and Bernice Rincón, challenged their male-dominated culture and the male-dominated wider society. They argued that within the struggle for labor improvement was embedded an equally important drive: for women to be seen as equal to men. They organized workshops, published newspapers and magazines, and spread their message widely. The result was an intellectual trend, especially evident in a literature called Xicanisma. This literary movement blossomed decades after *el movimiento* with writings by authors such as Gloria Anzaldúa, Ana Castillo, and Cherríe Moraga, all too young to have been a part of the Chicano Movement.

## Q: Who was Dolores Huerta?

A: Huerta was a co-founder of the National Farm Workers Association and a co-founder, with César Chávez, of the United Farm Workers. Born in Dawson, New Mexico, on April 10, 1930, she attended Stockton College in California. She and Chávez met through their work with the Community Service Organization and were both greatly influenced by founder Fred Ross. Along with Chávez, Huerta led marches, sit-ins, and boycotts. In 1966 she negotiated a contract between striking grape workers and Schenley Wine. This was a historic moment: the first time that farmworkers had successfully represented themselves and negotiated their own contract with an agribusiness. Huerta's work culminated in the landmark Agricultural Labor Relations Act of 1975. Passed by the California legislature, this act was the nation's first legislation protecting farmworkers' right to organize and bargain for their rights.

Throughout her career as nonviolent activist, Huerta has been in prison approximately twenty times. In 1988, while protesting a visit to San Francisco by the then vice president George H. W. Bush, she was beaten by a police officer with a nightstick. The attack was caught on videotape. In a settlement, the San Francisco Police Department paid Huerta $850,000 and was forced to implement stricter crowd-control policy.

Huerta established a foundation under her own name to advance the training of leaders from low-income communities. She has served on the University of California Board of Regents, was inducted to the National Women's Hall of Fame, and was given the Eleanor Roosevelt Award by President Bill Clinton in 1998.

Dolores Huerta, a leader of the Chicano movement and co-founder of the United Farm Workers, urges citizens to vote against certain ballot initiatives harmful to immigrants in the 2005 California Special Election.

> “ Misguided men, who will chastise
> a woman when no blame is due,
> oblivious that it is you
> who prompted what you criticize. ”
>
> —SOR JUANA INÉS DE LA CRUZ, SEVENTEENTH-CENTURY MEXICAN NUN AND INTELLECTUAL

# CHAPTER 5

# THE CARIBBEAN

The Spanish-speaking Caribbean is a string of islands, each with its own political history and social and religious composition. Puerto Rico became a satellite of the United States during the Spanish-American War and Puerto Ricans were given U.S. citizenship in 1917. The island became a commonwealth in 1950. The Dominican Republic achieved independence in 1843 but has since been governed primarily by military dictatorships that have done a poor job of managing the economy, leading to large-scale emigration. Fidel Castro, the bearded rebel who overthrew the Cuban government in 1959, turned Cuba into a communist state with ties to the Soviet Union. Over time, the Cuban Revolution and its aftershocks, including strained and punitive relationships with the United States, sent roughly one million people into exile—primarily to south Florida, where they created another Cuba, *la Cuba de afuera* (the Cuba outside Cuba). Diasporas of Puerto Ricans, Dominicans, and Cubans are essential and influential components of the Latino minority in the United States.

Left: This 1898 map of the West Indies shows an independent Dominican Republic, and a soon to be independent Cuba.

# *Nuyoricans*

**Q: What is the history of Puerto Ricans in New York?**

**A:** Puerto Ricans differ from other Latino migrants in that they are already U.S. citizens, which gives them the right to vote and makes them eligible for important government programs, including health care, education, and welfare. They are seen as neither refugees nor immigrants, but as a distinct kind of migrant.

Before the 1917 Jones Act and the Puerto Rican migration in the early twentieth century (see chapter three), New York had Puerto Rican settlers. Mostly, they were *tabaqueros*, cigar workers, from the educated segment of the working classes. (Cigar companies commonly hired a *lector*, or reader, who read the newspapers, literature, and major works in social and political thought to the cigar rollers.) Many Puerto Ricans were also employed in munitions factories. The diaspora population grew after the Spanish-American War, when Puerto Rico became closely linked politically with the United States. As their numbers grew, though, working conditions declined and they were subject to racial discrimination and harsh labor conditions. Bernardo Vega, a *tabaquero* born in 1885 who moved to New York in 1916, became a labor activist, journalist, and diarist.

His autobiography, *Memoirs* (published posthumously in 1977), meticulously describes the contemporary urban social and political landscape and is an invaluable ethnographic resource. Another important early figure, also interested in politics, was Jesús Colón, author of *A Puerto Rican in New York and Other Sketches*, first published in 1961. Colón was a columnist for the *Daily Worker*, the city's communist newspaper. He ran for the New York State Senate as a representative of the American Labor Party in 1954 and was defeated. He was also unsuccessful in his bid for the office of comptroller of the city of New York in 1969.

U.S. citizenship for Puerto Ricans and economic instability on the island increased migration to the mainland. After World War II, New York had the largest concentration of Puerto Ricans outside San Juan (Philadelphia, Chicago, and Newark, New Jersey, followed closely). This early-twentieth-century tide is known as the Great Migration. Out of the convergence of so many islanders sprang significant figures in music, art, and literature, including musicians Tito Puente and, later, Marc Anthony. Poet Julia de Burgos was intensely active in the New York literary scene in the 1940s, and her *El mar y tú* (*The Sea and You*, 1954) contains many poems about her relationship with the city. Poet Pedro Pietri picked up where de Burgos left off with his *Puerto Rican Obituary* (1962).

A 1907 view of Manhattan from the southeast. In the coming years, Puerto Rican migrants would populate East Harlem and the Lower East Side of Manhattan, as well as North Brooklyn and the South Bronx, merging Puerto Rican and urban American customs and eventually creating the vibrant Nuyorican subculture.

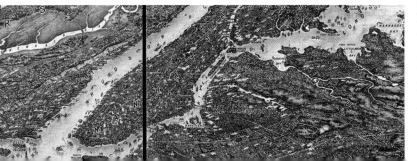

## Q: What is *La Loisaida* and who are *Nuyoricans*?

**A:** Puerto Ricans originally settled in East Harlem, North Brooklyn, the South Bronx, and the Lower East Side, an area of New York City populated by Jewish immigrants at the end of the twentieth century and prior to that by Irish new-comers. Photographer Jacob Riis depicted their lives in his provocative book *How the Other Half Lives* (1890), in which he showed the disastrous living conditions of the working class. The term *Loisaida* was coined in the 1970s by activists Chino García and Bimbo Rivas, to refer to the area of Manhattan where the greatest number of Puerto Ricans lived. It is Spanglish for Lower East Side, an area from Avenue A to the East River bounded to the north by 14th Street and on the south by Houston Street. The East Harlem section where Puerto Ricans lived came to be known as *El Barrio*. Literary representations of it include Piri Thomas's *Down These Mean Streets* (1967) and Edward Rivera's *Family Installments* (1982).

The term *Nuyorican* was born in the 1960s and denotes second- and third-generation Puerto Ricans living in New York City. Metaphorically, it refers to a double consciousness, one defined by a hybrid identity—that of belonging both to the American city and the Caribbean island. Originally, the primary users of the term, the ones who reduced its stigma and gave it a positive meaning, were the poets of The Nuyorican Poets Café, a Lower East Side institution that was established by Professor Miguel Algarín and a group of writers in 1973.

A mural by the artist Chico memorializes Pedro Pietri, a founding poet of the Nuyorican Poets Café, still a venue for edgy poetry but also a forum for music and the visual and performing arts.

## Q: What is the conflict surrounding Vieques?

**A:** Vieques is an island, also known as Isla Nena, off Puerto Rico's east coast. It became a municipality of Puerto Rico in 1843, but after the Spanish-American War the American government used it for military maneuvers, including the notorious testing of two bombs in 1999 that killed a Puerto Rican security guard and wounded four others. It has become a symbol of Puerto Ricans' fight for autonomy for their island. Protests by members of the local populace were staged to push the military out; some important American leaders, including Jesse Jackson, supported these actions. Ultimately, the U.S. Navy was forced to leave the island in 2003.

> **Ethnic problems move some people to act. They paralyze me.**
>
> —*Rita Moreno, the first Latina performer to win an Oscar, for her supporting role in* West Side Story

# Dominicans

**Q:** What is the history of the relationship between the Dominican Republic and the United States?

**A:** The Dominican Republic shares a border with Haiti; together, the two are the island Hispaniola, where Columbus

A fifteenth-century map of Hispaniola, where Columbus first attempted to build a Spanish settlement. Today the island is divided into French Creole-speaking Haiti on the west and the Spanish-speaking Dominican Republic on the east.

first tried to establish a Spanish colony. At various times, the Dominican Republic was under French, and then Haitian rule, but eventually the island's resistance movement threw off all colonial ties, gaining independence in 1843. A boom in the island's sugarcane crop in the following decades made annexation commercially appealing to the United States, but attempts by President Ulysses S. Grant encountered opposition in the U.S. Senate. In 1905, the island became a financial protectorate of the United States, and it was controlled by the American military between 1916 and 1924. If residents of the island voiced criticism of the occupation, they faced

cruel penalties, but the U.S. military also made some improvements in the island's infrastructure and sanitation systems. When the U.S. military government left, the power vacuum was filled by a dictator named Rafael L. Trujillo, who ruled from 1930 to 1961.

**Q:** What caused the flight of immigrants?

**A:** Although Trujillo was a vicious dictator, he was supported by the United States largely because he was a staunch anticommunist who sided with the Allies during World War II. He was one of the few Latin American leaders to admit Jewish refugees from Eastern Europe in the 1930s. This was part of his policy to "whiten" his island's population—the vast majority of Dominicans are a racial mix of Africans brought over as slaves, and American Indians. In 1937, the brutal Trujillo ordered the massacre of 20,000 dark-skinned Haitians who were living in the Dominican Republic. By contrast, he was considered to have made some improvements in the economic sector, allowing the middle class to steadily grow and expand economically. Although during his rule emigration was tightly restricted, Dominicans nevertheless found ways to flee the island. After Trujillo was assassinated in 1961—partly as a result of the revulsion caused by his killing of the Mirabal sisters, chronicled in Julia Alvarez's novel *In the Time of the Butterflies* (1994)—political and economic instability followed; Dominicans left the country in large numbers, primarily settling in Puerto Rico and New York City.

The New York community firmly established itself in the neighborhood of Washington Heights. A particular form of Spanglish, a hybrid of Spanish and English, called *Dominicanish*, is spoken there among the Dominican American community. The second and third generations retain a strong loyalty to the island of

their grandparents' and parents' origin. As in the case of Puerto Ricans, the interplay between island and U.S.-born Dominican Americans shapes their culture. In addition to Alvarez, the community has produced intellectuals, performance artists, and scholars, including Pedro Henríquez Ureña, Silvio Torres-Saillant, Josefina Báez, author Daisy Cocco de Filippis, and Frank Gutiérrez.

The Dominican Day Parade on August 8, 2004, brought out large numbers of Washington Heights residents carrying Dominican flags and portraits of patron saints, such as this one of Nuestra Señora de Altagracia (Our Lady of High Grace).

"I write in order to find out what I think."

—*Julia Alvarez*

# Cuba

Right: Cuban War Minister Fulgencio Batista with his wife and officers of her military women's legion, 1935–36. Batista was the power behind many of the Cuban governments between 1933 to 1959. However, he was officially president during only a portion of those years.

Below: Fidel Castro, age 31, waging guerrilla warfare against President Batista, from the Sierra Maestra in 1958.

**Q:** What kind of relationship has Cuba had with the United States since the Spanish-American War?

**A:** Though Cuba gained independence in 1898, the island's government was overseen by the United States for the first half of the twentieth century. During the tenures of both Gerardo Machado, a nationalist general in the war of independence, who ran as the Liberal Party's candidate for president in 1924, and Fulgencio Batista, a seditious sergeant who led repeated coups until becoming president himself (1940–44 and 1952–59), corruption was widespread.

Machado, though protecting Cuban goods and its economy, maintained a close political relationship with the United States. He persecuted and tortured his opposition. In 1930, in response to massive strikes and demonstrations, he suppressed constitutionally guaranteed rights. Once president, Batista initially did much to promote democratic principles. However, when he lost the presidential election twelve years later, he organized another coup d'etat to put himself back in power. That coup halted the campaign of a young aspirant for parliament—Fidel Castro.

**Q:** Who is Fidel Castro?

**A:** Arguably, no other politician and revolutionary in the whole of Latin America (with the possible exception of Simón Bólivar) has been more influential than Fidel Castro. He has served longer than any other world leader. Known since the 1960s as *el líder máximo* (the maximum leader), an appellation first given by the U.S. Central Intelligence Agency (CIA) that was later adopted by the Cuban population, he was born the son of a wealthy landowner in Oriente Province. After his frustrated run for a parliamentary seat in 1952, he began to organize a rebellion. In 1953, he and his brother Raúl staged a small and soundly defeated attack on the Moncada army barracks. He was sentenced to two years in prison, then exiled to Mexico, where he met the Argentine physician Ernesto "Ché" Guevara. Over time, Castro gathered more than seven thousand recruits in Cuba's Sierra Maestra and staged a revolution that sent Batista fleeing. On January 1, 1959, Castro and his supporters entered Havana in triumph.

Castro took swift revenge on Bastista's loyalists and nationalized approximately $1.5 billion worth of North American property, including sugar corporations and oil refineries. In 1960, the Soviet deputy premier visited Cuba and set up a four-year trading plan, thereby ousting the United States as Cuba's largest trading partner. A partial commercial embargo was established against Cuba in 1960 by President Dwight Eisenhower. The total economic embargo

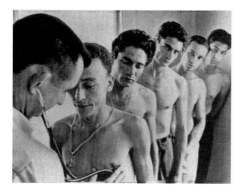

that has been in place since the Foreign Assistance Act of 1961 has had a significantly negative effect on the Cuban economy. During the presidency of John F. Kennedy, the CIA began a series of maneuvers to undermine and eliminate Castro, the most famous of which was the failed invasion of the Bay of Pigs, in which Cuban soldiers forced the surrender of the U.S.-backed exile army after three days of fighting.

## Q: How did Fidel Castro's revolution affect Latin America?

A: Castro's triumph was seen as proud resistance against a neighbor with a track record of foreign intervention. The political left supported Castro, and his ideology spread throughout Latin America. The current populist president of Venezuela, Hugo Chávez, embodies some of Castro's revolutionary principles. Ché Guevara left Cuba not long after the revolution to fight for the liberation of other Latin American countries. He was killed in Bolivia on October 9, 1967. While Castro has been portrayed in the U.S. mainstream media as a repressive dictator since the late 1950s, Guevara has been elevated to the status of a folk hero—not only in Cuba but throughout leftist circles worldwide, especially in the United States.

Left: Recruits, possibly Cuban refugees, line up for physical examinations in Miami, Florida, prior to the 1961 Bay of Pigs invasion.

Below: Ernesto "Ché" Guevera has become an iconic figure due to his leadership during the 1959 Cuban Revolution and subsequent involvement in liberation movements across Latin America. These portraits were taken less than one month before his October 1967 capture and execution.

> " Condemn me, it does not matter. History will absolve me. "
>
> —FIDEL CASTRO, DURING HIS TRIAL FOR SEDITION AFTER ATTACKING THE MONCADA ARMY BARRACKS IN 1953

# Little Havana

Thousands of Cubans have fled the island for Miami, just ninety miles away by boat. Here, refugees throw a line to a U.S. Coast Guard member in 1965.

**Q:** What kind of emigration took place after the 1959 revolution?

**A:** During the first three years of Castro's regime, the middle and upper classes stampeded off the island with all the possessions they could carry. The diaspora relocated in Puerto Rico, Mexico, Spain, Germany, and Scandinavia, but exiles primarily made their new home ninety miles away from their old, in Miami, Florida. New Jersey was another popular American destination. The exiles, many of whom had flourished because of Batista's close ties with the American economy, feared the loss of their assets and their political and religious freedom. Racially, whites made up the majority of the exiles.

In their exodus, these Cubans were joining a long procession of exiles, beginning with the forced conversion and expulsion of the Jews and Muslims from the Iberian Peninsula in the fifteenth century. In Latin America, prominent figures like Domingo Faustino Sarmiento, an early-nineteenth-century Argentine intellectual (and future president of his country) known for the canonical work *Facundo: or, Civilization and Barbarism* (1845), had lived in Chile to escape the tyrannical regime of Juan Manuel de Rosas. Cubans had only to look to José Martí to see exile in their own past; he lived in Key West, Florida, and New York City, while thinking about how to liberate his country from Spain.

The early wave of Cuban émigrés were members of the upper class. These Cuban refugees shop in a Miami department store three years after the 1959 revolution.

**Q:** How did the Cuban émigrés become part of American life?

**A:** Their arrival in the United States with the legal status of political refugees made Cuban exiles eligible for and recipients of government benefits (education and health care, for example) from which other Latino immigrants were barred. Their first years were spent waiting for Castro's regime to implode. When that failed to happen, the first generation of exiles, who tended to be highly educated, began gradually to assume roles as business executives, political leaders, journalists, teachers, and other professionals, while maintaining a tightly knit and virulently anti-Castro community.

**Q:** What kind of relationship does the exile community have with Havana?

**A:** The exiles in Miami are not well-regarded in Cuba. They are portrayed as CIA operatives eager to unsettle Castro's

made an effort to send them secretly and temporarily to the United States. Starting on December 26, 1960, some 14,000 unaccompanied children between the ages of six and eighteen fled Cuba in an effort organized by American headmasters of schools in Cuba. The United States supported *Operación Pedro Pan*, as it is known in Spanish, by waiving visa requirements for these children.

So many Cubans flooded Miami after the Cuban Revolution that the character of the city was significantly changed. Whole neighborhoods began to serve Cuban food and speak Spanish.

government. In turn, the Cuban exiles accuse the communist regime of abuse of power, corruption, intimidation, and torture. Sometimes members of the same family, separated by a stretch of just ninety miles of water, find themselves on opposite sides of this bitter conflict.

The program highlighted the tension between Cuba and the U.S. government. It was seen by Castro's regime as a psychological strategy to increase resistance to its power. Approximately 6,000 children ended up in the care of friends and relatives, while the remaining 8,000 were placed in the care of the federal government. Harrowing stories of separation, nostalgia, and reunion were and continue to be a fixture of the Cuban American community.

## Q: What was Operation Peter Pan?

A: With Castro's ascent to power, upper- and middle-class parents feared for the future of their children. They

> **Freedom is the right of every man to be honest, to think and speak without hypocrisy.**
>
> —*José Martí, from Carlos Ripoll's Martí: Thoughts/Pensamientos*

# Cuba and the Night

The U.S Coast Guard rescues six Cuban migrants from their unseaworthy raft just twenty miles off Cuba's coast in 2005.

### Q: What was the Mariel Boatlift?

A: In 1980 a public dispute took place between the Cuban government and the Peruvian Embassy, when a group of Cubans crashed a bus into the embassy, then demanded and received political asylum. The Cuban government responded by announcing that anyone wishing to leave Cuba could do so at will by going to the Peruvian Embassy to receive exit visas. Within two days, 100,000 people had massed in and around the embassy. The Cuban government then authorized a massive boatlift of its citizens to the United States, encouraging exiles in Miami to pick up their relatives in the port of Mariel. Reports of prisoners being released from jails circulated, resulting in a number of Cuban arrivals being detained by the U.S. Immigration and Naturalization Service. This generation of Cuban exiles is known as *marielitos*, a term that can be pejorative.

### Q: What is a *balsero*?

A: The word means "rafter" in Spanish. In their desire to escape the deprivations of Cuban life in the 1980s and after, caused by the slow decline of Cuba's trading partners (the Soviet Union and its satellites) and the strictly enforced U.S. economic embargo, Cubans sought any available means to leave, including building makeshift boats from empty oil drums, truck tires, wood, and any other object that would float. Miami is close enough to Havana that at night the lights of each city are visible to the other across the ocean. The number of *balseros* in any given season varies according to security levels and the weather. According to some estimates, approximately 17,000 *balseros* had arrived in the United States from Cuba by 1994.

### Q: What was the Elián González affair?

A: González was a six-year-old boy who, along with his mother Elisabet Brotons, left the island—and Elián's father, divorced from his mother—on a raft to come to the United States. The mother drowned at sea and the child was found floating in the ocean off the coast of Florida on Thanksgiving Day 1998. His rescue became an international issue as Miami relatives took Elián to their home and blamed Fidel Castro's regime for generating the kind of poverty and repression that resulted in *balseros*' risking their lives. Elián's father, supported by the Cuban government, demanded that the boy be returned. The Cuban exile community was fiercely opposed, while a majority of non-Cuban Latinos sided with the U.S. mainstream in their support of returning the child to his father. Eventually, Attorney General Janet Reno ordered federal officers to break into the relatives' house on April 22, 2000, and take the boy away. He was reunited with his father and they returned to Cuba in June of that year.

of the most well known and reproduced pieces is a symbolic poem "Dos patrias" ("Two Homelands") written in exile by José Martí. The poet uses the image of a widow to lament the fracture at the heart of the Cuban population, divided by the injury of exile. It opens with the following lines: "*Dos patrias tengo yo: Cuba y la noche.*" In English: "I have two homelands: Cuba and the night." Near the end of his life, Martí stated: "It is my duty to prevent, by search for Cuba's independence, the United States from spreading over the West Indies and falling, with added weight, upon other lands of Our America. All I have done up to now, and shall do hereafter, I do to that end . . . I have lived inside the monster and know its entrails, and my weapon is only David's slingshot." The Castro government has made Martí a hero because of his lifelong anticolonial stance.

Left: Elián González is held by one of the two men who rescued him from the ocean as armed federal agents seized the boy in order to return him to his father in Cuba.

Right: Dressed in his school uniform, Elián González sits next to Fidel Castro (not pictured) in Cardenas, Cuba, at an event commemorating his successful return to Cuba five years prior.

**Q:** How has the Cuban exile been represented in literature?

**A:** Bookcases have been filled with the novels, essays, stories, theater, and poetry depicting the experience of Cuban exiles. Works by Guillermo Cabrera Infante, Heberto Padilla, Reinaldo Arenas, and Zoe Valdés are among them. One

"I don't care if I fall as long as someone else picks up my gun and keeps on shooting."
— CHÉ GUEVARA, CLAIMED TO BE HIS DYING WORDS

# CHAPTER 6

# OUT OF MANY, ONE

Up until the 1980s, Latinos were parts of a perceived whole rather than a solidified ethnic minority; the national needs of Mexicans, Puerto Ricans, and Cubans pushed them in different directions. Population growth, along with the realization that strength is based on unity—*la unión hace la fuerza*—gradually contributed to a sense of partnership and a commitment to solidarity. The civil wars in Central America in the late 1970s to the mid-1990s sent hundreds of thousands of Central Americans north, where they settled into pre-existing Latino communities. National lines began to blur and blend. Brazil, although by far the largest country of Latin America in terms of land area, had previously been considered outside the Latino/Hispanic identity because of its cultural and linguistic colonization by Portugal. Recently, however, integration has increased; the introduction of Brazilians into the U.S.–Latino mix has infused the minority with fresh music, ideas, and customs.

Left: 1998 CIA map of Central America and the Caribbean.

Above: Police fire tear gas to disperse protesters in Izalco, El Salvador, in 1998.

# Contras and Refugees

**Q:** When did immigration from Central America reach its peak?

**A:** The civil wars in Guatemala, El Salvador, and Nicaragua in the 1980s forced their citizens to emigrate, with the United States being the most common destination. The immigrants' journeys were arduous and necessarily included crossing several borders.

**Q:** What is the history of these civil wars?

**A:** Guatemala has had a consistent history of political instability in the twentieth century. The nation's population, divided into Mayan Indians and mestizos, each speaking a different language and geographically isolated from each other, has long been in turmoil as a result of repeated coups d'etat as well as social and economic divisions. Guatemala endured civil war from 1961 to 1996. The war claimed nearly 200,000 victims. During the dictatorship of General Efraín Ríos

Montt in the early 1980s, many left—half a million, according to some estimates—often after being burned out of their villages. (The country had a total population of more than ten million.) Despite this violent history, a majority of Guatemalan Americans retain strong connections with their homeland.

The greatest immigration of Salvadorans to the United States occurred from 1979 to 1992, in response to El Salvador's civil war, which began with unrest over unequal civil rights and poor economic conditions. Coming on the heels of several military coups, the war ultimately killed 75,000 and displaced hundreds of thousands more. A guerrilla resistance movement, the Farabundo Martí National Liberation Front (FMLN), sprung up to fight the military. Although Salvadoran immigration had been minimal before the war, during the early years of the 1980s, nearly half a million refugees from El Salvador crossed into the United States; they remained largely undocumented as the Reagan administration refused to recognize them as political refu-

This map, drawn in 1890, shows the potential of the Nicaragua Canal connecting the Atlantic and Pacific Oceans.

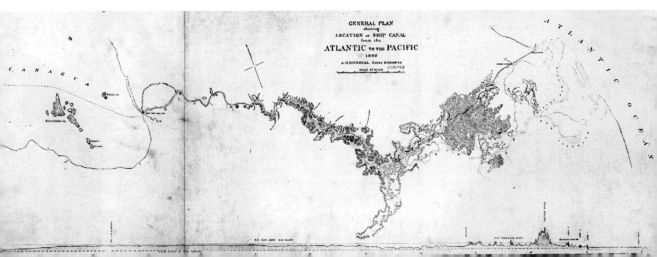

GENERAL PLAN
showing
LOCATION of SHIP CANAL
from the
ATLANTIC to the PACIFIC
1890
A.G.MENOCAL, Chief Engineer

established by the Sandinistas by backing antigovernment rebels, known as Contras.

Thousands of Sandinistas gather at the Plaza de La Fe in Managua, Nicaragua, in 2005 to commemorate the twenty-sixth anniversary of the downfall of the Somoza dynasty.

## Q: What was the Iran-Contra Affair?

A: After the Iran Hostage Crisis of 1979–81 (which followed Iran's Islamic Revolution and in which militant Iranians took sixty-six Americans hostage at the American Embassy in Tehran and held fifty-two of them for more than a year) was resolved, a newly elected President Ronald Reagan, some members of his cabinet, and some of his advisers attempted to orchestrate a counterrevolution against Daniel Ortega's Sandinista Nicaraguan government. The money for weapons came from illegal sales of arms to Iran, some of the proceeds of which were diverted to support the Contras, an anti-Sandanista group. The scandal caused by this circumventing of the Iran arms embargo and the diversion of funds almost brought down Reagan's presidency. During those years of U.S.-backed civil war, massive numbers of Nicaraguans fled north to the United States, where they were granted political asylum. A strong Nicaraguan community developed, especially in Miami.

gees. Accordingly, Salvadoran Americans remain among the poorest Latinos in the United States.

Nicaragua has been a strong focus of U.S. interest and foreign policy since the early twentieth century, in large part because it held the potential for a passage connecting the Atlantic and Pacific Oceans—the Nicaragua Canal. In 1912, U.S. marines invaded the country. Augusto César Sandino emerged as a leading figure of the opposition but was assassinated in 1934. Corrupt dictatorships led by Anastasio Somoza and his sons, Luis and Anastasio Jr., followed, crushing any opposition. In the 1970s the Sandinista National Liberation Front emerged as an alternative party for the poor and disenfranchised. After violent confrontations, the Sandinistas overthrew the dictatorship in 1979. The United States sought to bring down the government

# South America

**Q:** To what extent has the United States been involved in South American governments?

**A:** As the continent of South America is not as geographically close to the United States as Mexico, the Caribbean Basin, and Central America, historical interventions in South America have been fewer. However, the U.S. did support a coup and shored up a repressive government in Chile. On September 11, 1973, Augusto Pinochet, a Chilean general, orchestrated an insurrection against elected president Salvador Allende (who reportedly committed suicide), and ushered in a dictatorship. Even without military coups and other unrest, countries ranging from Colombia to Uruguay have experienced massive emigration because of badly mismanaged and looted economies and political strife.

The U.S. Census Bureau delineates South Americans as a category within Latinos. Of the foreign-born population calculated by the American Community Survey in 2005, 30.7 percent were from Mexico, 23.4 percent were from South and East Asia, 8.8 percent Central America, 6.8 percent South America, 3.4 percent Middle East, and 19.8 percent Other.

Two posters from the late 1970s express hatred for the regime of General Augusto Pinochet in Chile. Pinochet's coup overthrew the elected president Salvador Allende.

**NOT WANTED**

IN THE UNITED STATES – OR ANYWHERE ELSE ON EARTH

**GENERAL AUGUSTO PINOCHET**

**because of his crimes against humanity!**

**PROTEST VISIT OF CHILE'S HITLER TO U.S.**

**Wed., Sept. 7, 5:00 pm**

**Lan-chile** 6 W. 51 ST. at 5TH AVE.

SEND TELEGRAMS TO PRESIDENT JIMMY CARTER
THE WHITE HOUSE
WASHINGTON, D.C. 20500

FOR FURTHER INFORMATION CONTACT:
CHILE DEMOCRATICO/CHILE SOLIDARITY COMMITTEE
156 FIFTH AVENUE/NEW YORK/NEW YORK/10010
212/691-9025

Labor donated

**Q:** How have Colombian drug wars affected Colombian emigration?

**A:** By 2005, approximately three million Colombians had immigrated to the United States, largely in response to the violence and economic instability brought about by the powerful cartels that controlled drug trafficking—*el narcotráfico*—in the Western Hemisphere. People from all socioeconomic backgrounds moved north, not only from cities like Bogotá and Medellín but also from rural areas. They have settled primarily in Florida, New York, New Jersey, and Texas.

## Q: What factors have contributed to Venezuelan immigration?

A: Venezuela was a relatively stable country until the 1980s, when an economic crisis brought unemployment and people began to look for ways to escape. Inflation was followed by currency devaluation, coups d'etat, impeachment of the president, and, eventually, the election of a leftist leader, Hugo Chávez. As president, Chávez aligned himself with Fidel Castro's policies, presenting himself as a populist Latin American leader who sought to galvanize opposition to the United States for decades of abuse of power. Chávez's rhetoric has targeted President George W. Bush. In speech after speech, Chávez has painted himself as a kind of Robin Hood of the poor nations eager to fight the rich. His power rests not only on his ability to win the support of the people of Venezuela but also on Venezuela's considerable oil resources.

The country is a main provider of oil to several neighbors—from Brazil to Argentina; the country used to sell great amounts of crude oil to the United States but has recently sought other markets, significantly reducing its sales to the U.S. Many middle-class Venezuelans, fearing economic and social instability, emigrated to the United States in the 1990s, settling for the most part in Florida, New York, Texas, New Jersey, and California.

Above: Venezuelan President Hugo Chávez with his wife and daughter at a rally two months before his landslide reelection in 2000.

Left: Two Dragonfly aircraft of the U.S. Twenty-fourth Tactical Air Support Squadron training with the Colombian Air Force pass over the coast of Colombia in 1989.

# The Brazilian Beat

**Q:**  **Are Brazilians Latinos?**

**A:** Spain was not the only colonizer of the Americas. Portugal had a major colonial empire in the sixteenth century, as did France and the Netherlands. Each left an imprint on their colonies. A form of Portuguese is the language

Above: A 1671 map of Salvador, Brazil. Right: 1994 CIA map of the entire country.

of Brazil, which is the largest country in South America, both geographically and demographically. Its historical differences from the Spanish-conquered colonies have traditionally and culturally isolated Brazil on the South American continent. Dominican exile Pedro Henríquez Ureña campaigned to stop the use of the term *"América latina,"* claiming it was misleading. Instead, he suggested the use of the terms Hispanic and Luso (that is, Portuguese)

Americas—*la América hispánica y la América lusitana*. Such terms make clear the linguistic and cultural differences of the colonial pasts of various Latin American countries and cultures. Brazilians have a significant representation in the United States. In 2005, the Brazilian government calculated that

there were 1.3 million Brazilians living in the United States, just under the number of Cubans (1.4 million including foreign- and U.S.-born). Brazilians are both inside and outside the Latino minority: They share some demographic and cultural characterics with other

Latinos, but their national distinctiveness is evident in their colorful style of dress and their unique music, from samba to bossa nova. Issues of race are approached in Brazil with openness unmatched in other areas of Latin America—the country was involved in the Portuguese slave trade and incorporated many Africans into its population.

Brazilians have primarily settled in Florida, Massachusetts, California, New York, and New Jersey. New York City boasts a "Little Brazil" on 46th Street in Manhattan.

## Q: What caused Brazilian immigration?

A: Brazil used to be known as a destination for immigrants, not a departure point. Jews, Germans, Italians, Japanese, and other national groups arrived at various times before the mid-twentieth century. The reversal started with the Gétulio Vargas dictatorship (1930–45; 1951–54). During this period many working-age men and women migrated to industrial nations, including the United States. After 1954, the government encountered rising inflation and implemented a series of failed plans to stabilize the economy, which further encouraged people to leave.

The United States has been the home—temporary and permanent—of Brazilian intellectuals, politicians, and artists, ranging from Carmen Miranda and Candido Portinari to Antonio Carlos Jobim and Juscelino Kutitscheck.

## Q: Are U.S. Anglos aware of the nuances defining Latinos?

A: The Latin motto of the United States, *e pluribus unum* (out of many, one), was established in 1776, the year of the nation's declared independence. It has remained a touchstone ever since, first as a reference to the united thirteen colonies, then to the thirteen stars on the original flag of the United States. Over time it has come to be seen as an endorsement of pluralism. Latinos themselves are also a sum of parts. People of different backgrounds have converged in a single country and are shaping a dynamic identity. Non-Latinos have needed some time to recognize the plurality of Latino experiences and backgrounds. The case of Brazil exemplifies the complicated nature of a united Latino minority.

**" All generalizations are false, including this one. "**
—*MARK TWAIN*

# CHAPTER 7

# FAMILY

The family is the center of Latino life and helps form many cultural behaviors and beliefs. Latinos are traditionally family-centric, placing familial obligations above those of work and individual priorities. The stereotypical role of the mother is reflected in religious iconography and in the embrace of *marianismo,* a set of values encouraging women to be virtuous, humble, nurturing, and self-effacing. The stereotypical image of men corresponds with the concept of machismo, as men are the income-earning, protective heads of households. Various customs surround pregnancy and childbirth, depending on specific cultural backgrounds. Like all Americans, Latino youths experience adolescence as a transitional stage; in some inner-city neighborhoods, poverty, the sale and use of drugs, and gangs can lead to troublesome behavior. Adulthood offers more hopeful prospects, although poverty and low education levels among Chicanos and Puerto Ricans may continue the cycle of poverty, truncated education, and disenfranchised youths.

In general, old age is a respected stage of deceleration and congeniality. Latinos often live in multigenerational households in which grandparents are part of daily family life.

Left: Marcelo Jimenez cares for his baby while his wife and her teammates play soccer in Chesterfield, Virginia.

Above: A Latino family —wife, husband, and child—in New Mexico in 1943, reads a letter announcing that the husband has won second prize in the state stock show for the best ram.

# *La Familia*

**Q:** What is the Latino concept of family?

**A:** While the stereotype is that *la familia latina* adheres to traditional principles, the truth is that various cultures display significant differences across national, ethnic, geographical, and economic lines. These differences are also often related to the kind of work the family does. Agricultural families tend to be more traditional, whereas urban families tend to participate to a greater extent in the American mainstream. Also, significant differences exist in the degree of traditional values held by families of newly arrived immigrants and those whose roots in the United States date back one, two, or three generations. The traditional ideal of a Latino family is one in which the familial unit is privileged over individual needs and desires. The father is the respected head of the family, while the mother is the caring heart. These attitudes stretch back to indigenous ideas of interdependence, modified by Spanish ideas of chivalry and heterosexuality.

Such familial roles are reflected in religious iconography. In Hispanic Catholicism, the mother is fundamental. For example, in Mexico, the Virgin of Guadalupe is the most important religious symbol, surpassing even Jesus Christ. Likewise, millions of Mexican Americans in the United States consider themselves *guadalupanos* (worshippers of the Virgin of Guadalupe). The same kind of religious figures are found in Hispanic Caribbean cultures, which offer myriad motherly icons, such as *La Virgen de la*

Right: A 1940 fiesta in New Mexico celebrating Hispanic folk dances.

*Caridad del Cobre* (the Virgin of Charity), the patron saint of Cuba. The virginity of a household's young women is highly prized and fiercely guarded.

In transitional families, such as first- or second-generation Latinos, women have increased their overt power by becoming wage earners. This may create conflict between couples if the husband struggles with relinquishing the role of complete financial provider for the family.

Above: In Latino families, mothers are considered the central nurturing and spiritual figure.

Left: An altar for Our Lady of Guadalupe—the central figure of Mexican and Mexican American religious and national spirit—surrounded by plants and candles.

“ **To win, one must play like a family.** ”

—*Roberto Clemente (1934–72), legendary Puerto Rican baseball player for the Pittsburgh Pirates*

# Gender Roles

**Q:** What vision of manhood did the Iberians carry to the New World?

**A:** The conquistadors, explorers, and missionaries from the Iberian Peninsula were predominantly men from the region of Extremadura. They highly valued loyalty and bravery and were extremely loyal to their king and devout in their faith. Unlike the British *Mayflower* colonists, they were not escaping religious persecution and did not consider themselves settlers eager to build a new civilization free from national religious authority. The mission of the Spanish was to turn the Americas into ideological and financial satellites of the Spanish Crown. As single men, the conquistadors and explorers engaged freely in sexual relations with indigenous female populations. The result was a large number of children with an Iberian father and an Indian mother: the birth of the *mestizo* civilization.

Christopher Columbus bids farewell to the Queen of Spain as he leaves for the New World on August 3, 1492. Thousands of Spanish colonizers followed in his wake, bringing Iberian Catholic ideas of faith and manhood with them.

**Q:** What is machismo?

**A:** The stereotype of the macho man is not exclusive to Hispanic society. It is pervasive in most Mediterranean civilizations—from Portugal to Spain, Italy, and Greece. Machismo projected itself onto the Americas through the conquest and colonization of Native American populations. The attitude of a macho man usually is represented as aggressive, domineering, and self-confident, in contrast with the caring, gentle, and weaker nature of women. Its representations are everywhere in movies, TV, literature, and art.

**Q:** What is *marianismo*?

**A:** The opposite of machismo is *marianismo*, a philosophy of female self-sacrifice. Its roots are in Iberian Catholicism, which gave women in the Middle Ages and the Renaissance the choice of becoming a nun or a wife. The literature, steeped in abnegation, sacrifice, and total devotion to Jesus Christ—urging women to emulate the virtues of the Virgin Mary in her purity and loyalty—has to some extent transformed *marianismo* into a fountain of religious and spiritual strength. In this tradition, Latina mothers are represented as a center of spirituality.

**Q:** What is the prevalence of single-parent families and divorce among Latino families?

**A:** A number of factors determine the solvency of the Latino family, among them economics, immigration, health, gender, and education. As divorce rates rise among the general American population, comparisons have been made to Latinos and Latino national subgroups. The most significant factor affecting marriage stability is migration patterns. Populations with a continuous influx of new immigrants, especially those of the Catholic faith, such as the majority of Mexicans, tend to adhere more strongly to traditional unions. Migration and adapting to new ways of life also increase stress levels, which in turn destabilize marriages. Among Puerto Ricans, for example, migrant women have much higher rates of divorce than women born on the island who raised their families there. The majority of Latino single-parent families are headed by women; those headed by men are fewer than 10 percent.

In 2004 the Pew Hispanic Center released a report on assimilation and language. Interesting differences were highlighted among families who spoke varying degrees of English. For example, 47 percent of Spanish-dominant Latinos considered divorce acceptable, compared to 63 percent of bilinguals, 67 percent of English-dominant and 72 percent of non-Latinos. In this case, with increased English-dominance came values that closely mirrored mainstream non-Latino Americans. Interestingly, when asked about having children without

The symbolism of the Virgin Mary and Child runs deep in Hispanic Catholicism.

being married, Spanish-dominant Latinos and non-Latinos thought similarly; just 49 percent of the former deemed it acceptable compared to 55 percent of the latter. Bilingual and English-dominant Latinos were more accepting—60 percent among the former and 67 percent among the latter. Language is linked to social values in complex ways.

**In order to give orders, one needs to know how to obey.**

—*Teresa de Avila,*
*sixteenth-century Spanish saint*

# Impressions of Childhood

A Latino father plays the guitar with his daughter in San Antonio, Texas, in 1934.

Education is a priority among many Latino families, but linguistic and cultural limitations often prevent Latino children from taking full advantage of school. Public school systems are often unequipped to deal with non-native English speakers.

**Q: How do Latinos regard *la niñez* (childhood)?**

**A:** Hispanic cultures respect and prize children and their relationships with their mothers. Childhood is understood as an impression-able, developmental stage, in which the individual absorbs the moral values needed to function in a series of societal institutions: the family (first and foremost), the school, and the religious center. Children are surrounded by a kind of reverence in some cultures, addressed in the formal form of Spanish, and referred to as *mamá* (mommy) and *papá* (daddy).

**Q: How do Latino children differ from children in other populations?**

**A:** As a result of the growth of the Latino community in the United States, the number of children of Hispanic descent has increased faster than any other ethnic group. In the first decade of the twenty-first century, 35 percent of the Latino population will be composed of children. This number is expected to remain steady at least until 2025.

Poverty is the most significant factor affecting the lives of Latino children. In 2000, a stunning 27 percent of Latino children under the age of eighteen lived in poverty. In these children's families,

linguistic and cultural limitations often give rise to difficulty at school and increase the risk of creating high school dropouts. To survive financially, often both parents work two or even three jobs.

**Q: What illnesses affect Latino children?**

**A:** Highly correlated with poverty and directly caused by poor diets (large amounts of sugar and fast food) and lack of activity, diabetes is on the rise among all children in the United States. However, Latino children are more severely affected than other populations. As immigrants adopt the common U.S. diet, they increase their risk of obesity. In addition, Latinos also live, for the most part, in cities where

play spaces are limited and may not be located in safe areas. Also, the transition from a home culture to a strange environment where familiar language and customs are little known often leads to anxiety and disorientation.

## Q: Is there child labor among Latinos?

A: The history of Latino children working in factories and in the fields is not well documented but extends back to *bracero* children who were employed in agriculture in the World War II era and *jíbaro* children who emigrated in the mid-twentieth century. Today almost all farmworkers in the United States are Latino, with nearly 80 percent Mexican. The Fair Labor Standards Act permits children to work in the fields with a parent at age twelve and by themselves at age fourteen. According to the United Farm Workers Union, around 800,000 underage children were employed in the United States in 2000. The General Accounting Office put it at 300,000, and the Census Bureau at 155,000. Many of these child laborers suffer work-related injuries; children account for nearly 20 percent of farm fatalities. They are also exposed to harmful pesticides. As pesticide-level standards are set by the EPA for adults, children who are much smaller are, accordingly, more greatly affected. Sanitary conditions are often poor, and work may interrupt schooling.

Note that child labor is not illegal; however, certain types of work are proscribed and children's hours are limited. For example, children are not allowed to operate or work near heavy machinery, nor can they work during school hours.

A 1910 photo of eight-year-old Peula Amava working in cranberry fields while school is in session in Delaware.

# Las Gangas

Public spaces are targets for gang members marking territory. This particular column is freshly tagged daily.

**Q:** **What are the roles and prevalence of gangs among adolescent Latinos?**

**A:** Adolescence is a period of transition. As the body undergoes changes, the individual also seeks to understand what place he or she might have in society. With the increasing number of broken families among the poor, adolescents look for ways to validate their identities by forming alliances with other disadvantaged youths. In cities large and small, the result is often the creation of groups with hierarchical structures, sometimes violent initiation processes, strong group loyalty, and the special function of a clan or family. These groups often engage in illegal activities. This phenomenon is known among Latinos as *gangas*, the Spanglish word for gangs.

Several hundred Los Angeles gang members, gathered in an auditorium during a "gang truce" rally in 1996, turn their heads to view information about health, educational, and legal advice.

Gangs have political, aesthetic, moral, gender, and psychological components. Reacting to the poverty and oppression within their environment—and perhaps the lack of opportunities to engage positively in the larger society—these urban youths are eager for attention. Some scholars contend that Latino gangs date back to the early parts of the twentieth century when seditious, sometimes revolutionary outlaws resisted and reacted to the Treaty of Guadalupe Hidalgo, the Spanish-American War, and other experiences in Latino history, in unorthodox and illegal ways.

Gangs often dismiss political channels as a way to express their grievances; their frustrations might be too vague to find a political target. Their primary interests are loyalty, tradition, and turf. Latino gangs fight for control of a particular territory, especially when several gangs are in close proximity. Many gangs that began as local entities, like many fraternal social organizations, have spread nationwide and can be found in urban, suburban, and rural areas. Gangs are commonly involved in the drug trade or some other income-earning illegal activity. Leaders are honored through a system of gifts and "taxes." Gangs distinguish themselves through their choice of dress, public symbols, and a type of self-created graffiti language with which they mark public spaces.

## Q: Are all gangs the same?

A: Since the 1980s, and the rise of gang cultures, gangs have diversified considerably in their aims, clothing style, initiation rites, inclusion or exclusion of females (some gangs are women only), governance, and leadership. Considerable differences exist between West Coast and East Coast gangs, and between Chicano and Puerto Rican gangs, for example.

## Q: How have Latino gangs been represented to the public?

A: Latino gangs have received considerable publicity since the 1980s and 1990s, including a few key books and movies that both informed mainstream Americans about Latino gangs and fed into stereotypes of Latino youths as aggressive and violent. Movies include *Boulevard Nights* (1979), *American Me* (1992), and *Blood In, Blood Out: Bound by Honor* (1993); books include *Always Running: La Vida Loca, Gang Days in L.A.* (1993) by Luis Rodriguez. Perhaps the forerunner was *West Side Story* (1961), originally a Broadway musical by Arthur Laurents, Stephen Sondheim, and Leonard Bernstein that opened in 1957. Gang formation and participation appears to be higher among ethnic minorities—Chicanos, Puerto Ricans, blacks, American Indians, and Filipinos—than Caucasians. In the early part of the twentieth century, however, the Irish, Jews, and Italians were also heavily involved in gangs. Economic exclusion and disenfranchisement, and the need for an ethnic group to "stick together" for protection, play large roles in the formation of gangs; these factors are a greater influence than membership in any particular ethnic group. In the case of adolescent gangs, surging hormones and the normal desire of young people to belong to a prominent group also play an important part.

Top: Chita Rivera dances with Ken Leroy in the Broadway hit *West Side Story*. Bottom: Rita Moreno singing "America" in the movie version of *West Side Story*.

# Views on Sexuality

A young woman at her first communion, c. 1900.

men are allowed, even encouraged, to experiment sexually. The Pew Hispanic Center has found that when other variables such as country of origin and years lived in the United States are removed from the equation, language remains a defining factor when it comes to social values. Spanish-dominant Latinos have more conservative views about homosexuality (only 16 percent find it acceptable, compared with 38 percent of English-dominant Latinos); and 95 percent of the former group think children should live at home until married, compared with 52 percent of the latter group.

**Q:** What is the approach to abortion and birth control?

**A:** Religious, particularly Catholic, upbringing among Latinos creates opposition to abortion; nevertheless, using numbers from the Alan Guttmacher Institute, the group Hispanic Americans for Life calculated that in the year 2000 Latinas accounted for 20.1 percent of abortions, although they make up only 12.8 percent of the nation's women of childbearing age. The Latino community has various opinions about abortion. For example, Cuban Americans tend to be more pro-choice than other Latinos.

Several methods of birth control are available to women. Surveys find that although one-quarter of Latinas between the ages of fifteen and forty-four use birth control pills regularly, Hispanic and black women are more likely than white women to be sterilized. Neither of these

**Q:** Is sexuality a forbidden topic in Latino cultures?

**A:** The typical Catholic Latino family culture tends to be a tight, conservative nuclear unit. Religion tends to keep the topics of sexuality and eroticism from general discussion. Although extramarital sex is not sanctioned, a double standard sometimes exists: Women must remain virgins until they are married, but single

methods control the spread of sexually transmitted diseases, however, and 65 percent of Latinas with HIV report having contracted the virus through unprotected sex.

## Q: In general, how do Latinos understand homosexuality?

A: Homosexuality is commonly viewed as the reverse of machismo. Gays, both female and male, may be ridiculed, ostracized, and even attacked by members of their families, acquaintances, and strangers. In the past ten to fifteen years, gay and lesbian organizations have had some success in reducing discrimination in Latino communities. A number of artistic, literary, and theatrical representations of gay and lesbian life have helped educate the public. The difficulty of being homosexual and Latino is discussed in books like Gloria Anzaldúa's *Borderlands/La Frontera* (1987), Achy Obejas's *We Came All the Way from Cuba So You Could Dress Like This?* (1994), John Rechy's *City of Night* (1963), Jaime Manrique's *Eminent*

*Maricones* (1999), Luis Alfaro's plays, and the essays of Richard Rodriguez.

## Q: Who is Richard Rodriguez?

A: Born in 1944, Richard Rodriguez, a gay and devoutly Catholic Mexican American, is one of the most controversial contemporary Latino intellectuals. He has written an autobiographical trilogy in which he challenges many liberal ideas and discusses the roles of religion and homosexuality in his life. His debut volume, *Hunger of Memory* (1982), contained an attack on bilingual education and affirmative action. He wrote two more books, *Days of Obligation* (1992) and *Brown* (2002). Rodriguez is a cultural commentator for radio and a public television (PBS) nightly news program.

A 2004 scene from a *quinceañera*, a fifteenth birthday party and welcoming into adulthood for Latina girls. Each rose held by attendants will later be given to the celebrant's mother, thanking her for giving fifteen years of her life to the raising of her child.

A sign at a year 2000 anti-abortion protest in Managua, Nicaragua, reads, "They are forgetting someone."

# Old Age and Death

Bottom, left: Dominoes is
a favorite pastime among
older Caribbean Latinos.

Bottom, right: Two 1943
scenes from the family
of the mayor of Trampas,
New Mexico. The mayor's
wife spins wool by the
fire (top) and his father,
ninety-nine years old, sits
in the living room.

**Q: How are the elderly treated
in Latino families?**

**A:** The nuclear Latino family remains
significantly stronger than the contemporary American model, and separation
of parents and children is much less
frequent. The elderly tend to live with
relatives as respected members of the
household. They are called to participate
in child care, cooking, religious, and
educational activities.

**Q: Is there a unified conception
of death among Latinos?**

**A:** Latinos comprise many ethnicities
and are members of many religions,
thus they have no single idea or
concept of death and the afterlife.
Pre-Columbian tribes like the Nahuatl
believed profoundly in the afterlife.
Aztecs, like many Christians, believed
that the way a person lived dictates
their experiences after death. Soldiers

A Day of the Dead altar in a Mexican home, complete with sweets and offerings for deceased family members.

who perished on the battlefield were believed to enter a special sphere, as did women who died during pregnancy or while giving birth. Indigenous views changed in the five hundred years of interaction with and domination by Roman Catholic Iberian culture. The Spaniards were engaged in rituals based on the story of Christ: To suffer in life is to achieve a better life after death. Belief in the afterlife and a desire to communicate with deceased relatives have produced holidays like the Mexican *Día de los Muertos*, the Day of the Dead, also known as All Saints' Day, celebrated on November 1 and 2. Mexican Americans spend the nights eating, chatting, and celebrating at the cemetery where relatives are buried.

**Q: What kinds of representations of death are available in Latino art and letters?**

**A:** The *calavera* (skeleton) is a pervasive pop icon in Latino culture. It appears on stickers, posters, key chains, cartoons, piñatas, and T-shirts. It is also present in murals and paintings, such as the artwork of Frida Kahlo. Death as a character shows up in *pastorelas*, Nativity plays staged during the Christmas season. In movies, the *calavera* is present in Luis Valdez's *Zoot Suit* (1981), and in literature it is explored in books like *The Labyrinth of Solitude* by Octavio Paz (1961) and *The Hispanic Condition* by Ilan Stavans (1995).

A "Catrina" sculpture, invented by José Guadalupe Posada, the father of the Mexican *calavera,* or skeleton icon. "Catrina" is a sarcastic name for a wealthy person.

**CHAPTER 8**

# RELIGION

Faith plays a major role in the lives of Spanish-speaking people around the world. Strict Iberian Catholicism was brought by Spaniards and Portuguese to the New World, but its encounter with indigenous practices in the Americas resulted in a religious transculturation—elements of the conqueror's saints and beliefs intermingled with the rituals and world views of the conquered. Enter a church in San José, Medellín, or Caracas and you will see the graphic suffering of Jesus Christ. Also present is an abundance of saints with dark skin, indigenous features, and names unknown to Iberian Catholicism. This kind of religious hybridization is reflected in the Catholicism that Latino immigrants have brought with them to the United States. Latin America has seen Protestant and evangelical sects making significant inroads in its cities and towns, while Spanish-language churches have sprung up in Latino neighborhoods in the United States. Latinos also practice faiths other than Christianity, including Judaism, Islam, and Buddhism. In all cases, religion helps define everyday life—from education to sexuality.

Left: Cuban pilgrims walking from the shrine of *La Virgen de la Caridad del Cobre* in Cobre, Cuba.

Above: 2006 Nigerian Osun Oshogbo Festival.

# Saints and Crosses

**Q:** What was the status of Catholicism in Spain in 1492?

**A:** When Columbus set sail, Spain was bringing to a close *La Reconquista,* the religious and territorial "reconquest" of the land from the Moors. The Holy Office of the Inquisition offered forced conversions or death to any remaining Moors, Jews, and pagans—including suspected witches. Once in the New World, the ostensible quest of the conquistadors and missionaries was to spread the Christian gospel; through the teaching of the doctrine of salvation through Jesus Christ, they hoped to convert and "civilize" the Indians, who were, in the eyes of the Spanish, idolatrous and barbarous. Spaniards committed themselves to *catecismo* (catechism).

Right: The Santo Domingo church in San Cristóbal de las Casas, Chiapas, Mexico.

Below: The preserved ruins of the Alhambra, the last Moorish stronghold to fall to Catholic Spain, lit up at night.

The first explorers, all Catholic, of what are now the states of Florida, Louisiana, Texas, and California established hundreds of missions. Accordingly, by the mid-nineteenth century, when the Treaty of Guadalupe Hidalgo and the Gadsden Purchase were signed, the population of the Southwest was predominantly Catholic.

**Q:** What kinds of pre-Columbian religion existed in the Americas, and how did those belief systems adapt to the imposition of Catholicism?

**A:** In the mid-fifteenth century, the two largest empires in the Americas were the Aztecs in central Mexico and the Incas in the Andean region. The Maya, once a powerful regime in Mesoamerica, had already been reduced to a small force in the Yucatán Peninsula. The indigenous religions were polytheistic, worshipping numerous deities believed to control the natural world and the afterlife. Many aspects of daily life were ritualized and based upon precise astrological alignments; like the ancient Greeks, American Indians created altars for specific gods at which they worshipped them and tried to please them with offerings. During the colonial period, with Catholicism thrust upon them, indigenous populations adapted their gods to fit the images of Catholic saints. Religious iconography in the New World was far more graphic; depictions of the crucifixion of Jesus tend to emphasize his wounds, to include visible signs of suffering, and to display more blood. Over time, indigenous peoples adopted some Catholic beliefs, while maintaining meaningful ancient practices.

Through the missions like the one in Saint Augustine, Florida, where Native Americans were primarily used for manual labor, Iberian priests taught their new subjects Catholic ethics and brought them to the Christian faith. Until the Mexican Revolution, they commonly used Pérez de Pineda's version of the Bible. A number of other translations, mostly produced in Spain, have since been used in the United States. The so-called *Reina Valera,* translated in 1909, is considered by millions of Spanish-speaking Catholics to be "*la palabra de Dios en español*" ("the word of God in Spanish").

## Q: What Spanish versions of the Bible circulated in the New World?

A: In 1551, an edict by the Holy Office of the Inquisition forbade the translation of the Old and New Testaments into Spanish because the church considered Latin the only language appropriate for communicating with the divine and the only language holy enough to communicate about the divine. Nevertheless, the Bible was translated into Spanish. The earliest Spanish version (originally published in Basel, Switzerland, in 1569) used in the Americas is known as *La Biblia del Oso*; the translator was Casiodoro de Reina.

Cover of *La Biblia del Oso*, the first Spanish-language Bible used in the Americas, translated by Casiodoro de Reina.

**Fanaticism is redoubling your efforts when you've forgotten your aim.**
—GEORGE SANTAYANA, FROM LIFE OF REASON *(1905)*

# *La Virgen*

## Q: What is *guadalupanismo*?

**A:** Mexican Catholicism centered on the Virgin of Guadalupe, and its further expression in *guadalupanismo* translates into the worship of the Virgin and the social and nationlistic use of her image. Her image was widespread during colonial times but acquired nationalistic overtones during the war of independence against Spain in 1810. Father Miguel Hidalgo y Costilla, the leader of the revolution, literally rang the bell of freedom—*el grito de Dolores*—and marched with a banner of the Virgin. Subsequently, her image was used by Pancho Villa, Emiliano Zapata, and other revolutionary figures. Politicians, too, embraced her. Her iconography touches every aspect of society, and her image appears on calendars, in movies, and on cigarette boxes, to name a few.

The Virgin of Guadalupe

## Q: What is the legend behind the Virgin of Guadalupe?

**A:** On December 12, 1531, about a decade after the fall of Tenochtitlán, the Aztec capital, the Virgin, eventually called "Queen of Mexico" and "Empress of the Americans" (other names include *La Virgen de Tepeyac, Santa María de Guadalupe, La Criolla, La Guadalupana, La Virgen Ranchera, La Morena, La Criolla,* and *La Pastora*), appeared to Juan Diego, an indigenous peasant, in Mount Tepeyac, near what is today Mexico City. She appeared in what was a shrine to the Aztec goddess Tonantzín. The apparition said she was the Virgin Mary and was accompanied by singing voices. Her silhouette and halo appeared a total of seven times. She told Juan Diego to visit the bishop of Mexico City, Juan de Zumárraga, and request the building of a temple in her honor. The temple, she said, would celebrate her embrace of the Mexican people: She promised to support them in their misery. Juan Diego visited Zumárraga but was sent away. He returned to the Virgin and told her of his rejection. She then asked him to pick some roses from a nearby bush that seldom bloomed at that time year, put them in his cloak, and take them to the bishop. When Juan Diego took them from his cloak in front of Zumárraga, the image of the Virgin materialized. A temple was subsequently built, and the Virgin of Guadalupe was canonized as the principal Catholic symbol of Mexico.

The Virgin Mary has small theological importance in the New Testament. The Trinity—the Father, the Son, and the Holy Spirit—command full attention, with Jesus Christ as the focus. The female half of the world is downplayed. Popular sentiment in Mexico, however, elevates the figure of Mary in her indigenous incarnation.

The most significant aspect of the Virgin of Guadalupe is that she is a *mestiza*. As is usual in this type of religious iconography, most of the body is covered except her face and hands, which are invariably brown-skinned. Thus, the Mexican variant of Spanish Catholicism adapted to the needs of a mixed-raced population. Additionally, her messages to Juan Diego establish her embrace of the humble and impoverished.

The Virgin's status as "Queen of Mexico" has expanded to "Mother of Chicanos." Her image appears in Mexican neighborhoods in the United States and broadly across the Southwest on Mexico's Independence Day, September 16, and also on César Chávez Day, March 31. Chávez displayed her image during labor strikes next to the UFW flag. In literature, she is famously represented in Rodolfo Anaya's *Bless Me Última* (1973).

Above: Statues of Juan Diego and Bishop Juan de Zumárraga in front of Los Angeles's St. Teresa of Avila church.

Left: Dolores Huerta (center in black jacket) joins UFW members during a Los Angeles rally on March 26, 2006, celebrating the birthday of César Chávez. An image of the Virgin of Guadalupe is displayed above the marchers.

# Santería

**Q:** What is Santería?

**A:** Also known as *Regla de Ocha*, Santería, which comprises Yoruba and Catholic elements, is a widespread Afro-Caribbean religion practiced in Cuba. During the colonial period, church-sponsored institutions, known as *cabildos*, formed; the church separated white and African groups but, significantly, permitted dark-skinned people to organize and govern their own *cabildos*. In these family-like institutions, the hybridization of Yoruba and Roman Catholic practices flourished. Saints, Jesus Christ, and the Virgin Mary were made parallel with Yoruba deities known as *orishas* or *santos* (saints). Almost every Catholic saint has a corresponding *orisha*. *Orishas* include *Ochún*, the goddess of water and sensuality; *Obatalá*, the god of purity and justice; and *Babalú Ayé*, a god of morality and healing. The central divine figure is *Olodumare*. Worshippers, called *santeros*, believe their prayers will cause divine intervention in natural and human affairs. High priests are called *babalaos*. Rituals include intense dancing and animal sacrifice.

**Q:** What important virgin figures have emerged from Afro-Caribbean religions?

**A:** *La Virgen de la Caridad del Cobre*, the Virgin of Charity, the patron saint of Cuba, is at the core of Afro-Caribbean religion. She became a national icon in 1916, after the Spanish-American War; Pope John Paul II officially acknowledged her on January 24, 1998, in Santiago de Cuba.

Below: Cuban drummers participate in a Santería ceremony.

Right: Pope John Paul II examines the statue of the Virgin of Charity of Cobre shortly before saying mass during his 1998 visit to Cuba.

Far right: A *santero* performs a ritual under the watchful eye of his *babalao*.

She is almost always portrayed with three children at her feet. Myth states that a statue of her was found around 1607 by three ten-year-old boys (the three Juanes), two indigenous and one black slave. They were on their way from the village of Barajagua to Nipe Bay in search of salt to cure meat. Once they returned to their village, they placed the statue in a hermitage. Seven times the statue disappeared in the night and reappeared in the morning. The villagers interpreted the event as a sign that she wanted to be placed in a better site. She was moved near the copper mines, where a basilica was built.

At times she is represented as a *mestiza*, others as a mulatta. The region where she was placed was inhabited by African slaves who imbued their prayers with animistic elements. *La Virgen de la Caridad del Cobre* is an incarnation of *Ochún*.

> **The indifference of the Mexican toward death is nurtured by his indifference to life.**
> —OCTAVIO PAZ, FROM THE LABRYINTH OF SOLITUDE *(1950)*

# Beyond Catholicism

**Q:** How common is Protestantism among Latinos?

**A:** Today, roughly 74 percent of Latinos are Catholics, though percentages vary across ethnic lines, while approximately 22 percent identify themselves as Protestant; the balance practice other religions or are agnostic or atheist. The influence of Protestantism in Latin America has been on the rise since the end of the nineteenth century. American soldiers brought varieties of Protestantism to the Caribbean Basin and Central America during the Spanish-American War and in subsequent invasions in the twentieth century. Evangelicals have made inroads, especially Pentecostals, through intensive missionary work. The use of TV as a messianic tool has been quite successful. At the end of the twentieth century, an estimated 15.5 percent of Mexican Americans were Protestants, 10.2 percent of Cuban Americans, and 10 percent of Puerto Ricans on the mainland. The expansion is partly a response to the corruption and sex scandals in the Catholic Church in the late twentieth century, but is also a reflection of the significant impact Protestants have made on Latin America.

**Q:** How common is Judaism in Latin America?

**A:** Approximately 400,000 Jews live in the Spanish- and Portuguese-speaking countries in the Western Hemisphere. The largest concentration is in Argentina, where a sizable immigrant wave from Eastern Europe (Poland, Lithuania, the Ukraine, etc.) and Russia settled between 1880 and 1920. The second- and third-largest populations are in Brazil and Mexico. In colonial times, Mexico and Peru were the most cosmopolitan centers in the hemisphere, and crypto-Jews—individuals who kept their Judaism secret out of fear of the Inquisition—were known to seek refuge in those countries.

**Q:** What percentage of Latinos in the United States are Jewish?

**A:** The U.S. Census Bureau does not classify people according to religion. According to other sources, the number is less than 1 percent. According to the Anti-Defamation League, a Jewish organization, close to 50 percent of Latino immigrants to the United States hold strong anti-Semitic opinions. That percentage decreases in the second and third generations.

A Protestant preacher in *La Casa de Jehová* (The House of God).

## Q: Are there Islamic Latinos?

A: Spanish cuisine, art, dance, and architecture demonstrate the enormous influence of Arabic/Moorish culture on the Iberian peninsula. Spanish words like *almohada* and *zanahoria* have Arabic roots. After the Crusades and *La Reconquista*, Islam was eradicated from the region and its contributions nearly erased. The Americas, through Spanish conquest, inherited some of these embedded contributions. In modern times, Muslims from Egypt, Syria, Lebanon, Iraq, and elsewhere have established themselves in Latin American countries, including Argentina, Colombia, and Mexico. Their communities are small, though Islam is gaining some converts among Latinos in the United States. Organizations like the Latino American Dawah (LADO), created in 1997 in New York City, are devoted to educating people about the Muslim world and its religion.

## Q: When was the Quran translated into Spanish?

A: The Quran was translated into Latin in the twelfth century by Peter the Venerable, abbot of Cluny, the first Christian to study Islamic sources. Part of the book was translated into Spanish for the first time in the nineteenth century.

Left: A rabbi in Catalonia, Spain, carries the Torah.

Right: Muslims prostrated in prayer in a Mexican mosque.

# Biographies

Throughout this book, path-breaking and important Latinos have been mentioned in the context of their historical period and areas of impact. In the following section, individuals who are not mentioned or whose importance is not sufficiently covered in the chapters are highlighted. These short biographies display not only the diversity of background but also of talent and vision among the heterogeneous Latino population.

## Arts and Letters

**Baca, Judith (b. 1946)**
Muralist, visual artist, arts administrator, and community and arts activist, Baca, a native of Los Angeles, is best known for her boldly colored and politically charged mural: *Great Wall of Los Angeles: A Site of Public Memory* (1976–83) in North Hollywood; it depicts a multiethnic history of the city from prehistoric times to the 1950s.

## Television, Film, and Theater

**Arnaz, Desi (1917–86)**
Cuban musician turned television star and executive. In 1940 he married actress Lucille Ball; in 1951 the couple premiered in *I Love Lucy*. They established Desilu Productions and produced several additional TV shows together until they divorced in 1960.

**Cantinflas (1911–93)**
Born Mario Moreno, Cantinflas was a Mexican comedian who became world famous. Early in his career he worked in vaudeville; by the 1940s, his Mexican comedies hit movie screens in the United States. He was wildly popular in the Southwest. Charlie Chaplin once called him "the funniest man in the world."

**Campeche, José (1751–1806)**
The preeminent Puerto Rican painter of the colonial era. Of Afro-Caribbean ancestry, Campeche was praised for his religious paintings but is best known as a portraitist who depicted well-known personalities and interior settings.

**Castaneda, Carlos (1925–98)**
Peruvian-born author most widely known for his best-selling book *The Teachings of Don Juan: A Yaqui Way of Knowledge* (1968), which was based on his apprenticeship with a Yaqui Indian shaman. His scholarship and authenticity later came to be questioned, and he is now a controversial Latino figure.

**Dorfman, Ariel (b. 1942)**
Argentine-born descendant of Eastern European Jews, Dorfman was a left-wing intellectual in Chile's Salvador Allende government. He was forced into exile after Augusto Pinochet's 1973 coup. He is the author of numerous books on popular Latin American culture; he has also published novels, poetry, and plays.

**Fornés, María Irene (b. 1930)**
Cuban theater pioneer. Her first play was staged in the United States in 1961. The author of more than thirty plays, including musicals, she often tackles issues of sexuality with mordant humor.

**Kreutzberger, Mario (b. 1940)**
Also known as Don Francisco, the Chilean Kreutzberger is the most-recognized Spanish-language TV personality in the United States. His shows include the three-hour *Sábado Gigante* (Huge Saturday), with an audience of nearly one hundred million. In 2001, he was honored with a star on the Hollywood Walk of Fame.

## Arts and Letters

**Ferré, Rosario (b. 1938)** Puerto Rican writer of novels, plays, poems, short stories, and essays with feminist themes. She publishes in both Spanish and English; the transition to the latter was well-noted by her Puerto Rican and Latin American fans. Her 1995 *House on the Lagoon* was nominated for a National Book Award.

**Hostos, Eugenio María de (1839–1903)** Foremost Puerto Rican reformer, essayist, and intellectual of the twentieth century. He championed the liberation of Puerto Rico and Cuba from Spain; the abolition of slavery; robust education for both sexes; and the formation of egalitarian democracies. He traveled in exile throughout Latin America and lived in New York City, establishing newspapers and, in the Dominican Republic, the first teachers' college.

**Lee, Muna (1895–1965)** Pioneering translator, author, Pan-Americanist, feminist, and government official. For more than twenty-five years she was married to Luis Muñoz Marín, future governor of Puerto Rico. A poet, she actively translated Latin American literature and published her work. In 1941, she was named cultural ambassador between the U.S. government and Latin American countries.

## Television, Film, and Theater

**Nava, Gregory (b. 1949)** Of Mexican and Basque ancestry, one of the most successful Latino filmmakers of his time. His initial acclaim came with the 1984 release of *El Norte* (The United States), about Guatemalan immigrants struggling to make it in the United States; the film won an Oscar for best screenplay. His successful crossover films include *Selena* (1997), which he directed, and *Frida* (2002)—he collaborated on the screenplay; Salma Hayek, who played the title character, won an Oscar.

**Marin, Cheech (b. 1946)** Irreverent Chicano humorist, actor, and private collector of Mexican American art, Marin is famous for his partnership with Asian American Tommy Chong and their low-budget, popular "Cheech and Chong" movies. After the duo split up, he directed and acted in several important Hollywood movies such as *Born in East L.A.* (1987) and *The Original Latin Kings of Comedy* (2003), which treat Latino themes.

**Quirarte, Jacinto (b. 1931)**
Specialist in the history and criticism of pre-Columbian, Latin American, and Latino arts. He has published an extensive body of scholarship; his seminal work, *Mexican-American Artists* (1973), was the first book devoted to the topic. Through the twenty-first century he has continued to publish on a variety of art forms, both European and Hispanic.

**Limón, José (1908–72)**
Acclaimed Mexican dancer and choreographer; founded the still-vibrant José Limón Dance Company in 1946. One work that explores his ancestry is *La Malinche* (the story of Hernán Cortés and his Indian mistress Doña María). He drew from several artistic sources and is noted for transforming the role of the male in American dance.

**Rivera, Chita (b. 1933)**
Rivera, an American-born Puerto Rican Broadway singer, dancer, actress, and winner of two Tony awards, was accepted into George Balanchine's American School of Ballet as a young woman. She performed in many popular Broadway plays including *West Side Story* in 1957. In 2002, she was the first Latino to be accorded the Kennedy Center Honors.

**Portillo, Lourdes (b. 1944)**
Acclaimed Chicana filmmaker, Portillo concentrates on Latino identity primarily through documentary films. An early apprenticeship with Cine Manifest served as both a filmmaking and political education. Her 1986 *Las Madres de la Plaza de Mayo* (The Mothers of the Plaza de Mayo), which tells the story of the mothers of those who were "disappeared" during Argentina's "dirty war" (1976–83), was nominated for an Oscar.

**Valens, Ritchie (1941–59)**
Valens, who had shortened his surname from Valenzuela to Valens, began his professional career in 1958. He died in a plane crash with Buddy Holly in 1959 just shy of his eighteenth birthday. Despite such a short recording career, his influence is still felt in rock 'n' roll, especially his great hit *La Bamba*, a *son jarocho* song from Veracruz, Mexico. In 1987, producer Luis Valdez made a movie of the performer's life.

## Science and Politics

### Alvarez, Luis Walter (1911–88)

Nobel Prize–winner in physics in 1968 for developing the liquid hydrogen bubble chamber and detecting new resonant states in particle physics, which eventually led to the theory of quarks, Alvarez, of Spanish descent, had previously been part of the Manhattan Project that created the first atomic bomb.

### Chavez, Linda (b. 1947)

A New Mexico native, Chavez began her career with the American Federation of Teachers. In 1983, while she was still a Democrat, President Reagan appointed her to be staff director of the U.S. Commission on Civil Rights; in 1985 she switched her party affiliation to Republican. She was President George W. Bush's first choice for secretary of labor, but personal issues caused her to withdraw from consideration. Currently, she is a conservative political analyst for Fox News, radio talk show host, and chair of the Center for Equal Opportunity.

## Sports and Music

### Bauzá, Mario (1911–93)

Founder and leading figure of Afro-Cuban jazz, a musician, composer, and arranger, Bauzá was born in Cuba, settling in New York in 1930. Classically trained and with big-band experience, he wrote "Tanga," considered to be one of the first Afro-Cuban jazz pieces, in 1943.

### Canseco, José (b. 1964)

Cuban-born and Miami-raised, this baseball star was the first big-league hitter to hit forty home runs and steal forty bases in a season (1988). He helped lead the Oakland Athletics to a World Series in 1989. Controversial but popular, Canseco, after he retired, admitted he had used steriods.

**Mas Canosa, Jorge (1939–97)**
A rags-to-riches Cuban immigrant who had fled Castro's revolution and became the most influential Cuban American in the United States, Mas Canosa founded the Cuban American National Foundation (CANF) in 1981 to promote the transition from communism to democracy in Cuba. He politically enabled the start-up of Radio Martí (a Miami-based station designed to create anti-Castro sentiment in Cuba) and successfully lobbied for the tightening of economic sanctions against his home country.

**Muñoz Marín, Luis (1898–1980)**
Son of a Puerto Rican politician, Muñoz Marín grew up in Puerto Rico, New York, and Washington, D.C. He married translator, feminist, and government official Muna Lee in 1919. In 1938 he founded the Popular Democratic Party in Puerto Rico and was elected to the Senate in 1940. He championed commonwealth status for the island and was its governor for four terms (1940–64).

**de la Hoya, Oscar (b. 1973)**
The son and grandson of Mexican boxers, de la Hoya won the National Junior Olympic 119-pound championship in 1988. In the 1992 Olympics, he won the only U.S. gold medal in the boxing competition. He is also a singer and was a 2000 Latin Grammy nominee.

**Colón, Willie (b. 1950)**
Bandleader, trombonist, singer, composer, and producer of Puerto Rican descent, Colón was a key figure in the New York City–based development of salsa. He incorporated Puerto Rican *salsero* and superstar-to-be Héctor Lavoe into his band. Recording his first album for the new Fania album when he was sixteen years old, Colón has since produced more than forty albums.

**D'Rivera, Paquito (b. 1948)**
Sensational Cuban bandleader and saxophonist who had played with his country's top musicians by the age of fifteen, D'Rivera is regarded as the most influential Latin jazz saxophonist playing today—especially since his move to New York City. He is also renowned as a clarinetist.

## Science and Politics

**Ochoa, Ellen (b. 1958)**
Scientist, engineer, and first Latina astronaut in history, Ochoa has traveled into space at least four times. Earlier in her career, she worked for a NASA research center where she developed optical systems and computer programs. She has received many scientific and civic awards.

## Sports and Music

**Lavoe, Héctor (1946–93)**
A Puerto Rican salsa vocalist known to his fans as *"El Cantante de Los Cantantes"* (The Singer's Singer). In New York City in 1967 he was introduced to Willie Colón, and they subsequently had an extremely productive eight-year partnership. Their lyrics explored Puerto Rican and Nuyorican subcultures. Lavoe became a successful solo artist as well as a member of the Fania All Stars (1968–88).

**Estefan, Gloria (b. 1957)**
Cuban pop music sensation who topped both Latin and English music charts in the 1980s and 1990s, Estefan got her start as part of the group Miami Sound Machine with her husband. They had their breakout hit, *Primitive Love,* in 1981; she has produced twenty-four albums and won five Grammy Awards since.

**Kid Chocolate (1910–88)**
Born Eligio Sardinias-Montalbo, Kid Chocolate was a legendary boxer who, in 1931, became the first Cuban to win a world championship title. He faced discrimination in the United States because of his dark skin. In 1994 he was post-humously inducted into the International Boxing Hall of Fame.

### Molina, Mario (b. 1943)

First Mexican-born winner of the Nobel Prize for chemistry (1995). Molina and Sherwood Rowland (who was also named by the Nobel committee) were on the cutting edge of studying the harmful effects of chlorofluorocarbons (CFCs) on the ozone layer in 1974. In 1994 he was appointed scientific adviser to the Clinton administration. He is professor emeritus at the Massachusetts Institute of Technology.

### Pantoja, Antonia (1922–2002)

A Puerto Rican activist and education pioneer, Pantoja founded the advocacy organization Aspira and the Universidad Boricua in Washington, D.C. Originally a teacher in rural Puerto Rico, she founded the Puerto Rican Forum in 1957 to attempt to reform the education of her fellow migrants. President Clinton awarded her the Presidential Medal of Freedom in 1996.

### Sosa, Sammy (b. 1968)

A Dominican baseball legend who signed with the Texas Rangers at age sixteen, Sosa broke a record in 1998 when he hit sixty-six home runs and was named the National League's MVP. He repeated the more-than-sixty feat in 1999 and is the only player to have done so in two seasons. In 2005 he became number five on the all-time record list for lifetime home runs. Some controversy surrounded his career, including accusations of spousal abuse and using a corked bat.

### Santana, Carlos (b. 1947)

Santana, a Mexican-American guitar virtuoso and rock icon, was influenced by blues musicians and Latin jazz artists. His break came in 1966 when he was invited to jam at a concert, promoted by Bill Graham, at Fillmore West in San Francisco. Graham gave Santana and his band a chance to perform at the 1969 Woodstock Festival. In 1970, their second album, containing "Black Magic Woman" and *"Oye Como Va"* by Tito Puente, was a quadruple-platinum seller. Santana received his first Grammy in 1988; in 2000 he took home eight.

### Puente, Tito (1923–2000)

A musical prodigy—percussion, piano, vibraphone, saxophone—and seminal figure in the history of Latin music, Puente made 120 recordings ranging from original Cuban *sons* to Americanized Latin music. He developed a huge fan base for Latin music; in the 1950s he was crowned *el rey de mambo* (the mambo king) by fans, and he later contributed significantly to Latin jazz. When a young Carlos Santana recorded Puente's *"Oye Como Va,"* the composer gained worldwide fame.

# Milestones

The early chapters of this book depict the eras of colonization and early integration of Latinos into the United States, but many chapters are arranged thematically. The following chronology spans the entire course of Latino history in the United States, drawing attention to the works and achievements of individuals, as well as events with large-scale impact such as the Spanish-American War, the Zoot Suit Riots, the Chicano Movement, and laws marking significant legal changes for Latinos and other minorities. A cross-section of cultural, political, legal, literary, and athletic events are represented here in order to give a broad picture of the Latino experience. It is far from complete, but we hope it informs and piques further curiosity.

**1492 January 2:** The last Moorish sultan, Muhammad XI (*Boabdil* in Spanish), surrenders the city of Granada to the Spanish monarchs Isabel of Castile and Ferdinand of Aragón, ending seven centuries of Moorish presence on the Iberian Peninsula. The campaign known as *La Reconquista* comes to a close.

Queen Isabel of Castile

**1492 End of July:** An edict by King Ferdinand of Aragón and Queen Isabel of Castile expels the Jews from Spain.

**1492 August 8:** Antonio de Nebrija publishes the first Spanish grammar.

**1492 October 12:** Christopher Columbus arrives with his caravels the *Niña*, the *Pinta*, and the *Santa María* on the island of San Salvador in the Bahamas.

**1493 November:** On his second voyage, Columbus finds the Virgin Islands and Puerto Rico.

**1494** Columbus establishes Isabela, the first permanent European establishment in the New World, on Hispaniola and sails to Jamaica.

**1508** Juan Ponce de León establishes friendly relations with the native chieftain of Puerto Rico, Agueibana, who presents him with gold.

**1510** Diego Velázquez de Cuéllar conquers Cuba despite several deadly raids by the Arawak chief Hatuey.

**1511** Velázquez is commissioned governor of Cuba, and the island's indigenous population is subjected to the *encomienda* system—soon to take over all of Spain's colonies—in which each Spaniard is given land and Native American slaves who are forced to work it.

**1512 December 27:** Laws of Burgos, the first European legal code for the colonies, is ratified in Burgos, Spain.

**1513** Juan Ponce de León lands on the shores of Florida.

**1518** Hernán Cortés sets out from Cuba to explore the mainland of Mexico in order to confirm reports of large native civilizations in the country's interior.

**1519** Aztec king Moctezuma receives conquistador Hernán Cortés.

**1520 July 1:** *Noche Triste* (Sad Night). The Spaniards are forced out of Veracruz by Cuitlahuac; Aztec king Moctezuma is killed.

Aztec calendar

**1521 August 13:** Cortés conquers Technotitlán and the Aztec Empire; he begins to build Mexico City on Technotitlán's ruins.

**1540** An estimated sixty-six Pueblo villages in the area of New Mexico grow corn, beans, squash, and cotton.

1542 Publication of *Chronicle of the Narváez Expedition* by Alvar Nuñez Cabeza de Vaca in which the explorer narrates his ten-year journey throughout the South and Southwest after being shipwrecked off the coast of Florida.

1564 Spanish missionaries introduce grapes to California.

1565 Establishment of mission in Saint Augustine, Florida—the oldest permanent settlement in the United States—by Spanish admiral Pedro Menéndez de Avilés.

1566 Spanish Jesuits begin building missions along the eastern seaboard from Virginia to Florida.

1580 European diseases have ravaged Puerto Rican Indians to near extinction.

1598 Juan de Oñate begins to colonize New Mexico and introduces livestock breeding to the American Southwest—the beginning of the *vaquero* (cowboy) culture.

1610 Santa Fe, New Mexico, founded.

1680 Pueblo Revolt against Franciscan missions in New Mexico; 21 Franciscans and 380 colonists are killed. The first royal *mercedes* (land grants) are granted to Spaniards in the fertile valleys of northern Mexico, just south of the present border.

1690 The first permanent Spanish settlement in Texas, San Francisco de los Tejas, near the Nueces River, is established.

1693 The Spanish Crown orders its colonizers to abandon Texas for fear of Indian uprisings.

1700 Jesuit missionary Eusebio Kino establishes a mission at San Xavier del Bac, near present-day Tucson, Arizona.

1716 The possibility of French encroachment prompts the Spanish to reoccupy Texas by establishing a series of missions; of these missions, San Antonio, founded in 1718, is the most important and prosperous.

1717 English and French slave-trading companies bring African slaves into Spanish lands in the Americas.

1738 The first free black community is established at Fort Mose in Spanish Florida.

1760 Large-scale cattle ranching in Texas begins with a grant by Captain Blas Maria de la Garza Falcón.

1766 King Charles III expels the Jesuits from the Spanish Empire. Franciscans become the primary missionaries in Spanish America.

1766 September 17: The presidio of San Francisco is founded, becoming Spain's northernmost outpost.

Junípero Serra

1769 Father Junípero Serra founds San Diego de Alcalá mission in Alta (Northern) California.

1770–90s African slaves numbering at least 50,000 brought to Cuba to work on the sugar plantations.

1770s The Age of Enlightenment sweeps Europe. Spain and its American colonies are slow to react.

1776 The American colonies declare their independence from Britain as the United States of America. The war lasts until 1783.

1790s–1820s Hispanic settlements thrives in *Pimería Alta* (California). At one point as many as a thousand Hispanics live in the Santa Cruz Valley.

1801 Haciendas with enormous herds of cattle take over the majority of northwest New Spain.

1803 April 30: Louisiana Purchase virtually doubles the size of the United States.

1804 President Thomas Jefferson funds the westward expedition of Lewis and Clark. Spain worries that the exploration foreshadows Anglo settlement of the West.

1810 Father Miguel Hidalgo y Costilla rings the bell of freedom (*el grito de Dolores*) to signal Mexico's will for independence from Spain.

1810 September 16: Spaniards withdraw their troops from the frontier presidios.

1811 July 30: Father Hidalgo is executed by a firing squad and his head displayed in Guanajuato.

1817–24 Simón Bolívar leads groups of revolutionaries calling for independence through present-day Venezuela, Ecuador, and Colombia.

1819 Spain cedes Florida to the United States.

1821 Mexico achieves independence from Spain.

1822 Joseph Marion Hernández becomes first Hispanic American in Congress; he is a delegate from the Florida territory.

1823 Erasmo Seguín, Texas delegate to U.S. Congress, helps pass a colonization act designed to bring more Anglo settlers to Texas. Between 1824 and 1830, thousands of Anglo families enter east Texas. They acquire hundreds of thousands of free acres and buy cheap land.

1823 Father Junípero Serra dies, but his Franciscan followers establish twelve more missions in California.

1823 December 2: Monroe Doctrine proclaimed; President James Monroe declares that European nations must not interfere in the activities of the Americas and the United States will reciprocate by not interfering in the affairs of Europe.

1824 Chumash Revolt against Franciscan missions in Santa Barbara, California, area.

1829 Slavery in Mexico is abolished under the new republic.

1834 After 350 years, the Holy Office of the Inquisition, active in Spain and the Americas, is officially abolished.

1830 Texas has 18,000 Anglo inhabitants and their African slaves, who number more than 2,000.

1836 March 6: Battle of the Alamo.

1836 May 14: Texas becomes an independent republic.

1843 The Dominican Republic achieves independence.

1846–48 Mexican-American War.

1848 February 2: Treaty of Guadalupe Hidalgo is signed between the United States and Mexico in which the latter cedes its northern half to the former.

1853 December 30: Gadsden Purchase Treaty is signed by the United States and Mexico in which the former gains a parcel of land known as the Mesilla region.

1855 In the new American state of California "greaser laws" are passed; they are attempts to eliminate the customs of Mexican Americans (derogatorily called "greasers").

1859 Cigar factories are built in New York and Louisiana. Many Cubans leave the island to find employment in the factories.

1862 The Homestead Act is passed; it allows squatters to settle vacant land (often owned by Mexicans fighting battles for their ranches) upon the condition of improving it.

1865 Chilean Philip Bazaar, member of the U.S. Navy, is the first Latino to receive a Congressional Medal of Honor, for service in the U.S. Civil War.

1870 All slaves who are the property of the Spanish government are freed in Puerto Rico and Cuba.

1871 Esteban Bellán is the first Hispanic to play on a professional baseball team in the United States, the Troy Haymakers.

1880s The Spanish government attempts to free all slaves in Cuba—a process that takes eight years.

The Alamo

José Martí

**1895 May 19:** José Martí is killed in an early battle in the Cuban War for Independence.

**1898 February 15:** The explosion and sinking of the USS *Maine* in Havana Harbor.

**1898 April 28:** President McKinley declares war on Spain.

**1898 December 10:** Treaty of Paris is signed between the United States and Spain. Spain gives sovereignty over Cuba, Puerto Rico, Guam, and the Philippines to the United States.

**1901** The Platt Amendment, which gives the United States control over Cuban foreign affairs and establishes an army base in Guantánamo Bay, is passed.

**1901** Puerto Rican labor union the *Federación Libre de los Trabajadores* (Workers Labor Federation)—or FLT—becomes affiliated with the American Federation of Labor, which changes its former policy of excluding nonwhites.

**1902** The Reclamation Act, a law in which the U.S. government "reclaims" land in the western states in order to fund irrigation projects, is passed. Dams are constructed on a large scale, and many Latinos are dispossessed of their lands through the federal right of eminent domain.

**1902** Cuba declares independence from the United States.

**1910** Mexican Revolution begins.

**1912** Brutality, including lynchings, against Mexican Americans in the Southwest is common. The Mexican ambassador formally protests.

**1917** The Jones Act grants U.S. citizenship to Puerto Ricans and allows more self-governance but does not change the island's colonial status. English is announced as the island's official language.

**1917 February:** Immigration Act of 1917 passes and institutes a literacy requirement for immigrants, inhibiting immigration from Mexico.

**1924** U.S.-Mexican Border Patrol is established to police the border.

**1926 July.** Rioting Puerto Ricans in Harlem are attacked by non-Latinos. By 1930 Puerto Ricans number 53,000 in Manhattan.

**1929** The Great Depression dramatically slows the immigration of Mexicans; many return to their home country.

**1929** League of Latin American Citizens (LULAC) is founded.

**1930** Rafael L. Trujillo becomes dictator of the Dominican Republic (until 1961) and citizens begin to flee the island.

**1933** The Roosevelt administration reverses the policy of English as the official language in Puerto Rico.

**1933** Mexican farmworkers in California's Central Valley cotton industry, supported by several groups of independent Mexican union organizers and radicals, go on strike.

**1933** Cuban dictator Gerardo Machado is overthrown.

**1933 September:** Fulgencio Batista leads a barracks revolt to overthrow Cuban provisional President Carlos Manuel de Céspedes y Quesada and becomes the dictator of the Cuban provisional government.

**1934** The Platt Amendent is annulled.

**1941** The Fair Employment Practices Act is passed, attempting to eliminate discrimination in employment.

**1941** Hispanics throughout the United States enthusiastically respond to the war effort as the country enters World War II. Approximately 375,000 Latinos serve in the armed forces during the war.

**1942 August 2:** Sleepy Lagoon incident; mass convictions of Mexican Americans do not occur until January 1943.

**1942 August 4:** The Bracero Agreement is signed between the United States and Mexico under which the United States admits thousands of Mexican workers to fill the wartime labor shortage in agriculture and public works.

1943 June 3: Initial Zoot Suit incident in Los Angeles leads to riots for the following four days.

U.S. servicemen with clubs during the Zoot Suit Riots.

1944 Operation Bootstrap is initiated by the Puerto Rican government to meet U.S. labor demands of World War II and encourage industrialization on the island; it stimulates a major migration wave of workers to the United States.

1947 American G.I. Forum is founded by Mexican American veterans in response to a Three Rivers, Texas, funeral home's refusal to bury a Mexican American soldier killed during World War II.

1949 Luis Muñoz Marín becomes the first elected governor of Puerto Rico.

1949 The first dark-skinned Cuban, Orestes "Minnie" Minoso, plays for the Cleveland major league baseball team.

1950 Beginning of the Puerto Rican "Great Migration" to the U.S. mainland.

1950 July: Under the leadership of governor Muñoz Marín the status of Puerto Rico is upgraded from a protectorate to a commonwealth.

1954 The Supreme Court rules in the landmark case *Hernandez v. Texas* that Hispanic Americans are not being treated as "whites." The court recognizes Hispanics as a separate class of people suffering profound discrimination, paving the way for Hispanic Americans to use legal means to attack all types of discrimination

throughout the United States. It is also the first U.S. Supreme Court case to be argued and briefed by Mexican American attorneys.

1950 José Ferrer is the first Latino to receive an Oscar for his performance in *Cyrano de Bergerac*.

1954-58 Operation Wetback is launched to deport Mexican *braceros* to their native country.

1959 January 1: Cuban Revolution; Fidel Castro ousts U.S.-backed dictator Fulgencio Batista, takes control of Havana, and institutes socialist changes. Nearly one million Cubans have since emigrated to the United States.

1961 April: Bay of Pigs invasion into Cuba fails.

1961 Passage of Foreign Assistance Act by U.S. government institutes economic sanctions on Cuba that continue to this day.

Rita Moreno

1961 Rita Moreno is first Latina to win an Oscar for her role in *West Side Story*.

1962 Reies Lopez Tijerina founds *La Alianza Federal de Pueblos Libres*, which aims to restore lands of Mexican Americans ceded by the Treaty of Guadalupe Hidalgo.

1962 Joan Baez is first Latino entertainer featured on the cover of *Time* magazine.

Joan Baez

1962 October: The United States blocks a Soviet plan to establish missile bases in Cuba. Soviet Premier Khrushchev agrees to withdraw the missiles if the United States declares publicly that it will not invade Cuba.

1964 Congress passes the Civil Rights Act of 1964, the first comprehensive civil rights law since the post-

Civil War Reconstruction period. "Affirmative action" programs are established. Title VII of the act prohibits discrimination on the basis of gender, creed, race, or ethnic background. Discrimination is prohibited in advertising, recruitment, hiring, job classification, promotion, discharge, wages and salaries, and other terms and conditions of employment. Title VII also establishes the Equal Employment Opportunity Commission (EEOC) as a monitoring device to prevent job discrimination.

1964 The Economic Opportunity Act (EOA) is the centerpiece of President Lyndon B. Johnson's War on Poverty. Programs for the poor include the Job Corps, the Community Action Program (CAP), and the Volunteers in Service to America (VISTA).

1965 Chicano Movement is founded when Filipino agricultural workers in Delano, California, begin a strike that is the start of an organization that becomes César Chávez's United Farm Workers.

1965 Immigration Reform Act eliminates all national-origins quotas.

1965 Crusade for Justice organization founded by Rodolfo "Corky" Gonzáles.

1966 Dolores Huerta successfully represents farmworkers in their negotiations with their employer (Schenley Wine) for the first time.

1966 Hundreds of Chicago Puerto Ricans riot, ostensibly in response to an incident of police brutality, but the underlying causes are linked to the broader problems of urban blight in their neighborhoods.

1968 Ten thousand Chicanos walk out of five high schools in Los Angeles.

1968 First Chicano Studies program established at California State University at Los Angeles.

1969 March: *"El Plan Espiritual de Aztlán,"* a manifesto for Chicano activism and independence emerges from the Chicano Youth Liberation Conference in Denver.

1970 August 29: Thirty thousand Chicanos march to protest the Vietnam War in the National Chicano Moratorium. Journalist Rubén Salazar is killed by a tear gas canister.

1971 The first Latina to hold a cabinet position, Ramona Acosta Bañuelos, is appointed U.S. treasurer.

1971 Geraldo Rivera named Broadcaster of the Year; in 1987 he is the first Latino to host his own talk show.

1973 Roberto Clemente is the first Latino baseball player to be inducted into the Baseball Hall of Fame.

1973 Nuyorican Poets Café is founded by Miguel Algarín.

1973 September 11: Salvador Allende's Chilean government is overthrown by Augusto Pinochet.

1974 Passage of Equal Education Opportunity Act by Congress gives Latinos the right to bilingual education.

1978–88 Latina participation in the workforce more than doubles, from 1.7 million to 3.6 million. In 1988, 56.6 percent of Hispanic women are in the workforce, compared with 66.2 percent of white women and 63.8 percent of blacks women. The proportion of Latino children living in poverty rises more than 45 percent. By 1989, 38 percent live in poverty.

Salvador Allende

1980 April 21–September 26: Mariel Boatlift from the port of Mariel, Cuba; more than 250,000 people flee the island by boat.

1980s Civil wars in Guatemala, El Salvador, and Nicaragua force millions of refugees to emigrate from Central America.

1986 Immigration Reform and Control Act is passed.

1987 The median income, adjusted for inflation, of Hispanic families below the poverty level falls from $7,238 in 1978 to $6,557.

César Chávez

1988 César Chávez's "Fast for Life"; he eats nothing and drinks only water for thirty-five days.

1988 President Ronald Reagan appoints the first Latino secretary of education, Lauro F. Cavazos.

1989 Oscar Hijuelos is the first Latino to win a Pulitzer Prize—for *The Mambo Kings Play Songs of Love.*

1989 Immigration from the Spanish-speaking Americas rises to 61.4 percent of total population. Mexico accounts for 37.1 percent of total documented immigration; the next highest number of immigrants is from El Salvador, at 5.3 percent.

1990 President George H. W. Bush appoints the first woman and first Latino surgeon general of the United States, Antonia C. Novello.

1990s Latinos debate usage of terms like "Hispanic," "Latino," "hispano," and subcategories like Mexican American, Cuban American, Dominican American, etc.

1991 March: Unemployment among Latinos reaches 10.3 percent, roughly double the rate for whites.

1991 October 23: President George H. W. Bush signs the Cuban Democracy Act, also known as the Torricelli Bill, heavily backed by Cuban Americans, which bans trade with Cuba by U.S. subsidiary companies in third-party countries and prohibits ships docking in U.S. ports if they have visited Cuba. The United Nations General Assembly condemns the U.S. for maintaining its 30-year embargo of Cuba.

1992 Quincentennial of the 1492 voyage of Columbus is celebrated worldwide amid a heated debate about its consequences.

1993 President Bill Clinton appoints Federico Peña secretary of transportation, Henry Cisneros secretary of housing and urban development, Norma Cantú assistant secretary for civil rights; all are the first Latinos to hold these positions.

Henry Cisneros

1993 April 23: César Chávez dies.

1994 North American Free Trade Agreement between Canada, the United States, and Mexico takes effect. *Maquiladoras* along the U.S.-Mexico border multiply.

1994 January 1: In Mexico, as many as one thousand Mayan guerrillas, calling themselves the Zapatista National Liberation Army, take over San Cristobal de las Casas and the towns of Ocosingo, Las Margaritas, and others in the state of Chiapas. After a cease-fire is established, the government and Mayan rebels sign a tentative thirty-two-point accord on March 2. In the following months, Mayan farmers seize some 75,000 acres of ranch lands, claiming that the lands had been stolen from them as far back as 1819.

1994 November 8: Californians pass Proposition 187 with 59 percent of the vote. The initiative bans undocumented immigrants from receiving public education and public benefits such as welfare and subsidized health care, except in emergency circumstances; makes it a felony to manufacture, distribute, sell, or use false citizenship or residence documents; and requires teachers, doctors, and other city, county, and state officials to report suspected and apparent illegal aliens to the California attorney general and the Immigration and Naturalization Service (INS). Governor Pete Wilson issues an executive order for state officials to begin following the initiative by cutting off government services to undocumented pregnant women and nursing home patients. On November 9, 1994, eight lawsuits are filed in state and federal courts protesting the measure.

1994 November 16: In Los Angeles, Federal District Court Judge William Matthew Byrne Jr. temporarily blocks the enforcement of Proposition 187, stating that it raises serious constitutional questions.

1998 Anthony Muñoz is the first Latino inducted into the Football Hall of Fame.

1998 Bill Richardson is the first Latino to be appointed secretary of energy, by President Clinton.

Bill Richardson

Los Angeles immigration rally.

1999 The Clinton administration expands travel to Cuba for aid workers, relatives, athletes, scholars, journalists, and religious groups—but not tourists.

1999 Spanish-language Internet presence grows in 1999 and 2000; Spanish versions of AOL and Yahoo!, among other sites, are created.

1999 Latino groups join the National Association for the Advancement of Colored People (NAACP) in protesting the lack of minority roles in prime-time shows. Studies show that 63 percent of Latinos do not feel that television represents them accurately. Latino groups urge viewers to participate in a national brownout of ABC, CBS, Fox, and NBC the week of September 12, Hispanic Heritage Week. The four major networks all publicly respond to the protest and quickly hire many minority actors for added-on roles.

2000 Elián González is reunited with father in Cuba upon orders of Attorney General Janet Reno.

2000 California makes César Chávez Day a full paid holiday for state employees. Texas and Arizona are working toward similar measures.

2002 Speedskater Derek Parra is the first Mexican American to win a medal during the Olympic Winter Games.

2002 Speedskater Jennifer Rodriguez is the first Cuban American to compete in the Olympic Winter Games.

2003 The U.S. Bureau of the Census announces that Latinos are the largest minority in the U.S. population. Publication of the first chapter of *Don Quixote of La Mancha* by Cervantes in Spanglish translation.

2003 U.S. Navy is forced to leave its base on the island of Vieques, Puerto Rico.

2003 Nilo Cruz is the first Latino to win the Pulitzer Prize in drama, for *Anna in the Tropics.*

2004 George P. Bush, nephew of President George W. Bush, gives Spanish and Spanglish talks before Latinos at rallies before the November election.

2005 As the war in Iraq continues, studies find that the percentage of African American and Latino casualties is disproportionate to their percentage of the United States population.

2005 Random House imprint Vintage *Español* announces its tenth anniversary and declares intentions to expand further into the Spanish-language book publishing market.

2006 April: Protests over immigration policy sweep the country, uniting Latinos and immigration advocates.

2006 November: The Seventh Annual Latin Grammys are held at Madison Square Garden in New York and filmed by Univision for the second year in a row.

# Demographics

Much has been made of the fact that Latinos are now the largest minority in the United States, that they are the fastest-growing ethnic/racial group, and that Spanish is the second-most-spoken language in the country. Clearly, the face of the nation is changing. In this section, the following charts (all courtesy of the Pew Hispanic Center) illustrate demographic changes and give a snapshot of the Latino population at this point in time.

Miami monument to Cuban independence leader and man of letters José Martí.

| POPULATION BY RACE AND ETHNICITY: 2000 AND 2005 | | | | | |
|---|---|---|---|---|---|
| | 2005 POPULATION | 2000 POPULATION | PERCENT OF 2005 | PERCENT CHANGE 2000-2005 | SHARE OF TOTAL CHANGE (%) |
| Hispanic | 41,926,302 | 34,494,801 | 14.5 | 21.5 | 50.3 |
| Native born | 25,085,528 | 20,488,299 | 8.7 | 22.4 | 31.1 |
| Foreign born | 16,840,774 | 14,006,502 | 5.8 | 20.2 | 19.2 |
| White alone, not Hispanic | 192,526,952 | 189,520,003 | 66.8 | 1.6 | 20.4 |
| Black alone, not Hispanic | 34,410,656 | 32,036,110 | 11.9 | 7.4 | 16.1 |
| Asian alone, not Hispanic | 12,331,128 | 9,893,205 | 4.3 | 24.6 | 16.5 |
| Other, not Hispanic | 7,203,781 | 7,693,277 | 2.5 | -6.4 | -3.3 |
| **Total** | **288,398,819** | **273,637,396** | **100.0** | **5.4** | **100.0** |

Note: "Other, not Hispanic" includes persons reporting single races not listed separately and those reporting more than one race. Pew Hispanic Center September 2006
Source: Pew Hispanic Center tabulations of 2000 Census and 2005 American Community Survey
Universe: 2000 and 2005 Household Population

The chart represents the population growth in the United States between 2000 and 2005 and what percentage of the growth came from each ethnic group.

## MEDIAN PERSONAL EARNINGS BY RACE AND ETHNICITY: 2005

|  | Median Earnings ($) |
|---|---|
| Hispanic | 20,000 |
| Native born | 22,000 |
| Foreign born | 18,000 |
| White alone, not Hispanic | 30,000 |
| Black alone, not Hispanic | 22,900 |
| Asian alone, not Hispanic | 30,000 |
| Other, not Hispanic | 22,000 |
| **Total** | **26,900** |

Note: Based on reported earnings, not adjusted earnings. Pew Hispanic Center September 2006
Source: Pew Hispanic Center tabulations of 2005 American Community Survey
Universe: 2005 Household Population with positive earnings

Median personal earnings among Hispanic, white, black, Asian, and "other" populations in 2005.

## SHARE OF HISPANICS FOR SELECTED STATES: 2000 AND 2005

|  | 2000 SHARE OF HISPANICS | 2005 SHARE OF HISPANICS | CHANGE IN SHARE OF HISPANICS |
|---|---|---|---|
| California | 31.1 | 29.9 | -1.2 |
| Texas | 18.9 | 18.8 | -0.1 |
| Florida | 7.6 | 8.2 | 0.6 |
| New York | 8.1 | 7.2 | -0.8 |
| Illinois | 4.4 | 4.3 | -0.1 |
| Arizona | 3.7 | 4.0 | 0.3 |
| New Jersey | 3.2 | 3.1 | -0.1 |
| Colorado | 2.1 | 2.1 | 0.1 |
| New Mexico | 2.2 | 2.0 | -0.2 |
| Other states | 18.8 | 20.3 | 1.5 |

Source: Pew Hispanic Center tabulations of 2000 Census and 2005 American Community Survey
Universe: 2000 and 2005 Household Population

The last column shows the slight changes (decreases, in general) in each of the listed state's share of the total U.S. Latino population between 2000 and 2005.

## DETAILED HISPANIC ORIGIN: 2005

| | Number | Percent of Hispanic |
|---|---|---|
| Mexican | 26,784,268 | 63.9 |
| Puerto Rican | 3,794,776 | 9.1 |
| Cuban | 1,462,593 | 3.5 |
| Dominican | 1,135,756 | 2.7 |
| Costa Rican | 111,978 | 0.3 |
| Guatemalan | 780,191 | 1.9 |
| Nicaraguan | 275,126 | 0.7 |
| Panamanian | 141,286 | 0.3 |
| Salvadoran | 1,240,031 | 3.0 |
| Other Central American | 99,422 | 0.2 |
| Argentinean | 189,303 | 0.5 |
| Bolivian | 68,649 | 0.2 |
| Chilean | 105,141 | 0.3 |
| Colombian | 723,596 | 1.7 |
| Ecuadorian | 432,068 | 1.0 |
| Peruvian | 415,352 | 1.0 |
| Uruguayan | 51,646 | 0.1 |
| Venezuelan | 162,762 | 0.4 |
| Other South American | 89,443 | 0.2 |
| Spaniard | 362,424 | 0.9 |
| All Other Spanish/Hispanic/Latino | 3,033,648 | 7.2 |
| **Total** | **41,926,302** | **100.0** |

Source: Pew Hispanic Center tabulations of 2005 American Community Survey
Universe: 2005 Hispanic Household Population

The percentages of U.S. Latinos according to country of origin.

| EDUCATIONAL ATTAINMENT BY RACE AND ETHNICITY: 2005 | | | | | |
|---|---|---|---|---|---|
| | Less than 9th grade | 9th to 12th grade | High school graduate | Some college | College graduate | Total |
| Hispanic | 5,445,635 | 3,742,845 | 6,121,196 | 4,577,331 | 2,784,588 | 22,671,595 |
| Native born | 932,599 | 1,432,188 | 2,919,444 | 2,748,266 | 1,503,847 | 9,536,344 |
| Foreign born | 4,513,036 | 2,310,657 | 3,201,752 | 1,829,065 | 1,280,741 | 13,135,251 |
| White alone, not Hispanic | 4,325,261 | 10,436,781 | 40,631,194 | 38,507,220 | 40,199,138 | 134,099,594 |
| Black alone, not Hispanic | 1,134,045 | 2,893,598 | 6,703,589 | 5,984,760 | 3,503,929 | 20,219,921 |
| Asian alone, not Hispanic | 679,081 | 516,628 | 1,428,716 | 1,645,826 | 4,146,216 | 8,416,467 |
| Other, not Hispanic | 206,109 | 400,755 | 1,022,398 | 1,149,895 | 743,832 | 3,522,989 |
| Total | 11,790,131 | 17,990,607 | 55,907,093 | 51,865,032 | 51,377,703 | 188,930,566 |
| Percent Distribution | | | | | |
| Hispanic | 24.0 | 16.5 | 27.0 | 20.2 | 12.3 | 100.0 |
| Native born | 9.8 | 15.0 | 30.6 | 28.8 | 15.8 | 100.0 |
| Foreign born | 34.4 | 17.6 | 24.4 | 13.9 | 9.8 | 100.0 |
| White alone, not Hispanic | 3.2 | 7.8 | 30.3 | 28.7 | 30.0 | 100.0 |
| Black alone, not Hispanic | 5.65.6 | 14.3 | 33.2 | 29.6 | 17.3 | 100.0 |
| Asian alone, not Hispanic | 8.1 | 6.1 | 17.0 | 19.6 | 49.3 | 100.0 |
| Other, not Hispanic | 5.9 | 11.4 | 29.0 | 32.6 | 21.1 | 100.0 |
| Total | 6.2 | 9.5 | 29.6 | 27.5 | 27.2 | 100.0 |

Note: "College graduate" refers to a person who has attained at least a bachelor's degree
Source: Pew Hispanic Center tabulations of 2005 American Community Survey Hispanics at Mid-Decade
Universe: 2005 Household Population age 25 and over

This chart details the disparity in educational attainment across racial and ethnic lines.

## HISPANIC POPULATION BY STATE: 2000 AND 2005

| | 2005 | 2000 | Change 2000-2005 | Percent change 2000-2005 |
|---|---|---|---|---|
| California | 12,534,628 | 10,741,711 | 1,792,917 | 16.7 |
| Texas | 7,882,254 | 6,530,459 | 1,351,795 | 20.7 |
| Florida | 3,433,355 | 2,623,787 | 809,568 | 30.9 |
| New York | 3,026,286 | 2,782,504 | 243,782 | 8.8 |
| Illinois | 1,807,908 | 1,509,763 | 298,145 | 19.7 |
| Arizona | 1,679,116 | 1,267,777 | 411,339 | 32.4 |
| New Jersey | 1,312,326 | 1,098,209 | 214,117 | 19.5 |
| Colorado | 895,176 | 718,956 | 176,220 | 24.5 |
| New Mexico | 827,940 | 746,555 | 81,385 | 10.9 |
| Georgia | 625,382 | 425,305 | 200,077 | 47.0 |
| Nevada | 557,370 | 389,336 | 168,034 | 43.2 |
| Washington | 546,209 | 434,747 | 111,462 | 25.6 |
| North Carolina | 544,470 | 367,390 | 177,080 | 48.2 |
| Massachusetts | 489,662 | 412,496 | 77,166 | 18.7 |
| Pennsylvania | 488,144 | 381,159 | 106,985 | 28.1 |
| Virginia | 440,988 | 324,314 | 116,674 | 36.0 |
| Michigan | 378,232 | 318,285 | 59,947 | 18.8 |
| Connecticut | 372,718 | 309,798 | 62,920 | 20.3 |
| Oregon | 360,000 | 267,017 | 92,983 | 34.8 |
| Maryland | 311,191 | 227,586 | 83,605 | 36.7 |
| Indiana | 273,004 | 210,189 | 62,815 | 29.9 |
| Utah | 264,010 | 197,315 | 66,695 | 33.8 |
| Ohio | 253,014 | 212,007 | 41,007 | 19.3 |
| Wisconsin | 230,715 | 187,205 | 43,510 | 23.2 |
| Oklahoma | 218,987 | 168,944 | 50,043 | 29.6 |
| Kansas | 218,244 | 182,827 | 35,417 | 19.4 >>> |

This chart shows the numbers of Latinos living in each state in 2005 and 2000, the population change, and the percentage of population change.

## HISPANIC POPULATION BY STATE: 2000 AND 2005

|  | 2005 | 2000 | Change 2000-2005 | Percent change 2000-2005 |
| --- | --- | --- | --- | --- |
| Minnesota | 185,464 | 139,259 | 46,205 | 33.2 |
| Tennessee | 171,890 | 113,610 | 58,280 | 51.3 |
| Missouri | 154,744 | 114,741 | 40,003 | 34.9 |
| South Carolina | 136,616 | 90,263 | 46,353 | 51.4 |
| Idaho | 135,733 | 97,765 | 37,968 | 38.8 |
| Arkansas | 130,328 | 82,155 | 48,173 | 58.6 |
| Louisiana | 126,856 | 107,541 | 19,315 | 18.0 |
| Nebraska | 124,504 | 90,881 | 33,623 | 37.0 |
| Rhode Island | 114,077 | 87,454 | 26,623 | 30.4 |
| Hawaii | 103,764 | 84,471 | 19,293 | 22.8 |
| Iowa | 102,047 | 77,968 | 24,079 | 30.9 |
| Alabama | 98,624 | 70,305 | 28,319 | 40.3 |
| Kentucky | 65,177 | 53,002 | 12,175 | 23.0 |
| Delaware | 50,007 | 37,185 | 12,822 | 34.5 |
| Mississippi | 48,795 | 34,543 | 14,252 | 41.3 |
| District of Columbia | 43,856 | 42,913 | 943 | 2.2 |
| Wyoming | 36,722 | 28,769 | 7,953 | 27.6 |
| Alaska | 29,219 | 23,992 | 5,227 | 21.8 |
| New Hampshire | 24,248 | 20,740 | 3,508 | 16.9 |
| Montana | 21,970 | 18,113 | 3,857 | 21.3 |
| Maine | 12,407 | 10,074 | 2,333 | 23.2 |
| South Dakota | 12,311 | 9,399 | 2,912 | 31.0 |
| North Dakota | 11,380 | 7,020 | 4,360 | 62.1 |
| West Virginia | 9,760 | 12,310 | -2,550 | -20.7 |
| Vermont | 4,474 | 4,687 | -213 | -4.5 |
| Total | 41,926,302 | 34,494,801 | 7,431,501 | 21.5 |

Source: Pew Hispanic Center tabulations of 2000 Census and 2005 American Community Survey
Universe: 2000 and 2005 Hispanic Household Population

# CHAPTER 9

# EDUCATION

Latinos represent more than 16 percent of the nation's school-age children, and the percentage of Latinos in public schools is rising faster than that of whites and African Americans. The story of Latinos in higher education is complex. Because Latinos are largely urban dwellers, most children attend elementary and high school in impoverished central cities. Four of the identified risk factors for low academic achievement among ethnic and minority groups are poverty, level of parents' education, level of English-language proficiency, and family structure (married couples versus single-parent families). The percentage of Latino children with two or more of these risk factors is five times greater than that of white children. Outmoded textbooks exacerbate the issue of educational attainment among Latinos; the textbooks used in many public schools are often outdated and do not include sufficient information about Latino history and culture. Although the numbers of Latinos entering two- and four-year colleges is rising, they still lag far behind the total population in attainment of college and postgraduate degrees: 11 percent compared with 25 percent. Some strides toward improved educational systems and processes for Latinos have been made; however, Latinos still underperform.

Left: Young student seated under a bilingual calendar. Above: First Lady Laura Bush stands with students during her visit to Sun Valley Middle School in Los Angeles in April 2005.

# Ethnicity and Bilingualism

**Q:** **What challenges face Latinos in primary and secondary education?**

**A:** The obstacles facing Latinos in the public school system are present from the start. One factor is lack of health insurance and subsequent lack of early childhood immunizations (only one-quarter of Latinos had insurance and received immunizations in 2000), which may lead to complications as they grow older. Of primary importance in the classroom is the ability to speak, read, and understand English; many children born to immigrant parents (who often speak exclusively Spanish at home) have difficulty in an all-English environment. Research has also found that parental behaviors such as reading to children and entering them early (age three) in preschool programs help significantly in preparing children for elementary school. Such behaviors are sometimes lacking among Latinos, partly due to poverty and lack of parental education. Access to technology, such as computers and the Internet, are problems for both Latino and African American students. Student alcohol and drug use, as well as involvement in street violence, inhibit classroom learning. The relative lack of role models from their ethnic and linguistic minority can also be dispirit-

Patient poster urges childhood vaccination. It reads: "Love them. Protect them. Vaccinate them."

**Ámelos. Protéjelos.**

**Vacúnelos.**

ing to Latino children. The movie *Stand and Deliver* (1988), which was based on the accomplishments of the students of California high school calculus teacher Jaime Escalante (played by Edward James Olmos), a Bolivian immigrant, was an inspiring example of a committed teacher who demanded excellence of his Latino students. The percentage of Latinos at higher levels of education administration is also low.

**Q:** **How has bilingualism defined the education of Latinos?**

**A:** Bilingualism is not a recent phenomenon in the United States. Through parochial schools, such as French Canadian Catholic schools in New England, immigrant communities have worked to maintain their native language in the service of cultural preservation while learning English in order to work and associate with the greater community. The strong push for bilingual education in the 1960s began in Florida among Cuban exiles waiting for the downfall of Fidel Castro. The program quickly grew and strengthened and transformed itself from a regional to a national program. A direct result of the civil rights movement, Title VII of the Elementary and Secondary Education Act, commonly known as the Bilingual Education Act, was passed in 1968. Its basic premise is that non-native

English-speaking immigrant children are entitled to schooling in their original language while they acquire English: Subjects like mathematics, geography, and social sciences are taught in Spanish by teachers fluent in the language; English-language classes are separate. When a child is competent in English, he or she is transferred to the mixed classroom. The right of children to learn in their native language during the transition to full English-language proficiency was upheld by the Supreme Court in 1974 in *Lau v. Nichols.*

Bilingual education, however, is hotly debated. Critics, such as conservative politician and commentator Linda Chavez, claim that the first major national review of bilingual education in 1977 concluded that Latino children in bilingual programs were neither learning English well nor scoring well on tests in subjects such as math and science taught in Spanish. In 1998, California organizer Ron Unz began to rally parents to sponsor English-immersion initiatives that mandated that all children be taught in classrooms where only English is spoken. The initiatives passed and Unz went on to sponsor similar successful initiatives in Arizona and Massachusetts. A 2002 referendum in Colorado failed, however. Supporters of bilingual education counter critics by stating that bilingual education fails because of understaffing and lack of funding.

A teacher in a bilingual classroom assists a student.

Linda Chavez, opponent of bilingual education.

"I find it offensive that some people think that those of us who have darker skin cannot take care of ourselves."

—LINDA CHAVEZ

# English Only, English First

**Q: Is English the official language of the United States?**

**A:** The United States does not have an official language. The Founding Fathers believed that the United States needed a flag, a currency, and a shared set of values, but they did not establish one language as the sole vehicle of communication. Over the past 230 years, several nativist movements to make English the official national language have been mounted, but all have failed.

**Q: What is the English-Only Movement?**

**A:** Many voter initiatives, lobbying efforts, and campaigns have been organized since the early 1980s to fight bilingual education and what was viewed as the threat of bilingual education—the erosion of "American" culture and the English language. One cohesive movement, the English-Only Movement, arose in response to the increasing Latino population, especially in Florida, Texas, and California, and to the Supreme Court case *Lau v. Nichols*. The term "English-Only" was coined in 1980 in Dade County, Florida, by opponents of an ordinance prohibiting "expenditures of any county funds for the purpose of utilizing any language other than English or

any culture other than that of the United States." The ordinance passed. Yet in 200 years of American history, not one congressional measure had sought to make English the official language of the United States. In 1981, Senator S. I. Hayakawa of California introduced the English Language Amendment in Congress; it failed. In 1983, however, Hayakawa continued his fight by co-founding the organization U.S. English with John Tanton. Although it found support in some states and was at one time headed by Linda Chavez, the organization has been plagued by scandal and charged with racism. Studies have shown that English-Only measures in

Senator S.I. Hayakawa, co-founder of U.S. English.

state legislatures have been supported by 90 percent of white state representatives, while 64 percent of black representatives have opposed them.

English-First is a variant of the English-Only movement. Supporters argue that English should be the only language of government communication, although the movement doesn't fight to eradicate other languages—as long as they don't pose a serious threat to the nation's cultural cohesiveness.

Michigan resident displays documents in Arabic and Spanish in May 2006 at the offices of the Michigan Civil Rights Commission.

A second-grade teacher in her dual-language classroom in Dodge City, Kansas, in 2005. Due to a dramatic increase in the Latino population, funding for bilingual programs was set to increase for the district.

# Going to College

**Q: Why are Latinos underrepresented in higher education?**

**A:** Historically, access to higher education has been severely limited for Latinos. Ivy League universities and prestigious liberal arts colleges enrolled few nonwhites in the post–World War II years—the era of Latino population expansion—and many even had racial quotas. Federal support in the 1950s and 1960s helped to create public two-year and junior colleges, often viewed as a stepping-stone to enrollment in a bachelor's program, but Latinos were not significantly affected. By 1970 whites still accounted for 87 percent of all college students. By the end of the twentieth century, the figures had shifted slightly: 69 percent of students were white, compared with 11 percent African American, 9 percent Latino, and 6 percent Asian. Latinos make up 14 percent of the nation's population, thus they are still underrepresented in higher education.

In 1965, passage of landmark legislation, the Higher Education Act, provided processes for federally funding underprivileged students and communities. In a 1992 reauthorization of the act, Congress identified a category of schools as Hispanic-Serving Institutions (colleges in which at least one-quarter of students are Latino), recognized that they were underfunded, and made these institutions eligible for federal grants and related assistance. Most of these schools are two-year programs and are located in states along the U.S.-Mexico border.

**Q: What effect did the Chicano Movement have on institutions of higher education?**

**A:** In the beginning, the Chicano Movement, defined in part by militant antiestablishment actions and manifestos, had difficulty gaining an audience among people of power in higher education. Gradually activists focused on the creation of Chicano studies programs; these programs would provide a sense of belonging for Mexican American students with little to no experience in traditionally white academic institutions, in addition to serving as a means to recruit more Latino students and secure financial aid. The

President Lyndon B. Johnson signs the Higher Education Act of 1965.

first Chicano studies program was established in 1968 at California State University, Los Angeles. In the ensuing decades, organizations devoted to serving Chicanos and Latinos in higher education were formed, including the National Association of Chicano and Chicana Studies and *El Movimiento Estudantil Chicano de Aztlán* (The Movement for Chicano Students of Aztlán).

Just five years after the creation of the first Chicano studies program, another dominant Latino group established a program to study their history and culture. The first Puerto Rican studies program was founded at Hunter College, City University of New York, in 1973. On the East Coast, further programs were established with a concentration on Caribbean (mostly Dominican) studies.

**Q:** What trends among high school students discourage application to and enrollment in institutions of higher education?

**A:** The challenge of graduating Latinos from four-year institutions begins in high school. First, Latinos have the highest drop-out rate of any ethnicity. Almost half of Latino high school seniors do not apply to college of any kind, compared with one-third of whites and one-quarter of Asians. Ethnic differences within the minority are clear: Enrollments are far higher among Cuban Americans than Mexican Americans and Puerto Ricans. The high school years are clearly troublesome—of Latino high achievers identified in eighth grade, only 70 percent later apply to college, the lowest rate of any ethnic group.

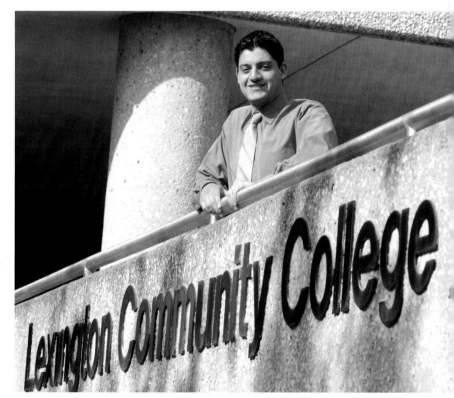

Jorge García, 19, a Mexican native, graduated from Lexington (Kentucky) Community College with an associate's degree in 2004. He will use this degree to transfer to the University of Kentucky to continue his education.

> "Action is an antidote to desperation."
> —JOAN BAEZ, SINGER/SONGWRITER

# Latino Studies

**Q:** How did Latino studies programs evolve?

**A:** After the establishment of Chicano studies programs in California and the Southwest and Caribbean studies programs in New York, New Jersey, and Connecticut, university departments began to cast broader nets—with the intention of studying systematically all Latino cultures and subpopulations in the United States. This quest was complicated because of the number of subpopulations of Latinos and the different methodologies that had been used to study Latinos since the Mexican-American War and the early waves of Caribbean migration. The struggle of Latinos studies departments has been to incorporate interdisciplinary approaches, including political science, economics, gender studies, popular culture, ethnomusicology (the musical history of an ethnic group), the arts, and foreign policy. Latino studies programs have grown enormously and are now established in many colleges and universities. In addition, many independent centers conduct important research into various areas of Latino experience in the United States.

Américo Paredes was a seminal figure in Chicano studies.

**Q:** Who were some groundbreaking scholars?

**A:** Many important independent scholars predated the creation of Latino studies programs. These trailblazers gave programs a base of material with which to work. The Henríquez Ureña family, immigrants from the Dominican Republic, are one famous example. Pedro Henríquez Ureña earned a doctorate from the University of Minnesota and expanded the debate on Hispanic culture through essays on history, language, and literature. He delivered the Charles Eliot Norton Lectures at Harvard University in 1940–41; they were published under the title *Literary Currents in Hispanic America*

(1945). Camila Henríquez Ureña taught at Vassar College; Max Henríquez Ureña was a specialist in *Modernismo* (Modernism). Another example is Ernesto Galarza. Born in 1905 in Puerto Vallarta, Mexico, Galarza was a pioneering Chicano scholar and militant activist for migrant labor rights. He wrote numerous articles and books on Latin American and Latino history, labor, and agriculture, and is famous for his memoir *Barrio Boy* (1971). Black Puerto Rican bibliographer and scholar Arthur Schomburg and translator and poet Muna Lee also did important work prior to World War II.

The recording of folkways and oral histories was one method used to preserve Latino history in the United States. Notable in this field were Auerlio and Gilberto Espinosa, as well as Américo Paredes, who published the landmark book *With a Pistol in His Hand: A Border Ballad and Its Hero* (1958). Paredes trained a generation of Mexican American scholars. Important figures in the field of literature include Tomás Rivera and Luis Leal, who devoted their careers to Mexican American authors from colonial times to the present.

Some scholars explored the Latino immigration experience, others produced seminal works on their own ethnic groups: Ramona Hernández and Silvio Torres-Saillant have focused on Dominican Americans; Louis A. Pérez, Gustavo Pérez Firmat, William Luis, and Ruth Behar have studied Cuban culture.

Muna Lee.

These pioneers helped create a path for Latino faculty today, though Latinos remain underrepresented. Nevertheless, their numbers have more than doubled since 1975, to more than 15,000 in 2000. Still, Latinos are only 2.4 percent of all college and university faculty nationwide.

> **Any history of Latinos stumbles at the start . . . There are many Edens, a thousand floods, discoveries and conquests in numbers beyond the capability of human memory.**
> —*Earl Shorris, from* Latinos: A Biography of a People *(1992)*

# CHAPTER 10

# SPANGLISH

Languages—their words and patterns that they follow—are in constant flux. Lexicography, the defining of words, must reflect the changing usage of words and expressions over time. The traditional pattern for immigrants to America has been to slowly give up their native tongues in favor of English. Irish, Italian, German, Finnish, Yiddish, and Polish disappeared as active languages in the United States. Spanish is not following this pattern. Because of the large Latino population and its several ethnic groups with different dialects, modes of address, and expressions, Spanish has widened its sphere, and the ability to speak the language has even become an asset, especially in Los Angeles, Miami, San Antonio, and New York—cities that have high concentrations of Spanish speakers. However, purists consider the Spanish spoken in these cities, and in pockets all over America, to be "contaminated." The language is being reshaped through its exposure to English, resulting in changes in syntax and vocabulary. In fact, a new language, not yet standardized, has emerged: Spanglish. Many wonder if it truly has a future. Is it a tool or an obstacle for Latinos in becoming part of the American mainstream? Some signs, such as recent television advertising, point to the mainstream's embrace of Spanglish.

Above: Jorge Almaraz, head chef of El Pocho Mexican Restaurant in Pikeville, Kentucky, mixes a pot of refried beans. He sends enough money home to support a wife and four children in Toluca, Mexico.

Left: A float rides along Market Street during the 2002 Latino Pride Parade in York, Pennsylvania.

# El español

**Q:** How did Spanish aid Iberian colonization?

**A:** The year 1492 is the *annus mirabilis* of Hispanic civilization. In that year, Columbus sailed his three caravels across the Atlantic in search of an alternative commercial route to the Indies; the Arabs and Jews were expelled from the Iberian Peninsula, thus allowing the Catholic monarchs, Isabel of Castile and Ferdinand of Aragón, the triumph of *La Reconquista;* and the first codified grammar of the Spanish language, written by the Salamanca philologist Antonio de Nebrija, was published. This third event is often overlooked, yet it had an enormous historical impact. As the Spanish Crown sought ways to expand its areas of influence, its unifying language became a crucial tool. *El español* had started as a regional dialect in Castile and competed, along with Catalan, Galician, and other dialects—all somewhat connected to the so-called vulgar Latin—for use in imperial endeavors. The Spanish spoken in Spain is often referred to as Castilian Spanish to differentiate it from, for example, Mexican Spanish, which has been influenced by American Indian languages. Spanish became the homogenizing force not only inside the peninsula but also in its colonies.

As Hernán Cortés, Francisco Pizarro, Pánfilo de Narváez, and other conquistadors and explorers took control of the Americas, the Spanish language and Catholicism were the principal tools of control and "civilization" of indigenous people. The Bible was forced upon the Indians in Spanish. And as the *mestizo* and mulatto populations emerged, and grew, the colonial effort made Spanish the hemispheric language of business transactions, politics, and religion.

In time each country developed its own variety of Spanish. While all share the same grammatical rules, certain characteristics distinguish the Spanish spoken in different countries. For example, *vos* is used in the River Plate region (Argentina and Uruguay) for the second-person singular, and a conjugation related to *vosotros* is then adapted, as in "*¿Vos venís mañana?*" ("Are you coming tomorrow?") In Colombia the second-person formal form, used to address a person respectfully, such as an elder or person of high social standing, *usted* is widespread, even in intimate relations. A daughter might say to her mother: "*Usted es mi madre.*" ("You are my mother.")

Statue of Antonio de Nebrija outside the National Library in Madrid.

Spanish spread at the expense of dozens of native languages. The conquistadors and missionaries portrayed their indigenous subjects as subhuman. Theologians used biblical references to suggest that the American Indians were closer to chimpanzees than to humans. Their languages were also considered primitive. A few Spanish thinkers and activists resisted these simplifications. One of the most celebrated was Fray Bartolomé de Las Casas, known for the so-called *leyenda negra*, the black legend. In works like *Brief Description of the Destruction of the Indies* (1542), he argued that the Iberian colonialists were engaged in genocide. He denounced their abuses and struggled to convince his readership in the Old World of the dignity of the aboriginal population. Other missionaries devoted themselves to codifying the pre-Columbian languages. Because of their work, we are able to have a modicum of understanding of indigenous languages.

Despite the efforts of those like de Las Casas, such was the scale of indoctrination that by the time the spirit of independence swept the Americas, from Mexico to Argentina, no language other than Spanish was possible as a collective means of communication. To be educated and to have access to civil and ecclesiastical power, one had to understand, speak, and write Spanish. In certain countries, indigenous languages remained widespread enough to continue to be used locally. In Paraguay, Guaraní is the country's de facto second language. In Bolivia, Inca, Quechua, and Aymara are still used. In Guatemala, dozens of indigenous dialects are spoken in remote areas. Yet these are exceptions. Only in the last decades of the twentieth century was instruction in Nahuatl, Quechua, Maya, Zapotec, and other indigenous languages allowed in Mexico, Guatemala, and elsewhere.

Mayan ruins at Palenque in Chiapas, Mexico.

**Language is the companion of empire.**

—*ANTONIO DE NEBRIJA*

# Spanish in *América*

Spanish is the second-most-spoken language in the United States and is taught in classrooms across the country.

**Q:** What has been the evolution of the Spanish language in the United States?

**A:** Like the languages spoken by the Iroquois, Cherokee, and Navajo, Spanish was a linguistic fixture of North America long before the landing of the *Mayflower* and English colonization. Iberian conquistadors and priests communicated among themselves and with American Indians in Spanish in missions and settlements from Florida to the states that today constitute the Southwest. However, Iberian Spanish itself was not "pure"—it reflected Moorish influence—and its use in the Americas was shaped by Nahuatl, Mayan, and, to lesser extent, by other indigenous pre-Columbian languages. Mexico's cession of half its territory to the United States under the Treaty of Guadalupe and the subsequent waves of Spanish-speaking immigrants from all over the Americas created varied forms

Founder, publisher, and editor in chief display their new magazine *Tu Ciudad* (Your City) in May 2005.

Spanglish-language magazines flood newsstands in big cities.

of Spanish throughout the United States. Today varieties of Spanish are plentiful. Spanish is the second-most-spoken language in the country.

The major Spanish-language newspapers include *El Diario* in New York, *La Opinión* in Los Angeles, *La Raza* in Chicago, and *El Nuevo Herald* in Miami. Spanish also boasts two full-fledged TV networks, Univision and Telemundo, reaching an audience of millions; in terms of advertising dollars, they are the fastest-growing networks in the television market. The number of radio stations is immense, and broadcast locations are widespread. In California alone, the number of Spanish-program affiliates is larger than those in all the countries of Central America combined. Additionally, the number of publishers of Spanish-language books continues to grow.

These media and, to a greater extent, Latino individuals employ an amalgamation of Spanish and English. In the same sentence both languages may be used, or an Anglicization of a Spanish word, such as *parquear* (to park), may be used instead of the original Spanish verb *estacionar*.

# The Sounds of Spanglish

**Q:** **What is Spanglish?**

**A:** Spanglish is a modality of speech used daily by millions of people in the United States. Users are mostly Latino, although non-Latinos (Anglos and other ethnic minorities) speak it, too. As a result of the global influence of American culture, one might also encounter Spanglish in Spain, the Caribbean Basin, and major metropolitan areas such as Buenos Aires, Caracas, Lima, and Bogotá.

Spanglish speakers engage in three traceable strategies: code-switching, automatic translation, and the coining of neologisms. Code-switching is the free-flowing transition from one language to another by someone familiar with both languages. A typical dialogue:

"Oye, Nicolás, wasup?"

"Notin' much. Mi vieja needs me to be en casa en la noche."

"Po'qué?"

"Cause ella necesita salir and someone has to keep un ojo on my sister."

These speakers are not necessarily fluent in either Spanish or English. In fact, Spanglish is often used by those with partial knowledge of their immigrant tongue whose immersion in the English-language environment is not yet complete. However, a large number of Spanglish speakers are completely fluent in both languages, but they enjoy the art of code-switching, a linguistic act that has been studied for decades.

Los Angeles disc jockey Nico Jones works at the 96.3 radio station which targets Latinos, using an English-language format.

## Q: What is automatic translation?

A: It occurs when a Spanglish speaker thinks in one language but uses another, resulting in syntax that shows signs of cross-fertilization. An example: "*Te llamo p'atrás.*" The expression means "I'll call you back." Syntactically, it makes no sense in pure, codified Spanish—"*p'atrás*" a contraction of *para atrás*, is a geographic locator meaning toward the back, as in toward the back of the room. The correct expression is "*Te devuelvo la llamada.*" ("I'll return your call"), but people living at the crossroads of Hispanic and Anglo civilizations use it less and less. Instead, they translate the English saying word for word.

## Q: What are Spanglishisms?

A: Neologisms, new words created to describe something that existing words can't capture, are not uncommon. They often are abbreviations. Spanglish speakers also are prone to creating new terms, such as "*wáchale*" for "watch out" and "*la migra*" for immigration patrol. The number of Spanglishisms in use today is enormous. Some are regional, others are used nationally. Some are used by one particular national group and not others. A handful come from adolescent lingo, sports, advertising, and the Internet, a language now known as cyber-Spanglish.

In 2003, a lexicon of approximately six thousand words was compiled and titled: *Spanglish: The Making of a New American Language.* Depending on where a Spanglish speaker lives, his or her age, nationality, and education, the sentence structure might be English-based sprinkled with Spanish terms, or vice versa.

Cuban Americans in Miami speak a type of Spanglish known as Cubonics. Other Cuban Americans elsewhere in the country—say Union City, New Jersey—might use a similar, though not identical, form of speech. Dominican Americans in Washington Heights, New York, have developed their own linguistic code, known as Dominicanish. Other forms include Nuyorican, Chicano Spanglish, Pachuco, and so on. As Spanglish is currently in transition from a purely oral form of communication to a codified one, it would be a mistake to describe it as defined language. At present it is closer to slang, although the speed with which it is establishing its own grammatical rules is astonishing.

Cartoonist Lalo Alcaraz

> **In el placete de La Mancha of which nombre no quiero remembrearme . . .**
> —Don Quixote de La Mancha *by Miguel de Cervantes, in Spanglish translation*

# Selling with Spanglish

**Q:** How do businesses and the media use Spanglish?

**A:** The recent dramatic growth of the Latino community in the United States has made Spanglish a cultural reality. Other immigrant groups also engaged in code-switching and verbal invention, but since their demographic numbers were smaller, their ways of communication have had little impact on the mainstream. At the dawn of the twenty-first century, Spanglish appears everywhere. It is essential in businesses like construction, restaurants, health care, and the legal profession in which Spanglish speakers are employees or clients. In cities like New York, Latino workers are omnipresent in kitchens; thus managers and owners are forced to engage in a mixed Spanish-English dialogue with their workers. Even at the college level, Spanglish is often considered appropriate between professor and student.

Large corporations and small companies alike are aware of the linguistic temperature of the country. MTV frequently uses Spanglish, and many radio stations from the Southwest to the Northeast use it sometimes or all the time. Brands and companies like Mountain Dew, Taco Bell, and Hallmark showcase their knowledge of cutting-edge culture by using Spanglish in their advertisements and greeting cards. Even the U.S. Army uses Spanglish in its recruiting ads. Novels, short stories, and collections of poems are available in Spanglish, including a partial translation of Cervantes's masterpiece *Don Quixote of La Mancha*. The most prominent venue for Spanglish exploration, however, is

Crossover reggaetón singer performs in Madison Square Garden.

George P. Bush greets his uncle, President George W. Bush, during a 2004 pre-election rally in Hobbs, New Mexico.

become the largest ethnic minority in the United States, this attitude is changing. Not only is Spanish being used by politicians at every level, from presidents (Bill Clinton) to state and local figures like Bill Richardson in New Mexico and Antonio Villaraigosa in California, but Spanglish too has been used to connect with Latino voters. In his first and second presidential campaigns, George W. Bush had his nephew, the son of Florida governor Jeb Bush and a fluent Spanglish speaker, deliver speeches to Latino audiences. Audiences have been receptive to these messages and are forgiving of someone whose use of the language—be it Spanish or Spanglish—is limited. On occasion, though, these political maneuvers backfire, in particular when a politician is not aware of linguistic nuances that distinguish expressions used in different ways in different subcultures.

music. For years Spanglish has been used by Latin singers in rhythms as diverse as *corridos,* salsa, merengue, *bachata,* and *reggaetón;* contemporary bands have continued this trend.

## Q: How is Spanglish used in politics?

A: Politicians embrace cultural trends. Spanish has been used regularly by Latino politicians since the colonial period, especially in New Mexico, Arizona, California, and Texas. In the late nineteenth century and throughout the twentieth, as Latinos were stereotyped negatively in the popular imagination, the language became associated with a lower class deprived of political clout. As Latinos

A court interpreter works with a man who speaks only Spanish and is waiting for his hearing.

# CHAPTER 11

# POLITICS

The Latino population of the United States is booming. While Latinos are still primarily concentrated in the states of the West and South and in major cities, the Southeast has the fastest-growing Latino populations. Even the states in the country with the least racial diversity, Maine and Vermont, contain pockets of Latinos, who are primarily employed in agricultural work. Economically, the vast majority of Latinos live under the poverty level, though income level varies by ethnicity, immigration status, and length of time living in the United States. Political issues that Latinos care most about, including health care, education, immigration, and labor, have traditionally had the majority of Latinos—Mexican Americans and Puerto Ricans—affiliating with the Democratic Party. The exception is Cuban Americans, most of whom, especially the older immigrants and first generation, care most about taking a hard line on Fidel Castro. Issues tied closely to religion, like abortion and gay marriage, have also complicated Democratic Party loyalties. The Voting Rights Act of 1965 made possible wider representation for Latinos; the Chicano Movement raised awareness of labor issues; and the immigration marches of 2006 galvanized many Latinos into becoming a part of the political process. Where Latino loyalties ultimately lie and whether they will unify into a single voting block remain to be seen.

Immigrants and immigrant advocates rally in downtown Los Angeles on May 1, 2006. The iconic figure of freedom fighter Ché Guevara appears on a poster above the crowd underneath words of the labor movement: *Sí Se Puede* (Yes, we can!).

# From Chicano to Latino

**Q:** **To what extent are Latinos a single political entity?**

**A:** The high concentration of Mexican Americans in the Southwest made New Mexico, Arizona, California, Texas, and Colorado the centers of Latino political power during the post–World War II Chicano Movement. Over time, Puerto Ricans established another political center in the Northeast, primarily in New York and New Jersey, while Cuban Americans developed a large presence and strong political clout in southern Florida. Although political bridges did exist between these groups, each national group responded to its own needs and worked toward its own aspirations. The demographic growth of Spanish-speakers from all over Latin America in the late twentieth century simultaneously brought about a concentration and a dispersion of Latino power. First under the category of Hispanic, then Latino, a new approach to ethnic politics slowly began to take shape. The need to combine the voices of several ethnic groups into one became more evident and grew as common priorities such as

A mother and child participate in the Los Angeles immigration rally in May 2006.

PLEASE LET US WORK

Wilfredo "Willy" Gort, former vice mayor of Miami, greets Al Cardenas, former representative of Bob Dole for President, during a meeting of Latino Elected and Appointed Officials in 1996.

education, health care, and employment opportunities were recognized. According to specialists, Latinos constituted "the shock of the new" in the American political landscape in the 1980s. Two decades later, though, Latinos as a whole are still working to organize. The attempts at unity are complicated by continual immigration, which brings different degrees of acculturation, English-language proficiency, and priorities. Newly arrived immigrants are first and foremost concerned about their citizenship status, economic opportunities, and education and health care for their children. Despite disagreements among subgroups, Latinos are often viewed as a homogeneous voting block by politicians unaware of cultural nuances. The interest in capturing Latinos' votes is evidenced by the many television and radio ads on Spanish-language stations. Is Latino political homogeneity possible?

# Noteworthy Politicians

**Q:** Who are some political luminaries in Latino history?

**A:** Mexican Americans have deep roots in this country and a long history of activism; however, the number of prominent figures from the community has been relatively small. One of the heroes of the Texas revolution—who also had a role in the slave trade—was Juan Napomuceno Seguín. In California, the influential Roybal family of Los Angeles—whose luminaries include Edward Ross Roybal, who served as a Democrat in the House of Representatives from 1963 to 1993, and his daughter Lucille Roybal-Allard, who currently represents California in the House and was the first Mexican American woman to be elected to Congress—gave a strong voice to Mexican American issues in the state in the twentieth century.

During the Civil Rights era, César Chávez, along with Dolores Huerta, Reies López Tijerina, and Rodolfo "Corky" Gonzáles, represented Chicano migrant workers. Figures like José "Cha Cha" Jiménez of the Puerto Rican Young Lords and Jorge Mas Canosa of the Cuban American National Foundation had a similar role in their respective national groups. Since the nineteenth century, Latinos have been state and national senators, repre-

Supporters of Los Angeles Mayor Antonio Villaraigosa celebrate on election night on May 17, 2005.

Edward R. Roybal.

Gonzales is the country's attorney general; Clinton's cabinet had the current governor of New Mexico, Bill Richardson, serving as secretary of energy, and Henry Cisneros, formerly mayor of San Antonio, as secretary of housing and urban development. In 2005, Antonio Villaraigosa was elected mayor of Los Angeles, the first Latino to serve in that position since 1872. Although all these men and others blazed important paths for Latinos, note that Latino presidential staff members were appointed by non-Latino presidents, not elected by a Latino base, and that Villaraigosa received only one-quarter of his votes from Latinos despite fully half the population of Los Angeles being Latino.

sentatives, and governors—though their numbers have been disproportionately small—but no one has achieved prominence as a national Latino leader. For example, none has achieved the status of the Reverend Jesse Jackson among African Americans.

**Q: What Latinos have recently been nationally prominent?**

**A:** In the 2004 congressional election two, new Latino senators won office, and the number of Latino representatives edged up to twenty-seven. Both President George W. Bush and former president Bill Clinton placed Latinos in positions of power. Currently, the conservative Alberto

New Mexico Governor Bill Richardson

**One cannot think while being angry.**

—*EDWARD R. ROYBAL*

# Organizing the Masses

Right: Former president Bill Clinton addresses the National Council of La Raza annual conference in July 2006.

**Q:** What are the prominent Latino political organizations?

**A:** Formed in 1921 in Corpus Christi, Texas, the League of United Latin Americans (LULAC) is the oldest Latino political organization in the United States. A lobbying group, LULAC engages in literacy and citizen awareness programs, develops corporate alliances, works to make technology accessible to low-income people, and works on housing and immigration issues. Other groups include the Congressional Hispanic Caucus (CHC) and the National Association of Latino Elected and Appointed Officials (NALEO). The former was founded in 1976 by five Latino Democrats in Congress, including Herman Badillo, the first person born in Puerto Rico to represent a mainland congressional district; CHC uses legislative channels to work for Latino issues. The latter group was also formed in 1976; it seeks to increase political participation and to implement programs on education, immigration, and community leadership.

Smaller, nationality-defined organizations are also active. Founded in 1968, during the Chicano Movement, the National Council of La Raza (NCLR), originally known as the Southwest Council of La Raza (SWCLA), focuses on issues specifically affecting Mexican Americans, although it has attempted to expand to represent Latinos in general. It has approximately 270 affiliates in about forty states, including Puerto Rico. The National Puerto Rican Coalition (NPRC), founded in 1977, is devoted to public policy issues of concern to the Puerto Rican community. The Cuban American National Foundation (CANF), founded

Former congressman Herman Badillo

in 1981, is a group with the objective of promoting democratic change and a free-market economy in Cuba. In addition, the Political Association of Spanish-Speaking Associations (PASSO), established in 1960, was originally conceived of as a national group but ultimately became better known as an influential Texas organization. The Council of Mexican American Affairs (CMAA), formed in 1953, as well as the Mexican American Political Association (MAPA), established in 1959, are both devoted to improving the standard of living of Mexican Americans.

League of United Latin American Citizens (LULAC) president Hector M. Flores.

# The Voting Booth

**Q:** What is the voter participation rate among Latinos?

**A:** Engagement in World War II was a significant political turning point for many Latinos. Mixing with other American soldiers, traveling, and participating in conflict on a worldwide scale increased political awareness. Many Latinos took advantage of the G.I. Bill to earn bachelor's and postgraduate degrees. A true benefit for Latinos and other minorities arrived in 1965 with the passage of the Voting Rights Act; signed by President Lyndon B. Johnson, this law opened the way for a larger number of Latinos to have political representation. The bill prohibited any "standard, practice, or procedure" that could result "in denial or abridgment of the right of any citizen of the United States to vote on account of race or color." Subsequently,

High school students work to get out the vote as part of a class civics program in a heavily Latino-populated East Boston neighborhood in 2004.

Congress made amendments, including one signed in 1975 for "minority-language citizens" without full proficiency in English. The amendment requires that bilingual ballots be made available in areas where a minority population exceeds 5 percent of the whole.

Nevertheless, the percentage of Latinos who vote remains small. For example, between the 2000 and 2004 elections, Latinos accounted for half the population growth in the United States but only one-tenth of the increase in total votes cast. This disparity has two major demographic reasons: Many Latinos are too young to vote and others are not eligible because they are not citizens. Thus, although the population increased by 5.7 million in the four years between presidential elections, only 2.1 million were potential voters. Of these potential voters, only 1.4 million cast ballots. Latinos lag behind whites and blacks significantly in the percentage of eligible voters: 39 percent compared with 77 percent for whites, 65 percent for African Americans, and 51 percent for Asians. The percentage of registered voters among Latinos is also small compared with other ethnic groups. At the time of the 2004 election 58 percent of eligible Latinos were registered to vote, compared with 75 percent of whites and 69 percent of African Americans. In general, American young adults are less likely to register to vote than middle-aged and older citizens. The relative youth of the Latino population helps explain the low percentage of registered voters.

President Lyndon B. Johnson signs the Voting Rights Act as Martin Luther King Jr. and other civil rights leaders look on.

**Q: What is the breakdown of foreign born versus native born in the Latino electorate?**

**A:** Native-born Latinos make up 75 percent of all Latino voters, or 12.9 million voters. Naturalized citizens (foreign-born who are now U.S. citizens) account for the remaining 25 percent, or 4.1 million voters. The fastest growth in the Latino electorate comes from the native born, especially second-generation (defined as having one foreign-born parent) youth, who account for 46 percent of the growth of the Latino electorate between the 2004 and 2006 elections.

A Latino teen engages in an immigration rally in Tucson, Arizona.

# Political Priorities and Parties

**Q:** What are Latinos' political priorities?

**A:** In the 2004 election, Latino voters—who represent only a fraction of Latino residents—were concerned with the same issues affecting mainstream Americans: education, health care, the economy, and the war on terrorism—though polls indicate education is more important to Latino voters than to other American ethnic groups. In addition, a majority of Latinos believe that the United States should provide health insurance for Americans who lack it and indicated that they would be willing to pay higher taxes or premiums to support such a program. Polls showed that the above priorities were of more concern than immigration policies in 2004. After the April 2006 immigration marches, however, a sea change occurred. Surveys report that Latinos are feeling more discriminated against, more politically energized, and more unified than before the marches. Two-thirds believed the marches signified momentum that would carry forward into a new and lasting social movement.

Supporters of Dominican Liberation Party candidate Lionel Fernández rally in Santo Domingo, Dominican Republic, in 1996. Dominicans living in the United States closely followed this election, and many cast absentee ballots.

**Q:** Do foreign-born Latinos participate in elections in their native countries?

**A:** One political attitude that sets Latinos apart from mainstream Americans is their attention to developments in their countries of origin. Latinos often watch Spanish-language news programs that cover sports, cultural events, and politics throughout Latin America. Given this degree of interest and attachment, some countries, the Dominican Republic and Mexico among them, have sought to provide absentee ballots to their citizens living abroad. Dominican Americans tend to follow their country's politics closely and vote in elections in both the Dominican Republic and the United States. Mexico's first attempt to capture the votes of its ten million citizens living in the United States during the July 2006 presidential election, however, was unsuccessful. Strict requirements and insufficient publicity hampered the Mexican government's efforts.

**Q:** Are Latinos Democrats or Republicans?

**A:** Political party affiliation among Latinos depends on many factors, including socioeconomic status and ethnicity.

A 2004 survey reported that Latinos are most likely to identify as Democrats (45 percent). Twenty percent say they are Republicans. The remainder report that they are independents (21 percent), "something else," or do not know. This breakdown in affiliation has remained steady since 1999. Swimming against the current of the overall Latino trend are citizens of Cuban origin, the majority of whom are Republican; this affiliation is strongly influenced by concerns about Cuban foreign policy and the desire to remove Fidel Castro from power. Few socioeconomic patterns distinguish Latino Republicans from Democrats except that Republicans tend to have higher incomes and a greater percentage are foreign born.

Florida Supreme Court Justice Raoul G. Cantero III, grandson of ousted Cuban president Fulgencio Batista, announces the 2003 launch of a Web site designed to broadcast the plight of political dissidents in Cuba.

" The government simply cannot provide work for everyone, education for everyone, insurance for everyone. The solution is to educate people. "

*—HERMAN BADILLO*

# Demographics

**Q:** How many Latinos live in the United States?

**A:** The mid-decade calculations conducted by the Pew Hispanic Center using information from the 2000 Census and the 2005 American Community Survey found that nearly 42 million Latinos live in the United States. Among these, 25 million are native born, with almost 17 million foreign born. The next largest minority, African Americans, number 34.5 million.

Broken down by ethnicity, Mexican Americans overwhelmingly outnumber the next-largest ethnic group, Puerto Ricans—63.9 percent compared with 9.1 percent. Cubans are 3.5 percent; Salvadorans, 3 percent; Dominicans, 2.7 percent; Guatemalans, 1.9 percent; Colombians, 1.7 percent; and Hondurans, 1.1 percent. All other Latin American nationalities account for less than 1 percent of the total Latino population, though the category "Other" claims 7.2 percent.

Latinos are the fastest-growing ethnic group in America. In 2005, the percentage of Latinas who had given birth in the past year was 9.2, compared with 6.3 for white, 7.4 for African Americans, and 7 for Asians.

**Q:** What states have the highest concentration and fastest-growing populations of Latinos?

**A:** More Latinos live in California, 12.5 million, than in any other state. But 43 percent of New Mexico's population is Latino, the highest percentage in the nation, compared with 35 percent in California and Texas. Some evidence has surfaced of very small outmigration (presumably to other states in the U.S., but the destinations are not known) of Latinos from states where they have traditionally been most highly concentrated: California, Florida, Texas, New Jersey, and New York. The fastest-growing Latino populations, with percentages in the high 50s and 40s between 2000 and 2005, are in the Southeast—South Carolina, Tennessee, Arkansas, North Carolina, and Georgia.

A Latino barrio clothing sale in the Los Angeles fashion district. Latinos make up half of the city's population.

A Latino man hoists his sentiments on a banner during an immigration rally in Nebraska.

# CHAPTER 12

# LA MÚSICA

Music is probably the most vibrant and widely known manifestation of Latino culture in the United States. From salsa to *plenas* to *reggaetón* to jazz, the possibilities of rhythm and style are infinite. Differences of race and class are often obliterated in the creation of music, new forms and old, as with Cuban icon Celia Cruz, who managed to unite Caribbeans of all backgrounds by simply shouting "*¡Azúcar!*" ("Sugar!"). Tito Puente made people spin on their feet with his drumbeats. Yet the music of Latinos is also an important historical record. The explosion of Latin music in New York City in the 1940s demonstrates the depth of cultural exchange with Cuba. The Mexican *narcocorrido* chronicles the adventures of drug traffickers, while the Dominican merengue tells of immigrants looking for a ticket to the American Dream. Pop singer Shakira combines her Lebanese, Colombian, and American ethnicities to sing about passion. Many argue that nothing can get a party going like a Latin beat.

Left: The guitar is ubiquitous in Latin music and can be elaborately decorated with paint, carving, and inlay. Above: Graffiti image of tango dancers in La Boca district of Buenos Aires.

# Musical History

**Q:** What music have Latin American immigrant groups brought to the United States?

**A:** Latino music manifests the same cultural traits as its immigrants: influences from Europe, Africa, and pre-Columbian America. Many of the most popular genres played today were and are heavily influenced by Cuba's musical traditions, as well as those of Puerto Rico, Brazil, Mexico, and Spain. Bolero, with roots in an ancient Iberian dance of ternary (three-beat) rhythms— even though today it has a binary (two-beat) form—is one of the most popular genres of Spanish music. It established itself in Cuba in the late nineteenth century. In the 1940s it crossed over to Anglo audiences, acquiring English-language lyrics and becoming a success in the United States. Caribbean immigrants and their descendants helped to make bolero widespread. The musical forms closest to the hearts of Puerto Ricans are the *bomba* and *plena*, which fuse European and African influences of the Caribbean Basin. Salsa, a fusion of Cuban, Puerto Rican, and New York City music and musicians, is arguably the most well known of all Latin American music. The music most often heard in the Dominican Republic is *bachata* and merengue, each of which has been slightly altered in U.S. mainland settings. In Mexico, *ranchera* music, often played by mariachi bands, is so prevalent as to be called an expression of the nation's psyche. *Ranchera* started as rural music, but in the second half of the twentieth century it migrated, along with

Also a martial art form, capoeira is just one example of the heavy influence of Brazilian traditions on Latin music.

its players, to urban settings—though the music still retains its rural roots. *Ranchera* has its songs and more experimental variations. Other uniquely Mexican music includes *corridos.* In the U.S.-Mexico border region, music known as *conjunto* and tejano has developed. Contemporary fusion music that reflects Latin American music influence includes *reggaetón*, jazz, and hip-hop. On the way to the United States from Latin America, some musical genres modified significantly. Lyrics now recount Latino experiences: the plight of immigrants; their quest to find a home away from home; loneliness; and the universal need for love and affection. New instruments were introduced, other traditions, such as Southeast Asian or American pop, influenced original forms, and a more diverse audience resulted in adaptations.

**Q: Which Latinos have trained in classical music?**

**A:** Some of the earliest exposure of indigenous Americans to Spanish classical music was through mission music, such as Gregorian chants and, later, baroque Catholic Masses. Some assert that in the nineteenth century the upper classes of Mexican Americans trained in and imitated European classical styles.

Louis Moreau Gottschalk, a pioneering classical composer and pianist, incorporated Latin American elements into his compositions. He subsequently trained Venezuelan Teresa Carreño, a sensational pianist and the first woman to conduct an opera. Spanish cellist Pablo Casals moved from Europe to Puerto Rico in 1956 and founded the Casals Festival.

Today, a number of Latino classical musicians have international reputations. Plácido Domingo, the acclaimed Spanish-born tenor from Mexico, has sung in and directed opera.

The list of Latino classical composers includes Pulitzer Prize–winner Mario Davidovsky, Orlando Jacinto García, Ricardo Lorenz, and Osvaldo Golijov. Working in more popular forms, Lalo Schifrin has scored movies, including *Dirty Harry* and the *Mission Impossible* series.

Mariachi players with violin and guitar in Old Town, San Diego.

# Playing in the Band

**Q:** **What instruments are used in Latino music?**

**A:** Across Latin American national and ethnic traditions, wind and string instruments—including flute, clarinet, and saxophone, as well as guitar, cello, harp, and bass—are common, with drums and percussive instruments of all shapes, sizes, and materials providing the beat. Accordions have entered some genres, as has piano. Each national tradition prizes different native instruments.

In Cuba, musicians use *batas* (hourglass-shaped hand drums), *batijas* (large, open-mouthed earthenware jugs), bongos (small hand drums), the *cajón* (hand-played wooden box), *chekere* (Yoruba instrument made from a dried gourd), claves (pair of sticks), congas (barrel-shaped hand drums), *guataca* (the blade of a hoe), *guiro* (hollowed and dried gourd open at the top and struck with a stick), *marimbula* (of Congolese origin, a wooden box with tonguelike slats plucked by the fingers), *palitos* (wooden sticks), and timbales (pair of cylindrical metal drum shells with tunable heads and open bottoms).

Mexico uses the marimba (a member of the xylophone family of African origin), *bajo sexto* (twelve-string guitar), and *gitarrón* (oversized six-string guitar). Puerto Rico employs the *bomba* (large barrel-shaped wooden drum), *cuatro* (string instrument, descendant of the Spanish guitar), *guicharo* (small, hollow dried gourd with serrated side scraped with a stick), and *panderetas* (small, flat, tunable hand drum like a tamborine). The Dominican Republic is known for the *guira* (lightweight metal instrument played by scraping the sides) and *tambora* (double-membrane tunable wooden drum).

Brazil's famous instruments include the *ago-go* (two small cowbell-like instruments), *berimbao* (a bow with an open-ended gourd on one end, both strung with metal wires), *cabasa* (dried gourd strung with beads), *chocalho* (metal shaker), *pandeiro* (considered the national instrument of Brazil, a single-membrane tunable tambourine with six groups of two-tin disks inside), and the *reco-reco* (hollow bamboo instrument scraped with a metal stick).

These instruments all evolved from different traditions and are increasingly used outside their traditional spheres as musicians experiment and play music that crosses national and ethnic boundaries.

The boxlike *cajón* is an example of international musical borrowing; originally a Peruvian instrument, it was adapted by the Spanish for use in flamenco music.

" "My dream as a child was to become another Jorge Negrete." "

—*Plácido Domingo*

Left: Most Latin music incorporates some kind of guitar.

Below: *Pandeiros* are used in Puerto Rican and Brazilian music.

Bottom: A set of congas, instruments essential to Cuban music.

# Border Ballads

**Q:** What is a *corrido*?

**A:** The word *corrido* comes from the Spanish verb *correr*, to run; a *corrido* is a border ballad (typically sung in the U.S.-Mexico border regions) about a legendary hero or historical event. The origin of the *corrido* may date back to the medieval Spanish *romancero* (romantic song). Some scholars believe that this tradition reaches into the pre-Columbian American past. Mexico has had *corridistas*, composers of *corridos*, since the war of independence in the early nineteenth century. Along the border can be heard famous songs that date from the time of the Spanish-American War; the songs recount deeds of outlaws like Gregorio Cortez and Tiburcio Vásquez and combine history and fiction.

The musical structure of a *corrido* is set: simple four-line stanzas that rhyme at the end and a chorus that carries a political message based on an individual's heroism. *Corridos* were created and sung anonymously, passed from one ballad-maker to another, and usually accompanied by a string instrument such as a guitar. *Corridistas* traditionally recited songs from memory, and so elements changed according to the singer's audience and ability to remember the music and words. The *corrido* tradition continues today with songs about President John F. Kennedy, César Chávez, and the martyred tejana singer Selena, for example.

A *corrido* songsheet from 1915.

# Q: What are *narcocorridos*?

A: The growth of the illegal drug trade in the Americas in the 1990s created a variant form of the *corrido*, especially among Mexican American laborers. *Narcocorridos* (literally drug *corridos*) focused on illegal immigrants, drug cartels, and encounters with the U.S. border police. Among the most famous *narcocorridistas* are Chalino and the group Los Tigres del Norte.

> *Voy a cantar un corrido, escuchen muy bien mis compas*

> *Para la reina del sur, traficante muy famosa*
> *Nacida alla en Sinaloa, la Tía Teresa Mendoza*

> I'm going to sing a corrido, listen well my friends
> For the queen of the south, a trafficker very famous
> Born in Sinaloa, Boss Teresa Mendoza . . .

> —Los Tigres del Norte, "La Reina del Sur"

Below left: *One Hundred Corridos: The Heart of Mexican Song* is one example of *corrido* anthologies being stocked in Mexican school libraries; the book's inclusion of *narcocorridos* has caused great controversy.

Below: Los Tigres del Norte are famous for their *narcocorridos*.

CIEN CORRIDOS
Alma de la canción mexicana

Mario Arturo Ramos

# Tex-Mex Rhythms

Santiago Jiménez Jr.,
center, recipient of
a National Heritage
Fellowship, plays the
button accordion at
an oral history series
in San Benito, Texas.
Accompanying him are
players of *el bajo sexto*,
left, and *el tololoche*.

**Q:** **What are
tejano and *conjunto*
music?**

**A:** In Spanish
the word *conjunto*
can be understood
to mean "band."
*Conjunto* music
includes elements
of Mexican music
from the northern
(*norteño*) part
of the country
and south Texas.
However, *conjunto,* also known as
Tex-Mex music, has also been influenced
by the music of African Americans and
immigrant groups such as Czechs, Poles,
Germans, and Italians; polka music has

been a distinct influence on *conjunto*.
At heart, a *conjunto* band includes an
accordion and a *bajo sexto* (twelve-string
bass guitar). Tejano music has come to
be more closely associated with pop and
country styles.

An accordion player
performs at a *Día de
los Muertos* (Day of
the Dead) celebration
in Los Angeles.

**Q:** **Who was
Selena?**

**A:** Selena, née
Selena Quintanilla,
was born in
Houston in 1971
and became
a famous and
talented tejana
singer with a soul-
ful soprano voice.
From a humble
background, she
began singing
in her family's
restaurant. When

she moved to Corpus Christi, she formed a group, Selena y los Dinos, with her sister and brother. She mixed tejano music with *cumbias,* the Latin American "tropical" music played in Colombia. She also performed polkas, ballads, and romantic music. Her first record, *Ven Conmigo* (Come with Me), was released in 1990; her second, *Amor Prohibido* (Forbidden Love), came out four years later and was a huge success. In 1995 a former employee who had been president of her fan club and had been suspected of stealing money shot her at a hotel in Corpus Christi. At the time of her death she was about to release *Dreaming of You,* a crossover album designed to expand her English-language audience. The record appeared posthumously. A movie about Selena, with Latina Hollywood icon Jennifer López in the starring role, was released in 1997.

Selena Quintanilla, shortly before her 1995 murder.

# From Bomba to Salsa

**Q:** What are *plenas*?

**A:** *Plena* is a popular Puerto Rican form of music composed of syncopated rhythms and call-and-response vocal cadences; the songs are usually about current social issues. *Plena* is a Spanish relative of the African-influenced *bomba,* another native Puerto Rican form. The first *plena* was recorded in New York City around 1927 by a group led by Manuel "El Canario" Jiménez. Other more popular rhythms, like salsa and merengue, have eclipsed *plenas.*

**Q:** Is there a difference between the merengue and *bachata* played in the Caribbean and those played the United States?

**A:** Merengue, originally rural music played in the Dominican Republic and now recognized as that country's national folk music, has been described as the prime maker of ethnic identity for Dominicans in the diaspora. Musicians in New York City use the basic features of typical Dominican merengues, originally played with string instruments such as guitars, but have made significant changes. Merengues in the United States now include accordions and drums and other percussion instruments, feature call-and-response style, and incorporate elements from other Latino and American genres. Lyrics can be nostalgic or recount stories of assimilation. A similar phenomenon occurred with *bachata,* which Juan Luis Guerra and his group Los 4.40 turned into an international sensation. Their music is about displacement and uncontrollable passion.

**Q:** What influence has Brazil had on Latino music?

**A:** Brazilian rhythms and genres such as samba, bossa nova, *baião, tropicália,* and others have exerted a powerful influence on many forms of Latin American music heard

Since their explosion onto the music scene in the 1960s and 1970s, salsa bands are now as varied as the musicians that compose them and the instruments they use, culled from all over Latin America and the United States.

in the United States today. Brazil itself, like the Caribbean, combines musical influences from Africa and indigenous populations in a fusion at once traditional and invigorating. Samba, popularized by Hollywood star Carmen Miranda, highlights the racial and cultural mix of Brazilian music. The extraordinary talent of Brazilian musicians like Caetano Veloso, Gilberto Gil, Chico Buarque, Jorge Ben, and Milton Nascimento have helped define Latino music in the United States.

The "Queen of Salsa," Celia Cruz, waves at the Third Annual Latin Grammy Awards in 2002.

**Q:** **What are the different types of salsa?**

**A:** Salsa is not a particular type of music. Rather, it is, as the musicologist Cristóbal Díaz-Ayala says, "a mode of making music." Salsa, which means "sauce" in Spanish, essentially derives from the Cuban *son*, but also incorporates elements of blues, pop, *plena*, *bomba*, and *guagancó*, an Afro-Cuban rhythm with sexual undertones, among others. Salsa exploded onto the music scene in New York City in the 1960s and 1970s. Famous salseros are Celia Cruz, Charlie and Eddie Palmieri, Johnny Pacheco, Ray Barretto, La Lupe, and Rubén Blades. Each developed a different repertoire. For example, the Spanish-Harlem style of Willie Colón and Daniel Santos differs from the Cuban approach of the Buena Vista Social Club.

**Q:** **Who was the "Queen of Salsa"?**

**A:** Born in Havana on October 21, 1924 or 1925 (sources differ), Celia Cruz became immensely popular for her talent and charisma; she was famous for shouting *¡Azúcar!* to enliven her audience. As a young woman, she joined La Sonora Matancera, a famous Cuban band, and established her international reputation. She left the island in 1960, after Fidel Castro's revolution, and settled in the United States. She recorded some seventy albums and established herself with songs like "Burundanga" and "*La negra tiene tumbao.*" Her Afro-Caribbean background demonstrates that in Latino music ethnic and racial borders are easily blended and sometimes erased. Her 2003 funeral in Miami was attended by millions.

> **I examined myself and realized I'm Panamanian and my eyes would not become blue . . . I had to deal with the reality of being myself.**
>
> —*RUBÉN BLADES, SALSA LEGEND AND SINGER, SONGWRITER, AND ACTOR*

# *Fusión*

**Q: What is Latino hip-hop?**

**A:** Sometimes ridiculed as simply hip-hop recorded by Latino musicians, Latino hip-hop pays tribute to the Puerto Rican roots of the rhythm, which took form in the 1970s in New York City, along with the "gangsta" developments of rap and graffiti. Latino hip-hop is widely played by DJs adapting the music of Tito Puente and others.

**Q: What is *reggaetón*?**

**A:** Also spelled *reguetón*, it is a type of music with origins in Panama that combines Jamaican dance-hall music with *bomba*, *plena*, and hip-hop. It started in the late 1990s and reached its height early in the twenty-first century.

**Q: Who are the leaders of Latin jazz?**

**A:** The jazz scene has been invigorated by the infusion of Latin jazz, an offshoot of more traditional American jazz; it incorporates elements of salsa, merengue, and other Latin rhythms. A fusion of Dizzy Gillespie, Charlie Parker, and Miles Davis set in an Afro-Cuban context, the form has evolved to include other national traditions. Latin jazz musicians dislike the

Both Charlie Parker (left) and Dizzy Gillespie (right) were huge influences in the formation of Latin jazz.

Tango, the most beloved musical genre in Argentina, has become a popular dance all over the United States.

label given to their music because they feel it indicates that they are not as legitimate as standard jazz musicians. Brazilian bossa nova injected a wild beat into jazz in New York City in the 1960s and 1970s. Bebo and Chucho Valdés, Danilo Pérez, Chico O'Farrill, Paquito D'Rivera, Gonzalo Rubalcaba, and Omar Sosa have pushed the form to astonishing heights.

**Q:** Do these muscial forms have accompanying dances?

**A:** Almost every musical rhythm comes with its own deliberate steps, often arranged for couples. The varieties of dance range from *montuno, guaracha, jarabe,* mambo, cha-cha, *danzón, cumbia, guajira, charanga, plena, bomba,* and merengue. As in the case of the music, the different types of dance are directly linked to their countries of origin. The dances found in the Dominican Republic—meringue and *bachata*—are not practiced in Mexico. Likewise, the *jarabe* is from a particular province of Mexico and remains unknown in the Dominican Republic.

As assimilation has proceeded in the United States, these dances have undergone changes that reflect the impact of Anglo civilization. The merengue danced in New York City is based on the one in the Dominican Republic, but the stories the musicians sing are about immigrants and the physical movements are a bit more inhibited.

Dance clubs are a feature of any Latino environment. Depending on national and ethnic background, one might come across clubs specializing in *conjunto,* salsa, tango, *música tropical,* merengue, rock, and *technobanda* (techno).

> **I love living on that stage. Without that, I die.**
>
> —Celia Cruz

# CHAPTER 13

# SPORTS

The tradition of sports in Latin America stretches back to pre-Columbian times. Today, playing and watching sports of all kinds is a favorite pastime of Latinos. Like many Anglo Americans, Latinos are often more interested in the outcome of a baseball game than the results of a political election. In Latin America, from Mexico to Argentina, children grow up watching *el fútbol* (soccer) on TV and playing the game in the streets and fields. When Latinos immigrate, they carry this passion with them. Historically, the most talented players, such as Pele (born Edson Arantes do Nascimento in Brazil) have come from Latin America. U.S. soccer teams today showcase numerous Latino players—some imported from Latin America but the majority native born. Baseball is wildly popular in the countries with a coast on the Caribbean, from Cuba and the Dominican Republic to Venezuela, Colombia, and Panama. The major leagues have a multitude of Caribbean legends, starting with Puerto Rican Roberto Clemente. Apart from these sports, Latinos have distinguished themselves in tennis, golf, and boxing, and play many others recreationally.

Left: Soccer, or *el fútbol*, is considered the national sport in most Latin American countries. Above: Enthusiastic Mexican fans dressed in indigenous and mariachi costumes prior to their country's second-round playoff game during the 2002 World Cup.

# Playing Ball with the Ancestors

**Q:** Were sports played by pre-Columbian populations?

**A:** When the Spanish conquistadors and missionaries arrived, they found a diverse, multifaceted civilization in good physical condition. Not only were religion, politics, astronomy, and organized warfare fundamental aspects of life, so were athletics. One sport in particular, *Tlachili*, known in Spanish as *pelota* (ball) was immensely popular. In Mesoamerica, a region that begins in Mexico and reaches through Guatemala to Belize and Honduras, *pelota* was a sophisticated ballgame with religious implications. A match was usually preceded by acrobats, dancers, and other performers, as well as by musicians with flutes, whistles, trumpets, and drums. A hard rubber ball was used on a stone court with two stone rings protruding from opposite high walls. Athletes were allowed to use any part of their bodies except their hands to pass the ball through the rings. They wore shin and elbow pads to protect themselves from their opponents and from the hard ball and court. Many scholars believe that the game was a battle between the forces of the sun and the forces of the moon. When the game was complete, one team was ritually sacrificed to the gods; scholars debate whether the sacrificed were the winners or the losers. The sites of Mayan ruins—such as Chichén Itzá and Uxmal in the Yucatán Peninsula—have amazingly well-preserved and elegant courts. The game, still played occasionally as a tourist attraction in the Mexican states of Yucatán and Quintana Roo, spread south to El Salvador and northwest toward the American Southwest. *Pelota* was played by the Maya, the Olmecs, Zapotecs, Toltecs, and Aztecs in stadiums filled with spectators. Since rubber was unknown in Europe at the time of the conquest, Hernán Cortés and his soldiers were mesmerized by the ball. Eventually they took samples back to Spain.

Soccer, known through the Anglicized word *el fútbol* and its less popular equivalent *el balonpié*, is Latin America's most famous sport. It is said that two entertainments capture the attention of all Spanish-language speakers: soccer and soap operas. In nations with unstable regimes and economies, governments often invest in these distractions as a balm for the citizens.

The Caribbean Basin is one region where soccer takes a backseat. There, *el beisbol*, also known as *el juego de pelota*, has been the favorite in the Dominican Republic, Cuba, Puerto Rico, and also in Panama and the coastal regions of Venezuela and Colombia since the mid-nineteenth century. Historians believe that the game came to some other countries—Nicaragua, for instance—when the U.S. military invaded them. Legend has it that a student returning from the United States brought a bat and ball to Cuba in 1864. It's likely that American troops played baseball during the 1847 invasion that was part of the Mexican-American War.

The stone "goal" in the ball court at the Mayan ruins of Chichén Itzá. The ball was made of hard rubber and players could use all body parts but their hands to send the ball through the goal.

" The man who sent the ball through the stone ring was surrounded by all . . . He was given a very special award of feathers or mantles and breechcloths, something very highly prized. But what he most prized was the honor. "

—FRAY DIEGO DURÁN, SIXTEENTH CENTURY SPANISH CLERGYMAN AND AZTEC ETHNOGRAPHER

# El fútbol

In Latin American countries, boys start kicking the ball around at young ages and in all kinds of settings—in backyards, parks, and the streets.

## Q: How is soccer part of Latino culture in the United States?

A: Within the United States the growth of *el fútbol* is relatively recent, and much of its popularity can be attributed to the increasing Latino population. For more than a century in the streets of Buenos Aires children have begun to kick the ball when they are still in diapers; however, the American Youth Soccer Organization wasn't formed until 1964. In the 1970s and 1980s, organizers and entrepreneurs sought to inject vitality into the sport by establishing the North American Soccer League and hiring, with expensive contracts, international stars such as Carlos Alberto,

Marinho, the world-famous Pele from Brazil, and Roberto Cabanas and Julio Cesar Romero from Paraguay. But not until the 1990s, when the U.S. team started to perform well in the World Cup and women embraced the sport at the professional

National and international soccer matches of Latin American teams are closely followed by Latinos.

Los Angeles native Oscar de la Hoya waves the Mexican and American flags after winning the gold medal in lightweight boxing at the 1992 Olympics.

level, did the culture around soccer begin to put down deeper roots in U.S. soil. Latin American immigrants and second- and third-generation Latinos are avid soccer fans and attend American stadiums regularly, although in general they still prefer to follow south-of-the-border teams, especially those of their place of origin. Proof of their interest comes from the televised matches broadcast in Spanish by Univision and Telemundo. Major League Soccer organizes special matches during Hispanic Heritage Month.

## Q: How are sports covered in Spanish-language media?

A: Arguably, the sports pages of newspapers like *La Opinión* in Los Angeles, *El Nuevo Herald* in Miami, *La Raza* in Chicago, and *El Diario/La Prensa* in New York are the ones that attract the largest readership. The same goes for channels like Fox News en Español and programs such as "*República Deportiva*" (Sports Republic) on Univision. Spanish-language stations have begun to broadcast NASCAR races as well as boxing, a sport that has Hispanic roots reaching back

to early-twentieth-century California. Latino interest in boxing eventually paved the way for 1992 Olympic gold-medal winner Oscar de la Hoya, a Los Angeles Mexican American. One might even argue that sports and the media attention given to them create a unifying identity for Latinos in the United States. The fact that Latinos of different national origins might embrace an athlete because of his Latin American or Latino background enables the population to build internal social and communal bridges. Ideological differences might be forgotten, even erased, during an athletic match. Add to this the often idiosyncratic and humorous descriptions of the plays and scores—the famous "Goooooooooooooooool!" comes to mind—of Spanish-language broadcasters and the result is a distinct Latino sports culture.

# El beisbol

Puerto Rican baseball legend Roberto Clemente was the first Latino to be enshrined in the Baseball Hall of Fame.

**Q:** **When did Latinos enter the major leagues?**

**A:** No Latino equivalent to the Negro League was ever established in the United States because leagues in Venezuela, Cuba, Puerto Rico, the Dominican Republic, and Cuba have been active, to some degree, since the late nineteenth century.

The first Latin American to play on an American team was likely Esteban Bellán, who joined a U.S. semipro league in 1869. During the early half of the twentieth century, dark-skinned Caribbeans played in the Negro Leagues, while some fairer Latin American players, such as the light-skinned Cuban Adolfo Luque, played in the majors. In 1947 Jackie Robinson broke the color barrier in baseball. Two years later, the first dark-skinned Latin American, Cuban Orestes "Minnie" Minoso, played

Red Sox players David Ortiz, right, and Manny Ramírez share a laugh during a July 2006 game.

most major league teams was astonishing, reaching 40 percent in some cases. The passion for baseball among Latinos and the increasing number of Hispanic players has greatly increased Latino attendance at ballparks. Teams recognize this enthusiasm by staging Spanish-language events.

for Cleveland; the first modern-day Dominican player was Osvaldo "Ozzie" Virgil. Among the biggest stars in baseball in general, and surely among Latinos, is Roberto Clemente, originally from Puerto Rico. He played with the Pittsburgh Pirates and was the first Latino to achieve the record of 3,000 hits. Clemente was active in philanthropic causes, speaking out for the poor and underrepresented. Tragically, he died in an airplane crash on New Year's Eve 1972.

By the beginning of the twenty-first century, the number of Latino players on

Just as black players have dominated basketball for decades, Latino baseball players have now become prized and hugely famous. A vast number of these men come from impoverished backgrounds. After growing up in poverty, entering the major leagues becomes an economic dream for an individual and his family, friends, and acquaintances. In countries like the Dominican Republic, players like Manny Ramírez and David Ortiz become not only role models but iconic figures.

" Every time I hit a home run, I touch my mouth with my fingers and say with my lips, 'To you, Mami.' "

—SAMMY SOSA

# Beyond Ballgames

**Q:** What other sports are popular among Latinos?

**A:** Like ordinary Americans, Latinos enjoy a variety of sports, including golf, swimming, tennis, fencing, running, and wrestling. Tennis is, for the most part, a sport played by the upper classes, and though the majority of Latinos are poorer than the average American, tennis has had its share of Latino notables, including Pancho Segura, Mary Jo Fernandez, and Richard "Pancho" Gonzáles. Similarly, golf, traditionally a sport of the wealthy, has had Lee Treviño in the 1960s and Nancy Lopez in the 1980s.

**Q:** What is special about Latino wrestling?

**A:** Latinos don't have an uncommon interest in the kind of wrestling most Americans are familiar with. However, an idiosyncratic variety of wrestling known as *lucha libre* (free wrestling) has caught Latinos' imagination. The wrestlers are usually masked with the exception of the eyes and mouth. The purpose of the match is to both outmuscle one's opponent and to unmask him. In Mexico, where the sport is immensely popular, the act of unmasking wrestlers posing as political figures was common when the ruling Partido Revolucionario Institucional (PRI) was in control (1929–2000). Every six years, as the presidential campaign got started, the current leader unmasked his successor in the ring, establishing who would carry the mantle thereafter. The act of masking also brings to mind rebel leaders like Subcomandante Marcos, leader of the Zapatistas in southern Mexico, who cover their faces to protect their identities. The act of hunting these rebels is sometimes seen as a form of unmasking. The *lucha libre* folklore includes Robin Hood–like urban heroes

A masked Mexican *luchador*.

Mexico. The sport appears frequently in the novels of Ernest Hemingway, significantly in *Death in the Afternoon*, but among Latinos bullfighting is not especially popular. The rodeo, on the other hand, is quite vibrant in the Latino Southwest, with national tournaments contested in cities like Las Vegas. Cowboy culture traces its roots to the Spanish colonial period. Much of the terminology—words like *laso*, *reata*, *vaquero*, and *rancho*—comes from Spanish.

Much of the cowboy, or *vaquero*, culture and language derives from Mexican ranching traditions in the Southwest.

who live in working-class neighborhoods like Tepito and Nezahualcóyotl in Mexico City and devote themselves to protecting the poor from abuse by the authorities. The sport has icons like El Santo (the Saint), whose wrestling career, thanks to B-movies and comic strips, has become the subject of urban myths. The legendary status of and passion for *lucha libre* wrestlers is also present among Mexican Americans. *Mucha Lucha,* a children's cartoon show on TV, draws on this Latino tradition.

## Q: Do Latinos participate in bullfighting or rodeos?

**A:** Bullfighting is a signature national sport in Spain and was imported to

## Q: What non-athletic games do Latinos enjoy?

**A:** The Aztecs played a board game called *Patolli*, which is similar to backgammon. Latinos today engage in board games popular south of the Rio Grande, such as *Serpientes y escaleras* (Snakes and Ladders) and, especially, *Lotería* (Lottery), a type of bingo using cards with images from popular culture. Children have *piñatas* at birthday parties. Street games include *rayuela*, played much like hopscotch, and *escondidillas*, a form of hide-and-seek. *Toma todo* (Take All) uses a six-sided top and is played by both children and adults.

# Athletic Latinas

**Q:** How has girls' and women's involvement in sports changed over the years?

**A:** Traditionally, sports were a masculine activity in Latin American and Latino cultures. For decades Latinas were reluctant to play on school-sponsored teams, despite the publicity of figures like tennis great Mary Jo Fernandez and golf Hall-of-Famer Nancy Lopez. Lack of participation has been attributed to negative stereotypes and to the belief that athletics are not feminine. Congress helped to open doors to competitive sport for all American women with the passage of Title IX in 1975, which prohibited gender-based discrimination in federally funded sports. Gradually, in the late 1980s, Latina participation began to increase.

Within the family setting, girls often had to overcome stereotypical expectations to participate in athletics, but as girls' and women's sports received more funding and support on the local, state, and federal levels, more females of all ethnicities have become more involved in sports. National studies show that girls who participate in sports are less likely to drop out of high school and more likely to go to college; these results have been borne out for Latinas as well.

Certainly, Latina sports stars have been great motivators for aspiring athletes. Lisa Fernandez, California-born of Cuban and Puerto Rican heritage, played softball for the University of California, Los Angeles, and became the most recognized female pitcher in the country. In the 2002 Olympics, speed skater Jennifer Rodriguez won two bronze medals. With increasing numbers of role models, the number of younger Latina athletes will grow as well.

Right: Softball pitcher Lisa Fernandez.
Opposite: Speed skater Jennifer Rodriguez.

# CHAPTER 14

# LETRAS

In addition to diaries, letters, and other historical accounts, the Spanish explorers and conquistadors expressed themselves and their lives in the New World though poetry and plays. In the late nineteenth century, English-language novels began to appear; they chronicled the fight for land as a result of the Treaty of Guadalupe Hidalgo and the Gadsden Purchase; they portrayed the Mexican American struggle for jobs, equal rights, and the preservation of their way of life. The political overtones in literary works also intensified among Caribbean intellectuals in the Northeast as the fight for independence from Spain took hold in Cuba and Puerto Rico. Literary depictions of immigration, ghetto and barrio life, and assimilation are elements of more recent Latino literature. Which language to publish in remains a dilemma for publishing houses in the United States; books are now released in Spanish, English, and bilingual format. Spanglish has recently become another literary force.

Left: Opening day of the Guadalajara Book Fair in 2003. Brazilian writer Rubem Fonseca (left) receives the Juan Rulfo Literature Award as Gabriel García Márquez (right) applauds.

Above: A page from *Travels of Father Kino and Other Jesuits to California and North America* by Juan Mateo Manje (1670–1727).

# Making Fiction

**Q:** What early Latino fiction was published in the United States?

**A:** Beginning in 1535, as the territories of what are today the states of the Southwest were being explored, Iberian chroniclers described the landscape and aboriginal population. Eventually more poetic books were written and published, like Gaspar Pérez de Villagrá's *Historia de la Nueva México* (History of New Mexico, 1610).

Only after the Treaty of Guadalupe Hidalgo was signed—when Mexicans suddenly became Americans—did the English language begin to take hold as a literary vehicle. Earlier, Anglo Americans had been the ones sparking readers' interest in Hispanic issues—for example, Washington Irving's *Tales of the Alhambra* (1832). The first novelist to explore the Mexican American experience in English was María Amparo Ruíz de Burton, whose first novel, *Who Would Have Thought It?*, appeared anonymously in 1872. Her most famous book is the now classic *The Squatter and the Don*, released in 1885 under the name "C. Loyal," meaning *Cuidano Loyal*, or Loyal Citizen.

*History of New Mexico*, by colonial explorer Captain Gaspar de Villagrá, was published in 1610.

Washington Irving piqued American readers' interest about the Hispanic world with his *Tales of the Alhambra*.

**Q:** Who was Felipe Alfau?

**A:** Knowing the odyssey of Barcelona-born Alfau is useful for understanding the publishing conundrums faced by Latinos in the early twentieth century. Alfau immigrated to New York City with his family before the Spanish Civil War. He wrote music criticism for *La Prensa*, a predecessor of the now merged *El Diario/ La Prensa*. He then decided to write novels, but switched to English to gain a wider readership. His *Locos: A Comedy of Gestures*, was finished in 1928, but it was not published until 1936. The novel resembles the work of Borges, Nabokov, and Pirandello, although, with the exception of the last, these authors had yet to make their mark in international letters. The immigrant Latino community in New York wasn't interested in the avant-garde explorations that Alfau was obsessed with. *Locos* was well received but went out of print until 1988, when it was rediscovered by Dalkey Archive Press, a small publisher in Normal, Illinois. Alfau wrote a second book in English, *Chromos*, but was unable to find a publisher. He also wrote poetry, which wasn't published until the 1990s. Had Alfau stayed in Spain and survived the Spanish Civil War, his career may very well have had a dramatically different trajectory: Writing books in Spanish in the United States limited his audience; yet choosing English limited his aesthetic and intellectual expression. As a result, he determined that his writing would reflect the perspective of an outsider looking in.

## Q: Who are the founding figures of twentieth-century Latino fiction?

**A:** Path-breaking Mexican American writers include María Cristina Chambers, who began publishing stories in New York magazines—at first for a primarily non-Latino audience—in 1913. Her later novels are set in Mexico. In the 1940s Mario Suárez of Tucson published several short stories about Chicanos in the Tucson barrios. Often considered the first modern Chicano novel is José Antonio Villarreal's *Pocho* (1959), a story of a youth torn between American and Mexican cultures. The Chicano Movement of the 1960s inspired many writers. Richard Vásquez published *Chicano* in 1970. Tomás Rivera published . . . *y no se lo tragó la tierra/ . . . and the Earth Did Not Devour Him* (1971). Rudolfo Anaya released his seminal *Bless Me, Ultima* in 1972, and Rolando Hinojosa-Smith wrote *Klail City Death Trip*, a series of novels, in the mid-1970s.

The first major contribution by a Chicana is considered to be Estela Portillo Trambley's *Rain of Scorpions and Other Writings* (1975).

A pioneer in Nuyorican literature is Nicholasa Mohr; her novel *Nilda* (1973) narrates the life of a girl growing up in East Harlem in the 1930s through World War II. Alongside Mohr was playwright and poet Miguel Piñero. He won an Obie in 1975 for his play *Short Eyes*. The late 1980s and 1990s brought widespread recognition to Latino writers of all ethnicities—Cuban exiles and their descendants, Dominican Americans, Puerto Ricans, Bolivians, Colombians, and others. Well-known authors and works include Sandra Cisneros (*House on Mango Street*, 1984), Julia Alvarez (*How the Garcia Girls Lost Their Accent*, 1991), Oscar Hijuelos (*The Mambo Kings Sing Songs of Love*, 1989), Junot Díaz (*Drown*, 1996), Cristina García (*Dreaming in Cuban*, 1992). In addition, playwrights María Irene Fornés and Cherríe Moraga have received considerable recognition.

Sandra Cisneros

> **Everyone needs a strong sense of self. It is our base of operations for everything that we do in life.**
> —*Julia Alvarez*

# Poetry and the Self

Right: Julia de Burgos

**Q:** What has been the evolution of Latino poetry?

**A:** While exiled in New York, Cuban José Martí wrote inspirational poetry that celebrated and instilled national pride. Another Cuban exile writer and poet, José María Heredia, published *Cartas sobre los Estados Unidos* (Letters on the United States) in 1826.

William Carlos Williams was not widely recognized as Latino during his time—his father was Anglo and his mother Puerto Rican—but he is a cornerstone of the genre. Born in Rutherford, New Jersey, in 1888, and dead in the same place at the age of seventy-nine, he was a doctor, poet, and essayist associated with the modernist school of poetry. His imagist poetry, his left-wing politics (he was appointed poet laureate consultant to the Library of Congress, but he didn't get the job because of his association with communism), and his probing explorations of American history in volumes like *In the American Grain* (1956) and in his *Autobiography* (1951) made him an inspiration to the Beat Generation.

William Carlos Williams

Another founding figure of Latino poetry is Julia de Burgos. She was born in Carolina, Puerto Rico, in 1914, and died in New York City in 1953. Her lyrical poetry plays with sexual, historical, geographical, and emotional images in a lucid, provocative fashion. She suffered from alcoholism and depression, and one of her famous poems, "Farewell in Welfare Island," was written in 1953 while in the hospital.

The Nuyorican Poets Café in New York City showcased the work of poet Pedro Pietri, famous for his "Puerto Rican Obituary." Tato Laviera was also a part of this community and coined the term "AmeRícan," describing the Puerto Rican mainland diaspora, in his collection of the same name published in 1985. Poets Sandra María Esteves, Lucky Cienfuegos, and Bimbo Rivas participated in the Café's scene as well. In 1994, Café founder Miguel Algarín and Bob Holman edited a volume titled *Aloud*, which offered samplings of the origins of this artistic movement but also related it to slam and hip-hop poetry in general.

Slam poetry is a movement that originated in 1984 in Chicago with construction worker and poet Marc Smith; it's designed to make poetry more accessible to audiences and is a competitive event with judges rating performances on a scale from one to ten. Hip-hop poetry is an outgrowth of the musical hip-hop culture; it is not necessarily competitive and consists of spoken-word verse.

In Chicano literature, important poets include Alurista, Lorna Dee Cervantes, and Gary Soto. Noteworthy Cuban-American poets include Virgil Suárez and Lourdes Gil.

Regis E. Gaines
performs at the Nuyorican
Poets Café.

# Memoirs

## Q: What has been the impact of Latino memoirs?

A: Ethnic literature is often defined by the tension between the individual and a foreign environment—the new and strange home. Autobiography can be a deeply emotional way to explore the personal trials of the immigrant as he or she acquires a new life. Examples of memoirists include Puerto Ricans Jesús Colon, Bernardo Vega, Piri Thomas, and Irene Vilar. Powerful Cuban exile memoirs include Heberto Padilla's *Self-Portrait with the Other* (1989) and Reinaldo Arenas's *Before Night Falls* (1993); the latter was turned into a movie starring Javier Bardem and

The port of Mazatlán, the Mexican town where Oscar "Zeta" Acosta disappeared.

Johnny Depp. Arenas's memoir was also important in the Latino gay and lesbian community as the author's homosexuality is a central theme. Cherríe Moraga wrote a memoir—*Waiting in the Wings* (1997)—about Latina lesbian motherhood. Well-known Chicano memoirists are Richard Rodriguez, with his three-part autobiography, and Oscar "Zeta" Acosta.

## Q: Who was Oscar Acosta?

A: Oscar "Zeta" Acosta was a lawyer, activist, and memoirist whose books— *The Autobiography of a Brown Buffalo* (1972) and *The Revolt of the Cockroach*

*People* (1973)—chronicle, using the language known as "Gonzo journalism" made famous by Hunter S. Thompson, the plight of Chicanos in the late 1960s and early 1970s.

Acosta adopted the *nom de guerre* "Zeta" as he came to recognize his role as a rebellious figure. Born in El Paso on April 8, 1935, Acosta moved with his family to Modesto, California, in 1940, where the Sleepy Lagoon Case and the Zoot Suit Riots left an imprint in his mind. After high school, he enlisted in the U.S. Air Force. He eventually became a lawyer and an activist and, while not part of the mainstream culture, argued important legal cases in the second half of the 1960s.

Acosta is the model for the 300-pound Samoan in Thompson's *Fear and Loathing in Las Vegas*. His death is surrounded by mystery. After an unsuccessful run for mayor of Los Angeles, Acosta traveled to the Mexican coastal town of Mazatlán, apparently in search of quiet in which to write. He was never heard from again. A mythical version of his disappearance claims he is hidden somewhere, plotting a takeover of the U.S. government along with other deceased Latin American guerrilla fighters such as Emiliano Zapata and Ernesto "Ché" Guevara.

> " **Brown is impurity.** "
> —*Richard Rodriguez*

# Literary Criticism

**Q:** Is literary criticism less common and less valued than fiction, poetry, and the personal essay in Latino literature?

**A:** A stereotype has Latinos as inveterate dreamers—rather than critical thinkers. When one thinks about Latin American literature, what comes to mind most readily is magical realism, a style popular in the 1960s but still in use today. This style interweaves dreams and reality. The most famous novel from this tradition is Gabriel García Márquez's *One Hundred Years of Solitude*, originally published in 1967. Other authors, including Jorge Luis Borges, Julio Cortázar, Carlos Fuentes, and Isabel Allende, also belong to this movement. Critical thinking in the form of literary criticism is less popular, although not necessarily less frequent. The Spanish-speaking Americas have certainly produced practitioners of

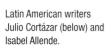

Latin American writers Julio Cortázar (below) and Isabel Allende.

the critical essay, from writers such as José Enrique Rodó in Uruguay to Octavio Paz in Mexico. In the United States, though, the number is small. Perhaps Latinos in the United States feel the need to enter the creative genres before moving into the critical sphere.

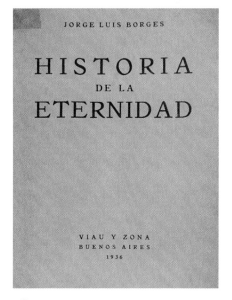

JORGE LUIS BORGES

# HISTORIA
## DE LA
# ETERNIDAD

VIAU Y ZONA
BUENOS AIRES
1936

## Q: What forms have literary criticism taken in the United States?

A: The evaluation and interpretation of literary works, including plays, by Latinos has taken three main forms in the United States: journalism, such as book reviews and critical essays; occasional and multimedia, such as prefaces and forewords to books and author interviews and speeches; and academic, whose audience is mainly limited to other academics. Most criticism being produced today contains itself to a particular ethnic or national group. Notable for breaking this mold was William Luis's *Dance of Culture*, which treated Dominican, Puerto Rican, Nuyorican, Cuban, and Cuban American work. Chicano literature, however, was not included. Another exception is the journal *Revista Chicano-Riqueña*, which takes a more Pan-American approach.

Within the field of Latino criticism, three main theories have emerged in the twentieth century. The first is border theory, which focuses on the link between culture and literature that exists across the U.S.-Mexico border; Américo Paredes's focus on border ballads is one example. The second is island theory, which, taking into account the multiracial heritage of Caribbean Latinos, sees culture and literature through the lens of replicating islands; for example, the Dominican-dominated barrio of Washington Heights in New York is a Dominican "island." A seminal book from this area is Antonio Benítez-Rojo's 1987 *La isla que se repite* (*The Repeating Island*). The third theory is feminist theory, two of whose main proponents are the creative writers Cherríe Moraga and Gloria Anzaldúa. Feminist theory highlights the fact that Latina history has been especially overlooked given historically prevailing machismo within Latino society, which itself, as a whole, has not been given the attention it is due.

Jorge Luis Borges's *History of Eternity*.

**A library is also a place where love begins.**
—*Rudolfo Anaya*

# Books *en español*

**Q:** Is there a Spanish-language book industry?

**A:** Publishing houses for Spanish-language works were active in urban centers (New York, Albuquerque, San Antonio) before the Treaty of Guadalupe Hidalgo was signed. California and New Mexico had printing presses in 1834. Authors like Juan B. Hijar y Jaro, José Rómulo Ribera, J. M. Vigil, Luis A. Torres, and more significant figures like the Chacón siblings, Eusebio (author of *Hijo de la tempestad*) and his brother Felipe Maximiliano, probed into the Mexican American experience in their works. By the end of the nineteenth century, works had been written in Spanish in the United States by Cuban and Puerto Rican exiles and refugees such as Eugenio María de Hostos, Lola Rodríguez de Tío, and Sotero Figueroa.

**Q:** Did the Latino publishing industry change with the Chicano Movement?

**A:** One offspring of *el movimiento* was a number of ethnic publishing houses, among them Arte Público Press and Bilingual

Press. Interestingly, these and other publishers of Spanish-language books formed in the aftermath of the Civil Rights era initially started as magazine ventures. It was recognized that Latinos lacked intellectual outlets in which to reflect on their history and identity.

The name Arte Público—the house was launched in 1979—is reminiscent of and even a tribute to a federally funded publishing effort in Mexico in the 1920s that is still active today: Fondo de Cultura

Nicholas Kanellos, director of Arte Público press.

Several other early-established presses are smaller in size. These include Tonatiuh-Quinto Sol (TQS), originally called Quinto Sol Publications and responsible for the Premio Quinto Sol prize. Editor-in-chief Octavio Ignacio Romano, a professor of public health at the University of California at Berkeley, died in 2005. In 1971 he edited a significant anthology of the Chicano Movement, *El Espejo/ The Mirror*.

The Latin American Literary Review Press, published by Yvette Miller in Pittsburgh, was originally launched in 1980 as a scholarly magazine, *Latin American Literary Review*. The press focuses primarily on publishing English translations of Spanish-language classics and Latin American literature, sometimes in bilingual format.

As the Latino population continues to grow, large publishing houses are beginning their own Spanish-language and Latino-focused imprints. Random House has Vintage *Español* and HarperCollins has Rayo. Other major houses are looking for ways to capitalize on the growing number of Latino readers.

Puerto Rican exile writer Lola Rodríguez de Tío.

Económica. Arte Público Press started in Gary, Indiana, and then moved to the University of Houston. Among its biggest sellers is Tomás Rivera's migrant classic *. . . y no se lo tragó la tierrá/ . . . and the Earth Did Not Devour Him*, considered to be the most influential novel by a Chicano published in the second half of the twentieth century. Founded in 1973, Bilingual Press publishes books in English, Spanish, and bilingually, including literature, scholarship, and art books by or about Latinos.

> **America belongs to the world, the greatest of all nations! America is noble, America is great! . . . Spread out your flag, let the light from your stars illuminate the entire world.**
>
> —LOLA RODRÍGUEZ DE TÍO

# CHAPTER 15

# ART AND TASTE

Is there a Latino sensibility, a unique aesthetic taste? Certainly Spanish-language TV and radio have been instrumental in the forging of a Latino identity; no other immigrant group has built a media infrastructure of equal significance, and media help shape behavior. Some Latino aesthetics, however, were formed long before the use of microphones and cameras. Folklore, in the form of stories, dance, song, and popular art, might well be the most vivid expression of Latinos' tastes. This folklore, Chicano, Caribbean, and South American, is evident in many places—from stand-up comedy, to cartoons, barrio bodegas, cuisine, and traditional celebrations.

Opposite page: Diverse indigenous cultures across Mexico are manifested in a wide variety of traditional dress and costume. Above: April Fair in Seville, Spain.

# Aesthetics

Below: Our Lady of Guadalupe is the inspiration for much Mexican American art.

Right: Gloria Estefan performs for the crew of a U.S. Navy aircraft carrier and their families.

**Q: Is there a Latino aesthetic?**

**A:** Aesthetics can be understood as a cultural approach to sensual perceptions. Or better, as a unified sense of taste shared by people of the same geographi-

cal, cultural, political, and artistic realm. The Hispanic world came into being from the fusing of the cultures of the Iberian Peninsula and the Americas; this fusion continues and adapts to new circumstances. In Mexico and Central America, the fusion has resulted in a *mestizo* aesthetic, whereas in Cuba, Puerto Rico, and the Dominican Republic, it has produced an Afro-Caribbean sensibility.

Such is the heterogeneity of Latinos that their aesthetics depend on class, race, ethnicity, generation, language preference, and geography. A working-class Chicano in San Antonio, while sympathizing with the Latino aesthetic, approaches it individually through *rascuachismo,* a term denoting a sense of empowerment about pop Chicano culture. For a Chicano, the Virgin of Guadalupe and Cantinflas might be icons. A middle-class Cuban American in Miami will likely embrace a different artistic constellation: Gloria Estefan and Santería. The approach in this case is *tropicalismo*—inspired by a Brazilian artistic movement around Oswald de Andrade's 1928 artistic manifesto "Anthropophagy."

In major urban centers, Latinos congregate according to national background. For example, Chicago has the Mexican American neighborhoods of La Villita and Pilsen, and Los Angeles has East Los Angeles (pronounced *Eeslos* by many Chicanos) among other neighborhoods; Florida's Miami-Dade and Broward counties have Cuban and Caribbean neighborhoods; and Dominicans congregate in New York

Its objective was for Latin American artists and thinkers to break away from their dependency on Spain. *Indigenismo*, an after-thought to the interpretations of José Enrique Rodó's groundbreaking book *Ariel* (1900), asks for a return to indigenous culture as a source of hemispheric identity.

Latinos have inherited these amalgamations. In turn, they have adapted them to their surroundings in the United States, giving rise to an altogether different sensibility that is part Hispanic and part Anglo. That sensibility is often contained in the concept of Spanglish. The aesthetic of Spanglish is about double con-sciousness. It embraces cross-cultural and multilingual cultures. It rejects purity and stresses the value of borrowings. It also elevates kitsch— derivative art produced for the consumption of the masses— as a legitimate form of expression.

A colonial-era painting representing *mestizo* culture—an example of a *pintura de castas* (a caste painting) that depicted people according to their racial heritage.

City's Washington Heights neighbor-hood. Although each of these areas is a center of a different ethnicity, they share common elements: language, a passion for music and sports, and a cuisine. However, none of them has yet convincingly articulated an aesthetic sensibility. Their various aesthetic roots can be found in many areas, including the *santos* and *devotos* of colonial art in the Southwest and south-of-the-border aesthetic movements like *Modernismo* and *Indigenismo*. *Modernismo* first formed in 1885 around the central figure of Nicaraguan poet Rubén Darío.

# Visual Arts

Poster for *The Three Caballeros* features Donald Duck, Panchito, and Joe Barioca with actress Aurora Miranda.

**Q:** **What is the history of Latino visual arts?**

**A:** Painting by Latinos in the United States is a centuries-old tradition. Religious art abounded in the Southwest during the colonial period. Christian iconography was a tool used to indoctrinate Native American populations. Religious art like *retablos*, small paintings of religious figures or miracles, incorporated indigenous elements. In New Mexico, perhaps the state with the oldest pictorial tradition, works in the European style were created, but there were also *santeros*, holy images created for altars in mission churches. Texas has similar artifacts.

Like language and literature, Latino visual art has evolved across national and geographic lines. For example, Martín Ramírez, a Chicano "naïf" artist—others would describe him as a folk artist—produces work that is wholly different from the Florida-based Cuban American artist Frank García, who evokes Italian Renaissance paintings. In turn, García differs from Nuyorican painters like Jean-Michel Basquiat, a graffiti artist of Haitian and Puerto Rican descent who defined his aesthetic in the context of the Afro-Latino influences in New York in the 1970s and 1980s. Such examples demonstrate that generalizations about Latino visual arts in terms of technique, themes, and political and religious content are nearly impossible.

**Q:** **What was muralism?**

**A:** Muralism was an ideological movement that consolidated in the Spanish-speaking world after the 1910 Mexican revolution. Signature artists of the movement—Diego Rivera, José Clemente Orozco, and David Alfaro Siqueiros—used public spaces—street walls, cafeterias, and music and civic centers—to call attention to *mestizos'* desire to find a place in the modern world. Thus, their work was intimately linked to Mexican nationalism. The muralists depicted important moments and figures in the country's history to raise political awareness. As their influence grew, Rivera, Orozco, and Siqueiros were invited to paint murals in the United States, in places like Detroit, Los Angeles, and New York. During the Civil Rights era, a number of Chicano artists adapted the muralists' art to the landscape of the Southwest.

An integral part of the Chicano Movement was the graphic art produced around strikes, marches, and other major gatherings. One of the legacies of the period is the astonishing array of public murals painted by Chicano artists such as Judith Baca, Marcos Raya, Xavier González, José

A mural completed in 1992 in South Beach, Miami, at the 11th Street Diner.

Aceves, René Yáñez, and Yolanda López. The Chicano muralists sought to explore history and myth in the same way as their forerunners, using public space to educate the masses. Los Angeles had posters about Aztlán and the Treaty of Guadalupe Hidalgo, with profiles of César Chávez and Dolores Huerta. Such posters and paintings also included images of the people, average Chicanos fighting for self-determination. Just outside of San Diego lies Chicano Park, an urban space of grass and concrete overpasses, in which nearly every inch of paintable space is covered in murals that carry the voices of a population.

Graffiti is a common form of street art in urban neighborhoods; for Latinos, the imagery often derives from expressions of the Mexican muralist movement.

## Q: How did graffiti evolve?

A: Muralism and graffiti are relatives. Graffiti—from the Italian word *graffito*, commonly defined as "crude scratching upon public spaces"—might not be as deliberately aesthetically pleasing as a mural, but it surely contains equally strong political statements. Its most common forms are aerosol paint and permanent marker on concrete and metal—though words and images can also be etched into metal and glass—applied illegally on public walls, trains, and other surfaces, usually at night. The act of making graffiti often needs to involve danger to be considered legitimate by the artist's peers. Graffiti artists are also called "writers" and "taggers."

Graffiti is a form of self-expression particularly popular among urban youth. It not only coincided with but is part of the same aesthetic that produced hip-hop. Writers sign as ALE, COMENT, FUZZ 1, LSD OM, and TAKI 183. Several artists are immigrants from Mexico, El Salvador, Honduras, and the Caribbean Basin. Some incorporated Aztec and Taíno elements into their art, while others reflected the plight of Latinos in the United States through references to historical and local figures.

## Q: Are Latinos figures in comic strips?

A: Walt Disney and Hanna Barbera created characters like the Three Caballeros and Speedy González. Latino toon-makers, however, produce outside the corporate world. The most significant artists are Lalo Alcaraz, the syndicated cartoonist who created *La Cucaracha*, featured in the *Los Angeles Times* and other publications, and the brothers Jaime and Gilbert Hernandez, known for the success of their comic *Love & Rockets* in the 1980s and 1990s.

**I paint self-portraits because I'm frequently alone and I'm the person I know best.**
—FRIDA KAHLO

# *Teatreros*

Right: Poster for a benefit concert at Carnegie Hall for the California Grape Workers and the National Farm Workers Service Center.

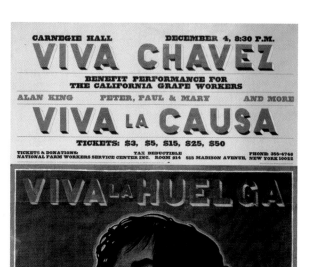

**Q:** What is the history of Spanish-language and Chicano theater in the United States?

**A:** Spanish-language theater has been present in the United States since the colonial period, when *actos* (one-act plays), *pastorelas* (Christmas plays), and other religious plays were enacted in the Southwest in plazas and missions. In the nineteenth century, *carpas*, itinerant theater troupes, entertained the poor with comic theater and vaudeville. In addition, professional companies from Spain and Latin America toured from one Spanish-language community to another.

A 1978 poster created by the Royal Chicano Air Force for a fundraiser for El Teatro Campesino.

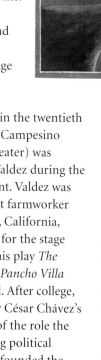

The growth of Latino theater took place in the twentieth century. El Teatro Campesino (The Peasant's Theater) was founded by Luis Valdez during the Chicano Movement. Valdez was born to immigrant farmworker parents in Delano, California, in 1940. He wrote for the stage in college, where his play *The Shrunken Head of Pancho Villa* was first produced. After college, he volunteered for César Chávez's UFW. Conscious of the role the arts had in creating political awareness, Valdez founded the theater with farmworkers. His objective was to make plays about the lives of Mexican Americans and support *la huelga*. In fact, his *actos* were performed to entertain strikers. Thus, his work had intra-ethnic, activist, and nationalist connotations.

Valdez is best known for *Zoot Suit*, a musical about the Los Angeles riots. After a run in Los Angeles, it went to Broadway and ultimately became a film starring Edward James Olmos, directed by Valdez himself. (He also directed *La Bamba*, the biographical movie about the singer Ritchie Valens.) Valdez's other plays include *La Gran Carpa de la Familia*

*Rascuachi* (The Big Top Circus of the Rascuachi Family), *Tiburcio Vasquez*, and *I Don't Have to Show You No Stinking Badges!* Along with lawyer Oscar "Zeta" Acosta and journalist Rubén Salazar, Valdez became legendary for his role in the Chicano Movement.

**Q:** **What theater companies developed in the Northeast?**

**A:** In the Northeast, the Caribbean community developed theater groups. The Repertorio Español (Spanish Repertory) was founded in 1973 in New York City. Many Hispanic actors were attracted to the company; one, Ofelia González, was the first to win an Obie without performing in English. The Puerto Rican Traveling Theater also began in New York City. Both companies are devoted to the dissemination of Hispanic plays, and they both perform in Spanish and English.

**Q:** **Who are important contemporary Latino playwrights?**

**A:** Chicano, Cuban, Dominican, and Puerto Rican playwrights have gradually made their mark with English-language plays on the American stage. They include Carlos Morton's *The Many Deaths of Danny Rosales* (1986), Dolores Prida's *Coser y cantar* (Sewing and Singing, 1981), María Irene Fornés' *Fefu and Her Friends* (1977), Miguel Piñero's *Short Eyes* (1974), René Marquéz's *La Carreta* (The Oxcart, 1954), and, more recently, Luis Alfaro's *Straight as a Line* (1998) and Nilo Cruz's *Anna in the Tropics* (2003). There is also *Dominicanish* by Josefina Baez and the political performance art of Guillermo Gómez-Peña.

Playwright and film director Luis Valdez.

# Screens, Big and Small

**Q:** How long have Latinos participated in American television?

**A:** The history of Latinos in American television may be divided into two parts: the presence of Latino characters in English-language programs, and Spanish-language TV. In the former category, the groundbreaker was the 1950s hit *I Love Lucy*, with Lucille Ball and her husband, Cuban American actor and musician Desi Arnaz, known on the show as Ricky Ricardo. The show lives on thanks to eternal reruns. In the 1950s Duncan Renaldo and Leo Carrillio were successful in *The Cisco Kid*. Many Latino actors performed in the dozens of John Wayne movies but mostly in stereotypical roles. Freddie Prinze, of German and Puerto Rican heritage, was a well-known stand-up comedian and starred in *Chico and the Man* from 1974 to 1977. Gradually Latinos began to escape the roles of *bandidos*, Latin lovers, victims, and drug pushers. Jimmy Smits made his television career with *NYPD Blue*, which began its run in 1993. Other examples of television shows with non-stereotypical Latino characters in the 1980s, 1990s, and moving into the twenty-first century include *Resurrection Boulevard*, *Miami Vice*, *The George López Show*, *American Family*, and *Mind of Mencia*. In the second category are the countless *telenovelas*.

Above: Lucille Ball and Desi Arnaz.

**Q:** What is a *telenovela*?

**A:** A *telenovela* is a Spanish-language soap opera, usually broadcast in prime time for an adult audience. The favorite topics are passionate love affairs, machismo and *marianismo*, illegitimate children, and revenge. They usually run for about twenty-five to forty episodes. Famous series have been *Simplemente María* (Simply María) and *Mi querida Isabel* (My Dear Isabel). Mexico produces the vast majority of *telenovelas* and captures the greatest audience around the globe, from Russia to Israel, and all of Latin America. Venezuela and Brazil also produce their own original material. Since the 1990s, Univision and Telemundo have been producing their own shows as well. The *telenovelas* produced in Miami and Los Angeles are exclusively geared to a Latino audience in the United States. The cast of actors might include Puerto Ricans, Colombians, Mexicans, Cubans, and Argentines.

**Q:** Is there a Latino cinema?

**A:** While Spanish-language TV and radio have grown dramatically since the 1960s, Hollywood remains fairly closed to Latino filmmakers. Nevertheless, Hollywood has produced important movies, including Robert Young's *The Ballad of Gregorio Cortez* (1982), León Ichazo's *El Super* (1979) and *Crossover Dreams* (1985), Ramón Menéndez's *Stand and Deliver* (1988), Gregory Nava's *El Norte* (1983), Luis Valdez's *Zoot*

*Suit* (1981) and *La Bamba* (1987), Patricia Cardozo's *Real Women Have Curves* (2002), Eric Eason's *Manito* (2002), and Sergio Arau's *A Day Without a Mexican* (1998, 2004). Their themes explore issues of isolation, acculturation, and self-affirmation. Considering the size and importance of the Latino population in the United States, it is striking that so few Latino directors have been able to explore relevant issues on the silver screen for an English-speaking audience.

The diversity within the Latino population also makes one ask: Can one talk of a truly Latino cinema? Would it not be more pertinent to explore the possibilities of Chicano, Puerto Rican, and Cuban film? This is the approach some film critics

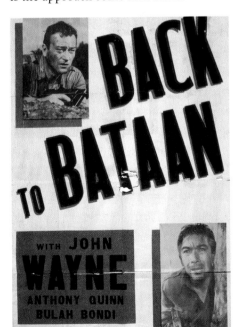

take. For example, the work of Luis Valdez is surely contained within the Mexican-American tradition.

**Q: Who are famous Latino actors in Hollywood?**

**A:** They begin with Rita Hayworth (née Margarita Cansino), Chita Rivera, Rita Moreno, Carmen Miranda, and Anthony Quinn and reach contemporary actors like Antonio Banderas, Jennifer López, Salma Hayek, and Benjamin Bratt. These actors' ethnicity might have been a springboard for them, but little of what they've tackled in their careers pertains to the Latino experience. Puerto Rican Rita Moreno was in *West Side Story* (1961), though many Puerto Ricans now object to the depiction of their culture in the play and film; Quinn, of Mexican descent, did *Viva Zapata!* (1952), with Marlon Brando, and *The Children of Sánchez* (1978); Banderas revived the *Zorro* (2005) franchise about a New Mexico folk hero of the colonial period; López played the tejana singer Selena; and Bratt played Miguel Piñero in *Piñero* (2001). Still, these efforts are not sufficient to constitute a group of Latino actors engaged in tackling Latino themes.

Rita Hayworth

Left: Poster for *Back to Bataan* starring John Wayne and Anthony Quinn.

# *Reporteros*

**Q:** How can Latino radio be described?

**A:** As in the case of TV, Latino radio, the "invisible" medium, ought to be divided into two categories: Spanish-language, and its English counterpart. The first decade of the twenty-first century boasted more than seven hundred Spanish-language radio stations in the United States, from urban centers like Los Angeles, San Antonio, Dallas, Houston, Chicago, Miami, Tallahassee, and New York, to rural areas from coast to coast. These stations broadcast news, sports, and entertainment. A series of corporations—Radio Unica, the Hispanic Broadcasting Corporation, Entravisión, and the Spanish Broadcasting System—own most of them. A number of important personalities, including El Cucú, have been listeners' favorites. The capacity of this media to mobilize audiences was tangible in the immigration marches of April 2006.

Today English-language radio stations targeting Latinos are fewer in number than their Spanish counterparts, but equally important. Programs like *Latino USA* on National Public Radio concentrate on politics and culture. Reporters Ray Suárez and María Hinojosa, both connected to TV as well, are leading newscasters. Their unquestionable ancestor is Rubén Salazar.

**Q:** Who was Rubén Salazar?

**A:** Rubén Salazar was a journalist for *The Los Angeles Times* during the Civil Rights era who refused to accept misrepresentation of Latinos and ignorance of issues affecting them—Mexican Americans, in particular. Salazar also pushed for a larger, more balanced ethnic representation in the American media. He was a visionary whose contributions opened up the profession to a more diverse perspective of American society.

Born in Ciudad Juárez, Mexico, on March 3, 1928, Salazar spent his childhood in Texas with his family. He joined the army in the early 1950s and eventually

CNN and NPR correspondent María Hinojosa.

(From left to right) New Mexico Governor Bill Richardson, CNN's Lou Dobbs, former Mexican Prime Minister Jorge Castañeda, the Reverend David Beckmann, and moderator Ray Suárez participate in the 2006 National Association of Hispanic Journalists luncheon.

got his B.A. from the University of Texas. He then worked for the *El Paso Herald Post* and later for a Santa Rosa paper, the *San Francisco News*. For the *Times* he covered the Vietnam War and became the Mexico City bureau chief correspondent, the first Mexican American ever to hold such a position at any American newspaper.

Speaking both English and Spanish and with a vast knowledge of the Mexican American community, he covered the Chicano Movement in a way that satisfied the community. But his sometimes explosive language made the newspaper uncomfortable and he was asked to tone down his language; eventually he became a target of FBI attention. In 1969, he became news director of KMEX, a Spanish-language TV station, while also writing for the *Times*. Through the two venues he was able to reach a large portion of the Los Angeles population.

**Q: How did Salazar die?**

**A:** He was killed during a 1970 march in Los Angeles organized by the National Chicano Moratorium in which some 30,000 protesters walked from Belvedere Park to Laguna Park. Salazar entered a café on Whittier Boulevard. Los Angeles Sheriff's Department Officer Tom Wilson also entered and fired a tear-gas grenade launcher. The ten-inch gas canister hit Salazar in the head. The killing was ruled a homicide, but Wilson was never prosecuted. Frank Romero painted a famous mural, *The Death of Rubén Salazar* (1986) that memorialized his death. The mural currently hangs in the Smithsonian Art Museum. The Santa Rosa public library is named after Salazar. By and large, he has become an emblem of resistance. Salazar brought a fresh, informed perspective to journalistic involvement in the Chicano Movement and broadened its scope.

# The Ways of *Mestizo* Folk

A *Cinco de Mayo* dancer
in St. Louis, Missouri.

**Q:** What are the varieties of folklore?

**A:** The term folklore was coined in
the 1840s by the British writer William
Thoms, who defined it as a people's "man-
ners, customs, observances, superstitions,
ballads, proverbs, etc." To a large extent,
these activities are a manifestation of a
collective psyche. As generations follow
one another, people tend to tread in the
footsteps of their ancestors, ultimately
allowing us to gain an understanding of a
people's character. With the multiplicity
of backgrounds within the Latino population in the United States, these activities
differ across national, class, and racial
lines. In Mexican American communities,
*quinceañera* parties, in which fifteen-
year-old girls salute their coming of
age, and *Cinco de Mayo* parades become
rich displays of folklore. Humor among
Dominican Americans has unique characteristics, as it does among Nicaraguan
Americans. Likewise, someone from a
working-class background will nurture a
set of beliefs and customs different from
those of the middle class.

**Q:** Who are the most
important ethnographers?

**A:** Américo Paredes, who taught at the
University of Texas at Austin for years,
spent his career studying, among other
issues, the border *corrido*. His book *With
His Pistol in His Hand: A Border Ballad
and Its Hero*, about the turn-of-the-nine-
teenth-century border outlaw Gregorio
Cortez, is one of the most significant

A row of crosses used in Santería practices.

contributions to American folklore in any ethnic group. Lydia Cabrera, a Cuban émigré who left her home after Castro's revolution and lived in Florida for years, devoted her attention to understanding African-based music, storytelling, religion, and politics in Cuba. Her book *El Monte*, loosely translated as *The Forest*, published in 1954, is an essential resource for the understanding and practice of Santería. These two scholars were rather unconventional ethnographers. Paredes also wrote fiction—he is the author of *The Hammon and the Beans* (1994) and *Uncle Remus con Chile* (1993)—and well understood the two sides of the creative process, as scholar and artist. His studies of Mexican folklore in South Texas defined a generation. Cabrera's style is even more impressionistic. Her deep knowledge of Afro-Cuban folklore persuaded her that the best approach to its sources was open-ended and nondogmatic. Her first book, *Cuentos negros de Cuba*, released in 1936, is a compilation of the Afro-Caribbean tales she heard as a child. These two scholars focused their attention on traditional popular culture, emphasizing the way memory is passed from generation to generation.

Lydia Cabrera

> It is worth transcribing on paper the teachings of the elders for the ones who will want to learn, and for rash people who are preyed upon by charlatans and exploiters.
>
> —*Lydia Cabrera*

# *América*, America

Interior of a Mexican restaurant.

Girl in traditional Peruvian dress.

Right: One of the most popular Spanish dishes: paella.

With the exceptions of Africans imported during the slave trade and the Chinese who labored on the railroads in the late nineteenth century, the majority of immigrants to the United States prior to World War II had departed from the Old World, places like Ireland, Italy, France, Germany, Scandinavia, Greece, and Poland. Racially, they were mostly Caucasian. Negative, nativist responses to their arrival were based on class, customs and foods, and religion. After World War II, an entirely different wave of immigrants, often darker-skinned and much less familiar than the previous groups, entered the country in increasingly large numbers: people from Korea and China, India and Pakistan, Vietnam and Cambodia, Nigeria and Senegal, Lebanon and Iran, the Francophone and Spanish-speaking Caribbean, and everywhere in Latin America. As a result, America has been continually redefining its national identity, one in which multiculturalism plays a central role. Metropolises like Los Angeles, San Antonio, Houston, Miami, and New York are now cities of multiple ethnicities, languages, and traditions. Similar social change has taken place, albeit more slowly, in rural areas, where ethnic minorities have grown in small but noticeable numbers.

In the past, acculturation was defined by renunciation: The newcomer let go of native culture and language so that he or she could take on "American" characteristics and ways of life. That was the theory of the melting pot: Different ancestries melted into one homogeneous American stew. The current approach replaces the concept of melting pot with the metaphor of the mosaic: In the age of multiculturalism, broadly speaking, America no longer forces the immigrant to leave behind native cuisine, customs, and ways of speaking; instead, society is composed of diverse communities unified by a common set of symbols (a flag, an anthem) and motifs (a shared sense of history, the belief in individual achievement, and the moral commitment to help those in need). Latinos are playing a unique role in this new era. From *América* to America, their current processes of transculturation are unlike the old models.

It is often said that in the twenty-first century the United States is being Hispanized; that is, Latinos are increasingly redefining

Right: Traditional Mexican clay masks. Below: Dictionaries reflecting the various linguistic influences throughout Latin America.

society through cuisine, music, sports, language, and political representation. An opposite trend is taking place south of the Rio Grande, where American culture has been infiltrating every aspect of life since the invention of television. When these two transformations are considered together, what is clear is that Anglo and Hispanic differences are slowly eroding, though some South American countries

are reacting to decades of U.S. influence by going their own route politically and economically. One dramatic counter-example to the fusion of Anglo and Hispanic cultures is the U.S.-Mexico border; once the site of vital cultural exchange, it has turned into a wound surrounded by wire fences. Thousands of people looking for a better life try to cross every day. Some make it, others are turned back, and a few perish in the attempt.

At this juncture, one might ask: When will Latinos be recognized as a truly essential component of the nation? Might there come a time soon when their history will be on display in a museum or with a monument in Washington, D.C., next to others recognizing slavery and the Holocaust, a museum where the rich and diverse contributions of indigenous American populations and their fusion with Iberian cultures are celebrated?

# Glossary

**ACTOS:** one-act plays.

**ADELITAS:** female soldiers.

**AFUERA:** outside.

**AZTLÁN:** mythical homeland of the Aztecs; became of spiritual importance to Chicanos and Latinos during the Chicano Movement.

**AZÚCAR:** sugar.

**BABALAO:** Santería high priest.

**BALSA:** raft.

**BALSERO:** rafter; specifically, Cubans who came to the United States on homemade rafts.

**BANDIDOS:** bandits.

**BARRIO:** neighborhood.

**BEISBOL:** baseball.

**BOMBA:** type of Puerto Rican music; also bomb.

**BRACEROS:** Mexican laborers brought to the United States under a formal 1942 agreement with Mexico to fill labor shortages caused by World War II.

**CABILDO:** colonial-era church-sponsored support group.

**CALAVERA:** skeleton; an image turned into a Mexican and Mexican American pop icon by José Guadalupe Posada.

**CALIFORNIOS:** Mexicans and, after the Treaty of Guadalupe Hidalgo, Mexican Americans living in California.

**CANCIÓN, LA:** song.

**CATECISMO:** catechism.

**CHICANISMO:** ideology of self-determination built upon the mythical, religious, and experiential motifs of Mexican American life.

**CHICANO/CHICANA:** United States–born descendants of Mexicans.

**COLONIAS:** Latino settlements, often temporary or unofficial, on the outskirts of large U.S. cities.

**CONJUNTO:** band. Also, a type of Mexican border music.

**CORRIDOS:** Mexican ballads about folk heros.

**CUBONICS:** Cuban American variety of Spanglish.

**CYBER-SPANGLISH:** variety of Spanglish used on the Internet.

**DOMINICANISH:** Dominican American variety of Spanglish.

**ESPAÑOL, EL:** the Spanish language. Also means a Spaniard.

**ESTADO LIBRE ASOCIADO:** literally, free associated state. Used to describe the status of Puerto Rico as a commonwealth.

**EXILIADO, EL:** an exiled individual.

**FAMILIA, LA:** the family.

**FÚTBOL:** soccer.

**GABACHO, EL:** foreigner.

**GANGAS:** Spanglish slang meaning gangs.

**GRINGO:** foreigner; used in particular for U.S. citizens.

**GUADALUPANOS/ GUADALUPANISMO:** worshippers of the Virgin of Guadalupe; a cult of Virgin worship that also embraces Mexican national identity.

**HACIENDA, LA:** large estate, ranch.

**HUELGA:** a labor strike.

**JÍBARO:** Puerto Rican peasant.

**JUSTICIA:** justice.

**LEYENDA NEGRA, LA:** The Black Legend. The stories of abuse of the American Indians by Spanish missionaries purposely spread by concerned clergy such as Fray Bartolomé de las Casas.

**LIBERTADOR, EL:** literally, the liberator. Used to describe Simón Bolívar.

**LÍDER MÁXIMO, EL:** the supreme leader. Used to refer to Fidel Castro.

**LOISAIDA:** The Lower East Side of New York City.

**LUCHA LIBRE, LA:** Mexican-style wrestling.

**MAQUILADORAS:** sweatshop-type factories located on the Mexico side of the U.S.-Mexico border that make items for export.

**MARIACHI:** a kind of Mexican folk music.

**MARIANISMO:** a set of attitudes that encourage women toward humility and self-sacrifice in emulation of the Virgin Mary.

**MARIELITOS:** a sometimes pejorative term referring to the generation of Cubans who arrived in the United States during the Mariel Boatlift of 1980.

**MERENGUE:** type of Dominican music.

**MESTIZAJE:** mixed-race group; originally coined to denote children of Spanish and American Indian parents.

**MESTIZO:** a mixed-race individual.

**MOVIMIENTO, EL:** the Chicano Movement.

**NARCOCORRIDOS:** Mexican ballads about narcotics traffickers.

**NORTE, EL:** the United States.

**NOVOMEXICANO:** a Mexican American from New Mexico.

**NUYORICAN:** a person or identity characterized by the fusion of New York City and mainland Puerto Rican cultures. Also used to describe the Puerto Rican variety of Spanglish used in New York.

**ORISHAS:** saints in the Cuban Santería tradition.

**PACHUCO/PACHUCA:** slang for a young Mexican American. Also used to describe a variety of Mexican American Spanglish.

**PALABRA, LA:** the word.

**PATRIA, LA:** homeland.

**PELOTA, LA:** ball used in sports.

**PICANTE:** spicy.

**PLENA:** type of Puerto Rican music.

**POCHO:** slang for Americanized Mexican. Also used to describe a variety of Mexican American Spanglish.

**POLÍTICO:** politician. Also used as an adjective.

**RANCHERA:** a type of Mexican music.

**RANCHO:** ranch.

**RAZA, LA:** literally, the race. Used to describe the Mexican American community.

**RECONQUISTA, LA:** literally, the reconquest. The centuries-long war waged by Roman Catholics to remove all Islamic Moors from the Iberian Peninsula. The last Moorish stronghold fell in 1492.

**REVANCHA DE MOCTEZUMA, LA:** Moctezuma's revenge. Used metaphorically when referring to the spreading of Hispanic culture in the United States.

**SALSA:** hot sauce. Also a type of Caribbean music.

**SANTERÍA:** A Cuban religion based upon the fusion of Roman Catholic and Yoruba beliefs and practices.

**SANTERO:** practitioner of Santería.

**SPANGLISH:** a hybrid language and culture resulting from the fusion of Spanish and English languages and Latino and American cultures.

**SUEÑO AMERICANO, EL:** the American dream.

**TABAQUERO:** cigar worker.

**TEJANOS:** Spanish-speaking individuals, originally of Mexican descent, from Texas.

**VIDA LOCA, LA:** literally, the crazy life. Used to mean the American way of life.

**WETBACKS:** Mexican laborers considered undesirable by the United States, which tries to deport them.

**ZOOT SUIT:** a clothing style popular among Mexican Americans in the 1940s characterized by a broad hat, long coat, ballooning pants, and narrow shoes.

# Further Reading

### Books

Acuña, Rodolfo. *Occupied America: A History of Chicanos.* 3rd ed. New York: HarperCollins, 1988.

Augenbraum, Harold, and Margarite Fernández Olmos. *The Latino Reader: From 1542 to the Present.* Boston: Houghton Mifflin, 1997.

Chávez Candelaria, Cordelia, ed. *Encyclopedia of Latino Popular Culture.* Westport, Conn.: Greenwood, 2004.

Darder, Antonia, and Rodolfo D. Torres, eds. *The Latino Studies Reader: Culture, Economy, and Society.* Malden, Mass.: Blackwell, 1998.

Davis, Mike. *Magical Urbanism: Latinos Reinvent the U.S. City.* New York and London: Verso, 2000.

García, John A. *Latino Politics in America: Community, Culture, and Interests.* Lanham, Md.: Rowman & Littlefield, 2003.

Gutiérrez, David G. *The Columbia History of Latinos in the United States since 1960.* New York: Columbia University Press, 2004.

Ramos, Jorge. *The Other Face of America: Chronicles of the Immigrants Shaping Our Future.* Translated by Patricia J. Duncan. New York: Rayo/HarperCollins, 2002.

Rodríguez, Richard. *Hunger of Memory: The Education of Richard Rodriguez.* Boston: David R. Godine, 1982.

Shorris, Earl. *Latinos: A Biography of a People.* New York: W. W. Norton, 1992.

Stavans, Ilan. *Spanglish: The Making of a New American Language.* New York: Rayo/HarperCollins, 2003.

———. *The Hispanic Condition: The Power of the People.* New York: Rayo/HarperCollins, 2001.

———. *Latino USA: A Cartoon History.* Illustrations by Lalo López Alcaráz. New York: Basic, 2000.

———, ed. *Encyclopedia Latina: History, Culture, and Society in the United States.* Danbury, Conn.: Grolier/Scholastic, 2005.

Suro, Roberto. *Strangers Among Us: How Latino Immigration Is Transforming America.* New York: Knopf, 1998.

Tobar, Héctor. *Translation Nation: Defining a New American Identity in the Spanish-Speaking United States*. New York: Riverhead, 2005.

Vélez-Ibáñez, Carlos G. *Transnational Latina/o Communities: Politics, Processes, and Cultures. With Anna Sampaio and Manolo González-Estay*. Lanham, Md.: Rowman & Littlefield, 2002.

## Web Sites

Latin American Network Information Center: www1.lanic.utexas.edu

Pew Hispanic Center: www.pewhispanic.org

San Diego Historical Society: www.sandiegohistory.org

Texas State Historical Association: www.tsha.utexas.edu

Thompson Gale Hispanic Heritage: www.gale.com/free_resources/chh

# Index

## A

ABC, 111
abolitionists, 21
abortion, 82, 83
accordion, *160*
acculturation, 10, 204
Aceves, José, 194–95
Acosta, Oscar "Zeta," 184–85, 197
*actos*, 196
*A Day Without a Mexican*, 199
"Adelita," *50*
adolescence, 73, 80–81
aesthetics, 192–93
Affirmative Action, 109
African Americans, 41, 43
Africans, 12, 56, 92–93, 105–106
Age of Enlightenment, 105
*ago-go*, 156
Agricultural Labor Relations Act, 51
agriculture, 16, 31, 33, 48, 79
Al Quaeda, 37
Alamo, 18–19, *106*
*Alamo, The*, 19
Alan Guttmacher Institute, 82
Alberto, Carlos, 170
Alcaraz, Lalo, *135*, 195
Alfaro, Luis, 83, 197
Alfau, Felipe, 180–81
Alfonso X "El Sabio," 11
Algarín, Miguel, 55, 109, 182
Alhambra, *88*
Alianza Federal de las Mercedes, 48–49
Alien and Sedition Laws, 30
Alinsky, Saul, 44
All Saints' Day, 85
Allende, Isabel, 186
Allende, Salvador, 68, 109
Almarez, Jorge, *129*
*Aloud*, 182
Alurista, 182
Alvarez, Julia, 56–57, 181
Alvarez, Luis Walter, 100
*Always Running: La Vida Loca, Gang Days in L.A.*, 81
*America is in the Heart*, 43
American Community Survey, 150
*American Family*, 198
American Federation of Labor, 35, 107
*American Me*, 81
American Labor Party, 54
*American Me*, 81
American Youth Soccer Organization, 170
AmeRícan, 182
*Amor Prohibido*, 161
Anaya, Rudolfo, 91, 181, 187
*Anna in the Tropics*, 111, 197
Anthony, Marc, 199
Anthropophagy, 192
Anti-Defamation League, 94
Anzaldúa, Gloria, 50, 83, 187
AOL, 111
April Fair, *191*
Arau, 199
Arawak, 104
Arenas, Reinaldo, 63, 184
Argentina, 94, 130
*Ariel*, 193
Arista, Mariano, 21
Arnava, Peula, *79*
Arnaz, Desi, 96, 198
art, 191–203
Arte Público Press, 188–89
assimilation, 129
astrology, 89
Austin, Moses, 16
Austin, Stephen F., 16, *17*
*Autobiography*, 182

autobiography, 184–85
*Autobiography of a Brown Buffalo, The*, 184
automatic translation, 134–35
Aymara, 131
Aztecs, 46, 84–85, 88, 104, 168, 175, 195
Aztec calendar, *104*
Aztlán, 42, 46–47, 195

## B

*babalaos*, 92
Baca, Judith, 96, 194
*bachata*, 137, 154, 162
*Back to Bataan*, 198
Badillo, Herman, 144, 149
Baez, Joan, 108, 125
Baez, Josefina, 57, 197
Bahamas, 5
*bajo sexto*, 156, 160
Ball, Lucille, 198
Ballad of Gregorio Cortez, The, 199
*balonpié*, 168
*balsero*, 62–63
Banderas, Antonio, 199
Bañuelos, Ramona Acosta, 109
Bardem, Javier, 184
Barretto, Ray, 163
*Barrio Boy*, 127
Baseball Hall of Fame, 109
baseball, 106, 168, 172–73
Basque, 130
Basquiat, Jean Michel, 194
*batas*, 156
*batijas*, 156
Batista, Fulgencio, 58–60, 107–108, *149*
Battle of Cerro Gordo, *15*
Battle of San Jacinto, 18–19
Battle of the Alamo, 18–19
Bauzá, Mario, 100
Bay of Pigs invasion, 59, 108
Bazaar, Philip, 106
Beat Generation, 182
Beckmann, David, *201*
*Before Night Falls*, 184
Behar, Ruth, 127
*beisbol*, 168, 172–73
Bellán, Esteban, 106, 172
Belvis, Segundo Ruíz, 33
Ben, Jorge, 163
Benítez-Rojo, Antonio, 187
*berimbao*, 156
Bernstein, Leonard, 81
Betances, Ramón Emeterio, 33
Biberman, Herbert J., 50
Bible, 89, 130
bilingual ballots, 146–47
bilingual education, 109, 120–21
Bilingual Education Act, 120
Bilingual Press, 188–89
biographies, 96–103
birth control, 82–83
Blades, Rubén, 163
*Bless Me Última*, 91, 181
*Blood In, Blood Out: Bound by Honor*, 81
Boabdil, 104
bolero, 154
Bolívar, Simón, *2*, 58, 106
Bolivia, 131
*bomba*, 154, 156, 162
bongos, 156
books, 179–189
border ballads, 158
border corrido, 202
*Borderlands/La Frontera*, 83
Border Patrol, 31, 36, 107
border region, 29, 36

border theory, 187
Borges, Jorge Luis, 186, *187*
Boricuas, 2
bossa nova, 165
Boston Red Sox, *173*
*Boulevard Nights*, 81
Bowie, James (Jim), 18–19
boxing, 171
Bracero Program, 29, 34–36, 39, 107
*braceros*, 2, 79
Brando, Marlon, 199
Bratt, Benjamin, 199
Brazil, 65, 70–71, 162–63
*Brief Description of the Destruction of the Indies*, 131
Brotons, Elisabet, 62–63
*Brown*, 83
Brownell, Herbert, 35
Buarque, Chico, 163
Buena Vista Social Club, 163
bullfighting, 175
Bulosan, Carlos, 43
Bush, George H. W., 51, 110
Bush, George P., 111, 137
Bush, George W., 69, 111, 137, 143
Bush, Jeb, 137
Bush, Laura, *119*
Byrne, William Matthew Jr., 110

## C

Cabanas, Roberto, 170
*cabasa*, 156
Cabeza de Vaca, Alvar Núñez, 8, *9*, 105
*cabildos*, 92
Cabrera, Lydia, 203
*cajón*, 156
*Cakewalk*, 42
*calavera*, 85
California Gold Rush, 16
California Grape Workers, *196*
California State University, 125
*californios*, 2
Campeche, José, 97
Canosa, Jorge Mas, 142
Canseco, José, 100
Cantero, Raoul G., *149*
Cantinflas, 96, 192
Cantú, Norma, 110
*capoeira*, *154*
Cardenas, Al, *141*
Cardozo, Patricia, 199
Caribbean, 3, 32–33, 53–63, 168
*carpas*, 196
Carreño, Teresa, 155
Carrillio, Leo, 198
Cart War, 16
*Cartas sobre los Estados Unidos*, 182
Casals, Pablo, 155
Castaneda, Carlos, 97
Castañeda, Jorge, *201*
Castilian Spanish, 130
Castillo, Ana, 50
Castro, Fidel, 53, 58–60, 63, 69, *92*, 108, 120, 149
Castro, Raúl, 58
Catalan, 130
*catecismo*, 88
Catholicism, 5–6, 10–11, 45, 74, 76–77, 82, 85, 87–90, 92, 94
Catrina sculpture, *85*
Cavazos, Lauro F., 110
CBS, 111
Central Intelligence Agency (CIA), 58–60
Cervantes, Lorna Dee, 182
Cervantes, Miguel de, 111, 135–36
César Chávez Day, 111
Chacón, Eusebio, 188

Chacón, Felipe Maximiliano, 188
Chalino, 159
Chambers, María Cristina, 181
Chapa, Juan Bautista, 9
Chavez
Chávez, César, 39, 42–45, 48, 51, 91, 109–110, 142, 158, 195–96
Chávez, Hugo, 59, 69
Chavez, Linda, 100, 121–22
*chekere*, 156
Chiapas, Mexico, 110
Chicago, 192
Chicanismo, 42
Chicano Movement, 13, 39–51, 109, 124, 139–140, 188, 194, 196–97, 201
Chicano Park, 195
Chicano Spanglish, 135
Chicano Studies, 109, 124–26
Chicano Youth Liberation Conference, 47, 109
Chichén Itza, 168, *169*
*Chico and the Man*, 198
childhood, 78–79, 119–123
child labor, 79
*Children of Sánchez, The*, 199
Chile, 68
Chinese Exclusion Act, 30
Chiule, 09
*chocalho*, 156
*Chromas*, 180
*Chronicle of the Narváez Expedition, The*, 8, 9, 105
chronology, 104–111
Chumash Revolt, 10–11, 106
Cienfuegos, Lucky, 182
cigars, 106
*Cinco de Mayo*, 202
cinema, 199
*Cisco Kid, The*, 198
Cisneros, Henry, 110, 143
Cisneros, Sandra, 181
*City of Night*, 83
Civil Rights Act, 109
Civil Rights era, 39, 142, 188, 194, 200
Civil War, 16, 30, 106
*civilización hispanica*, 3
classical music, 155
claves, 156
Clay, Henry, *17*
Clemente, Roberto, 75, 109, 167, *172*, 173
Clinton administration, 111
Clinton, Bill, 51, 110, 137, 143, *144*
CNN, *200-201*
Cocco de Filippis, Daisy, 57
code-switching, 134–35
college, 124–27
Colombia, 68, *69*, 130
Colón, Jesús, 54, 184
Colón, Willie, 101, 163
*colonias*, 33
colonization, 6–13, 70
Columbus, Christopher, *1*, 2, 5–7, 56, 88, 104, 110, 130
Columbus Day, 5
comic strips, 195
communism, 53
Community Action Program, 109
Community Service Organization, 51
congas, 156, *157*
Congressional Hispanic Caucus (CHC), 144
Congressional Medal of Honor, 106
*conjunto*, 155, 160
conquistadors, 6, *7*, 8, 76, 88, 130–32
Contras, 67
corridos, 137, 155, 158–59, 202
Cortázar, Julio, 186
Cortés, Hernán, 9, *12*, 104, 130, 168
Cortez, Gregorio, 158, 202
*Coser y cantar*, 197
*Cosmic Race, The*, 13
Council of Mexican American Affairs (CMAA), 145
Creole, 9, 12
Crespi, Juan, 8
Crockett, David (Davy), 18, *19*

*Crossover Dreams*, 199
Crusade for Justice, 49
Cruz, Celia, 153, 163, 165
Cruz, Nilo, 111, 197
crypto-Jews, 94
*cuatro*, 156
Cuba, 24–27, 53, 58–63, 74, 104–105, 110–111
Cuban American National Foundation (CANF), 142, 144–45
Cuban Americans, 135, 139–140, 149
Cuban Democracy Act, 110
Cuban Revolution, 53, 108
Cuban War for Independence, 24, 107
Cubonics, 135
*Cuentos negros de Cuba*, 203
Cuitlahuac, 104
*cumbias*, 161
Cyber-Spanglish, 135
*Cyrano de Bergerac*, 108

**D**

*Daily News*, 40
*Daily Worker*, 54
Dalkey Archive Press, 180
dance, 165
*Dance of Culture*, 187
Darío, Rubén, 193
Davidovsky, Mario, 155
Davis, Miles, 164
*Days of Obligation*, 83
de Andrade, Oswald, 192
de Anza, Juan Bautista, 8–9
death, 84–85
*Death in the Afternoon*, 175
*Death of Rubén Salazar, The*, 201
de Avila, Teresa, 77
de Avilés, Pedro Menéndez, 8, 105
de Burgos, Julia, 54, 182
de Burton, María Amparo Ruíz, 180
de Céspedes y Quesada, Carlos Manuel, 107
de Coronado, Francisco Vásquez, 8–9
de Elvas, Caballero, 9
de Escobedo, Alonso Gregorio, 9
de Hostos, Eugenio María, 33, 188
de la Cruz, Sor Juana Inéz, 51
de la Hoya, Oscar, 101, 171
de la Vega, el Inca Garcilaso, 9
de las Casas, Bartólome, *10*, 131
Democratic Party, 139, 149
demographics, 112–17, 147, 150
de Nájera, Pedro Castañeda, 9
de Narváez, Pánfilo, 8
de Nebrija, Antonio, 104, 130–31
de Niza, Fray Marcos, 8–9
de Oñate, Juan, 8–9, 105
de Pineda, Pérez, 89
deportation, 35, 108
Depp, Johnny, 184
de Reina, Casiodoro, 89
de Rosas, Juan Manuel, 60
de Soto, Hernando, 8–9
de Tío, Lola Redríguez, 33, 188, *189*
de Villagrá, Gaspar Pérez, 9, 180
de Zumárraga, Juan, 90–91
*Día de la Raza*, 5
*Día de los Muertos*, 85, *160*
diabetes, 78
*Diario de Rodrigo Ranjel*, 9
Díaz, José, 40
Díaz, Junot, 181
Díaz, Porfirio, 34
Díaz-Ayala, Cristóbal, 163
Diego, Juan, 90–91
diet, 78
*Dirty Harry*, 155
divorce, 76–77
Dobbs, Lou, *201*
Dole, Bob, *141*
Domingo, Plácido, 155, 157
Dominican Americans, 135, 149
Dominican Day Parade, *57*

Dominican Liberation Party, *148*
Dominican Republic, 53, 56–57, 106–107
Dominicanish, 57, 135
*Dominicanish*, 197
dominoes, *84*
*Don Quixote de la Mancha*, 111, 135–36
Dorfman, Ariel, 97
"Dos patrias," 63
*Down These Mean Streets*, 55
*Dreaming in Cuban*, 181
*Dreaming of You*, 161
D'Rivera, Paquito, 101, 165
drug wars, Colombian, 68, 69
Durán, Diego, 169

**E**

Eason, Eric, 199
East Los Angeles, 192
Economic Opportunity Act, 109
education, 78, 109, 115, 119–127, 148
Eisenhower, Dwight, 59
*El Barrio*, 55
*el coloso del norte*, 23
El Cucú, 200
elderly, *84*
*El Diario*, 133
*El Diario/La Prensa*, 171, 180
Eleanor Roosevelt Award, 51
Elementary and Secondary Education Act, 120
*El espejo/The Mirror*, 189
*El gallo: La voz de la justicia*, 49
*el lider máximo*, 58
*El mar y tú*, 54
*El Monte*, 203
El Movimiento Estudiantil Chicano de Aztlán, 125
*el movimiento*, 39, 50
*el narcotráfico*, 68
*El Norte*, 199
*El Nuevo Herald*, 133, 171
*El Paso Herald Post*, 200
*El plan espiritual de Aztlán*, 39, 47, 49, 109
El Salvador, 65, 66–67, 109
El Santo, 175
*El Super*, 199
El Teatro Campesino, 196
embargo, 59
eminent domain, 107
*Eminent Maricones*, 83
English-First Movement, 123
English-Only Movement, 122–23
Entravisión, 200
Equal Education Opportunity Act, 109
Equal Employment Opportunity Commission, 49, 109
Escalante, Jaime, 120
*escondidillas*, 175
Espinosa, Auerlio, 127
Espinosa, Gilberto, 127
Estefan, Gloria, 102, 192
Esteves, Sandra María, 182
ethnography, 202
etymology, 1–2
evangelicals, 94
explorers, 8–9
Extremadura, 76

**F**

*Facundo: or, Civilization and Barbarism*, 60
Fair Employment Practices Act, 107
Fair Labor Standards Act, 79
Falcón, Blas Maria de la Garza, 105
family, 73–85
Farabundo Martí National Liberation Front (FMLN), 66
Fast for Life, 44, 110
father, 74
F.B.I., 201
*Fear and Loathing in Las Vegas*, 185
*Federación Libre de los Trabajadores*, 107
*Fefu and Her Friends*, 197
feminism, 50

feminist theory, 187
Ferdinand of Aragón, 6, *7*, 104, 130
Fernández, Lionel, *148*
Fernández, Lisa, 176
Fernández, Mary Jo, 174, 176
Ferré, Luis A., 27
Ferré, Rosario, 98
Ferrer, José, 27, 108
fiction, 180–81
Figueroa, Sotero, 33, 188
Filipinos, 43
Firmat, Gustavo Pérez, 127
Flores, Hector M., *145*
folklore, 191, 202–203
Fonda de Cultura Económica, 188–89
Fonseca, Ruben, *179*
Font, Pedro, 9
Foraker Act, 26
Ford, John, 19
Foreign Assistance Act, 59, 108
Fornés, María Irene, 97, 181, 197
Fort Mose, 105
Fox network, 111
Fox News en Español, 171
Franciscans, 10
Fricke, Charles, 41
Friedan, Betty, 50
Fuentes, Carlos, 186
fusion music, 155, 164
*fútbol*, 167–71

**G**

Gadsden Purchase, 12, 21, 22, 47, 106
Gadsden, James, 22
Gaines, Regis E., *183*
Galarza, Ernesto, 127
Galician, 130
games, 175
Gandhi, Mahatma, 39, 44
gangs, 80–81
gangsta rap, 164
Garcés, Fray Hermenegildo, 9
García, Chino, 55
García, Cristina, 181
García, Frank, 194
García, Jorge, *125*
García, Orlando Jacinto, 155
Garrison, William Lloyd, *17*
Garza, Carmen Lomas, *42*
gays, 82–83
gender roles, 74–77
genocide, 131
*George López Show, The*, 198
G.I. Bill, 35, 146
G.I. Forum, 108
Gil, Gilberto, 163
Gil, Lourdes, 182
Gillespie, Dizzy, 164
glossary, 205–209
golf, 174
Golijov, Osvaldo, 155
Gómex, Máximo, 24
Gómez-Peña, Guillermo, 197
Gonzales, Alberto, 143
Gonzáles, Richard "Pancho," 174
Gonzáles, Rodolfo "Corky," 39, 47, 49, 109, 142
González, Elián, 62–63, 111
González, Ofelia, 197
González, Xavier, 194
Gonzo journalism, 185
Gort, Wilfredo "Willy," *141*
Gottschalk, Louis Moreau, 155
graffiti, *80*, 81, *153*, 195
Granada, 7, 104
grandparents, 73
grapes, 105
greaser laws, 106
Great Depression, 35, 107
Great Migration, 33, 54, 108
Guadalajara Book Fair, *179*
*guadalupanismo*, 74, 90–91

Guam, 25
Guantánamo Bay, 26, 107
Guaraní, 131
*guataca*, 156
Guatemala, 66, 109
Guerra, Juan Luis, 162
guerrilla warfare, 24
guest-worker program, 37
Guevara, Ernesto "Ché," 42, 58–59, 63, *139*, 185
*guícharo*, 156
*guiro*, 156
guitar, *153*, *157*
*gusanos*, 60
Gutiérrez, Frank, 57

**H**

haciendas, 105
Haiti, 56
Hallmark, 136
*Hammon and the Beans, The*, 203
Hanna Barbera, 195
HarperCollins, 189
Harvard University, 126
Hatuey, 104
Hayakawa, S. I., 122
Hayek, Selma, 199
Hayworth, Rita, 199
health insurance, 120, 148
Hearst, William Randolph, 24
Hemingway, Ernest, 175
*Herald Express*, 40
Heredia, José María, 182
*Hernandez v. Texas*, 108
Hernandez, Gilbert, 195
Hernandez, Jaime, 195
Hernández, Joseph Marion, 106
Hernández, Ramona, 127
Hidalgo y Costilla, Miguel, 16, 90, 105–106
higher education, 124–25
Higher Education Act, 124
high school, 125
Hijar y Jaro, Juan B., 188
*Hijo de la tempestad*, 188
Hijuelos, Oscar, 110, 181
Hinojosa, María, 200
Hinojosa-Smith, Rolando, 181
hip-hop poetry, 182
hip-hop, 155, 164
Hispanic Americans for Life, 82
Hispanic Broadcasting Corporation, 200
*Hispanic Condition, The*, 85
Hispanic Heritage Month, 171
Hispanic Heritage Week, 111
Hispanic-Serving Institutions, 124
Hispaniola, 56
*Historia de la Nueva México*, 9, 180
*Historia del Nuevo Reino de León*, 9
*History of Eternity*, 187
HIV, 83
Hollywood, 199
Holman, Bob, 182
Holy Office of the Inquisition, 88–89, 106
Homestead Act of 1862, 15, 106
homosexuality, 82–83, 184
Hostos, Eugenio María de, 98
House on Mango Street, 181
Houston, Samuel, 16, *17*, 18–19
*How the Garcia Girls Lost Their Accent*, 181
*How the Other Half Lives*, 55
Huerta, Dolores, 39, 51, *91*, 109, 142, 195
*Hunger of Memory*, 83
hunger strikes, 44, *48*
Hunter College, 125
Hussein, Saddam, 36

**I**

Ichazo, León, 199
iconography, 194
*I Don't Have to Show You No Stinking Badges!*, 197
illness, 78

*I Love Lucy*, 198
immigration, 29, 30–33, 36–37, 66–69, 110–11, *139*, *140*, 148, 204
Immigration Act of 1875, 30
Immigration Act of 1917, 30–31, 107
Immigration and Nationality Act, 31
Immigration and Naturalization Service (INS), 110
Immigration Reform Act, 31, 109
Immigration Reform and Control Act, 31, 109
immunizations, 120
*In the American Grain*, 182
*In the Time of the Butterflies*, 56
Incas, 88, 131
Indians, see Native Americans
*Indigenismo*, 193
Infante, Guillermo Cabrera, 63
Inscription Rock, *8*
instruments, musical, 156–57
Internet, 111, 135
Iran Hostage Crisis, 67
Iran-Contra Affair, 67
Iraq War, 111
Irving, Washington, 180
Isabel of Castile, 6, *7*, 104, 130
Isla Nina, 55
Islam, 6–7, 95
Islamic Revolution, 67
island theory, 187
Ivy League, 124

**J**

Jackson, Jesse, 55, 143
Jamestown, Virginia, 6, 10
*jarabe*, 165
jazz, 41, 155, 164–65
Jefferson, Thomas, 105
Jesuits, 10, 105
Jews, 104, 55–56, 94
*jíbaros*, 2, 33, 79
Jim Crow laws, 43
Jiménez, José "Cha Cha," 43, 142
Jiménez, Manuel "El Canario," 162
Jimenez, Marcelo, *73*
Jiménez, Santiago Jr., *160*
Job Corps, 109
Jobim, Antonio Carlos, 71
John Paul II, 11, 92
Johnson, Lyndon B., 49, 109, *124*, 146, *147*
Jones Act, 26, 32, 54, 107
Jones, William A., 32
journalism, 200–201
Juan Rulfo Literature Award, *179*

**K**

Kahlo, Frida, 42, 85, 195
Kanellos, Nicholas, *188*
Kennedy, John F. , 49, 59, 158
Key West, Florida, 2
Khrushchev, Nikita, 108
Kid Chocolate, 102
King Charles III, 105
King, Martin Luther Jr., 39, 43–44, *147*
Kino, Eusebio Francisco, 8, 105
Kit Carson National Forest, 49
*Klail City Death Trip*, 181
KMEX, 201
Kreutzberger, Mario, 97
Kutitscheck, Juscelino, 71

**L**

*La Alianza Federal de Pueblos Libres*, 108
*La Bamba*, 196, 199
*la Biblia del Oso*, 89
labor, 33–35, 44–45, 48–49, 50, 79
*Labyrinth of Solitude, The*, 85
*La Carreta*, 181
*la Cuba de afuera*, 53
*La Cucaracha*, 195

*La edad de oro*, 24
*La Florida*, 9
*La Florida del Inca*, 9
*La Frontera*, 36
*La Gran Carpa de la Familia Rascuachi*, 197
*la huelga*, 45, 48, 196
*La isla que se repite*, 187
*La Loisada*, 55
La Lupe, 163
language, 77, 120–23
*la niñez*, 78
*La Ofrenda II*, 42
*La Opinión*, 133, 171
*La Prensa*, 180
La Raza Unida Party, 49
*La Raza*, 133, 171
*la reconquista*, 6–7, 88, 130
*La Relación*, 8, 9
*Las adelitas*, 50
La Sonora Matancera, 163
Latin American Literary Review Press, 189
Latin Grammys, 111
Latino American Dawah (LADO), 95
Latino Pride Parade, *129*
Latino Studies, 126–27
*Latino USA*, 200
Latino, etymology of, 1–3
*Latinos: A Biography of a People*, 127
*Lau v. Nichols*, 121–22
Laviera, Tato, 182
La Villita, 192
*La Virgen de la Caridad del Cobre*, 74, *87*
Lavoe, Héctor, 102
Law of Burgos, 104
League of Latin American Citizens (LULAC), 17,
    107, 144, *145*
Leal, Luis, 127
*lector*, 54
Lee, Muna, 98, 127
Leroy, Ken, *81*
Lewis and Clark expedition, 105
lexicography, 129
*leyenda negra*, 131
Liberal Party, 58
Limón, José, 99
literacy test, 30
literary criticism, 186–87
*Literary Currents in Hispanic America*, 126
literature, 57, 63, 76, 127, 179–189
Little Havana, 60–61
*Locos: A Comedy of Gestures*, 180
López, Jennifer, 161, 199
Lopez, Nancy, 174, 176
López, Yolanda, 195
Lorenz, Ricardo, 155
Los 4.40, 162
Los Angeles, *80*
Los Angeles Police Department, 40–41
*Los Angeles Times*, 40, 195, 200–201
Los Tigres del Norte, 159
*Lotería*, 175
Louisiana Purchase, 105
*Love & Rockets*, 195
Lower East Side, 55
*lucha libre*, 174–75
Luis, William, 127, 187
Luque, Adolfo, 172
lynchings, 107

**M**

Maceo, Antonio, 24
Machado, Gerardo, 58, 107
machismo, 50, 73, 76
magical realism, 186
Major League Soccer, 171
*Mambo Kings Play Songs of Love, The*, 110, 181
Manhattan, *54*, 55
Manifest Destiny, 15, 20, 24
*Manito*, 199
Manje, Juan Mateo, *179*

*Many Deaths of Danny Rosales, The*, 197
maquiladoras, 29, 36, 110
maracas, *3*
mariachi, 154, *155*
marianismo, 73, 76
Mariel Boatlift, 62
*marielitos*, 62
*marimba*, 156
*marimbula*, 156
Marin, Cheech, 98
Marín, Francisco "Pachín," 33
Marín, Luis Muñoz, 32
Marina, Doña, *12*
Marinho, 170
Márquez, Gabriel García, 179, 186
Marquéz, René, 197
*Martí Thoughts/Pensamientos*, 61
Martí, José, 24–25, 33, 61, 63, 107, 182
Mas Canosa, 101
Maya, 66, 88, 110, 131–32, 168
Mayan ruins, *131*, 168
*Mayflower*, 1, 6, 76
Mazatlán, Mexico, *184*, 185
McKinley, William, 25–26, 107
media, 24, 40, 111, 133, 136, 135, 149, 171, 175, 191
melting pot, 204
memoirs, 184–85
*Memoirs*, 54
*Memoirs of the History of Texas*, 9
Mendoza, Teresa, *159*
Menéndez, Ramón, 199
*mercedes*, 105
merengue, 137, 153–54, 162, 165
Mesilla region, 106
Mesoamerica, 168
*mestizo*, 11–12, 76, 91, 130, 194, 202–203
Mexican American Political Association (MAPA), 145
Mexican Americans, 2, 22–23, 34–35, 39–51, 85
Mexican flag, *47*
Mexican Revolution, 34, 107
Mexican-American War, 2, 15, 20–23, 106, 126, 168
*mexicanos*, 2
Mexico, 16–19, 20–23, 149
Miami-Dade County, 192
Miami, Florida, 60–61
*Miami Vice*, 198
Miller, Yvette, 189
*Mind of Mencia*, 198
Minoso, Orestes "Minnie," 108, 172–73
Mirabal sisters, 56
Miranda, Carmen, 71, 199
*Mission Impossible*, 155
Mission of San Antonio de Valero, 18
missionaries, 5, 9, 88
missions, 8,10–11, 105, 155
*Mi querida Isabel*, 198
Moctezuma, 9, *12*, 23, 46, 104
*Modernismo*, 127, 193
Mohr, Nicholasa, 181
Molina, Mario, 103
Monroe Doctrine, 20, 106
Monroe, James, 20, 106
Montt, Efraín Ríos, 66
Moors, 104
Moraga, Cherríe, 50, 181, 184, 187
Moreno, Rita, 55, *81*, 108, 199
Morfi, Fray Juan Agustín, 9
Morton, Carlos, 197
mosaic, 204
mother, 74, *75*, 76, 78
Mountain Dew, 136
Mr. Polk's War, 21
MTV, 136
*Mucha Lucha*, 175
Muhammad XI, 104
multiculturalism, 204
Muñoz, Anthony, 110
Muñoz Marín, Luis, 27, 101, 108
muralism, 194–95
music, 153–165
Muslims, 95

**N**

Nahuatl, 84, 131–32
naïf artist, 194
*narcocorrido*, 153, 159
*Narrative of the Expedition of Coronado, The*, 9
NASCAR, 171
Nascimento, 163
National Association for the Advancement of Colored
    People (NAACP), 111
National Association of Chicano and Chicana Studies,
    125
National Association of Hispanic Journalists, *201*
National Association of Latino Elected and Appointed
    Officials (NALEO), *141*, 144
National Chicano Moratorium, 201
National Council of La Raza (NCLR), 144
National Origins Act, 31
National Public Radio, 200
National Puerto Rican Coalition (NPRC), 144
National Women's Hall of Fame, 51
Native Americans, 104–105, 130–32, 168
Native Americans, 6, 9–11, 13, 76, 88–89
nativism, 30, 204
Nava, Gregory, 98, 199
NBC, 111
Negrete, Jorge, 157
Negro League, 172
Neighborhood Youth Corps, 49
neologisms, 134–35
New Progressive Party, 27
New York City, 54–55, 57
*New York Journal*, 24
*New York Sun*, 24
newspapers, 133, 171
Nicaragua, 66–67, 109
Nicaragua Canal, 66, 67
Nieto-Gómez, Anna, 50
*Nilda*, 181
*Noche Triste*, 104
Nogales, Arizona, *29*
nonviolence, 39, 51
North American Free Trade Agreement, 110
North American Soccer League, 170
Novello, Antonia C., 110
novels, 179
*Nuestra Señora de Altagracia*, 57
Nuestra Señora de Dolores mission, 8
Nuyorican, 2, 54–55, 135
Nuyorican Poet's Café, 55, 109, 182, *183*
*NYPD Blue*, 198

**O**

Obeja, Achy, 83
Ochoa, Ellen, 102
O'Farrill, Chico, 165
official language, 122
oil, 69
old age, 73–85, 84
Olmecs, 168
Olmos, Edward James, 120, 196
Olympics, 111, 176
*One Hundred Corridos: The Heart of Mexican Song*, 159
*One Hundred Years of Solitude*, 186
Operation Bootstrap, 33, 108
Operation Peter Pan, 61
Operation Wetback, 35–36, 108
oral history, 127
Orden Hijos de América, 17
*orishas*, 92
Orozco, José Clemente, 194
Ortega, Daniel, 67
Ortíz, David, 173
Oscars, 108
Osun Oshogbo Festival, *87*

**P**

Pacheco, Johnny, 163
Pachuco, 135
*pachucos*, 40

Padilla, Heberto, 63, 184
paella, *204*
painting, 194
*Pa'lante*, 43
Palenque ruins, *131*
*palitos*, 156
Palma, Tomás Estrada, 26
Palmieri, Charlie, 163
Palmieri, Eddie, 163
Palou, Fray Francisco, 8
*pandeiro*, 156, *157*
*panderetas*, 156
Pánfilo de Narváez, 130
Pantoja, Antonia, 103
Paraguay, 131
Paredes, Américo, *126*, 127, 187, 202–203
Parker, Charlie, 164
Parra, Derek, 111
Partido Revolucionario Institutional (PRI), 174
*pastorelas*, 196
*Patolli*, 175
Paz, Octavio, 85, 93, 187
PBS, 83
Pele, 167, 170
*pelota*, 168
Peña, Federico, 110
Pentecostals, 94
People of Aztlán, 2
Pérez, Danilo, 165
Pérez, Louis A., 127
pesticides, 79
Peter the Venerable, 95
Pew Hispanic Center, 77, 82, 112, 150
Phillipines, 25
Pierce, Franklin, 22
Pietri, Pedro, 54, *55*, 182
Pilgrims, 6
Pilsen, 192
*Pimeria Alta*, 105
*piñatas*, 175
*Piñero*, 199
Piñero, Miguel, 181, 197, 199
Pinochet, Augusto, 68
*Pirates, Indians, and Spaniards*, 9
Pittsburgh Pirates, 173
Pizarro, Francisco, 130
Platt Amendment, 26, 107
plays, 179
playwrights, 197
*plena*, 154, 162
*Pocho*, 181
poetry, 179, 182–83
Political Association of Spanish-Speaking
     Organizations (PASSO), 145
political parties, 148–49
politics, 3, 137, 139–151
Polk, James K., *17*, 20–21
polytheism, 88
Ponce de Leon, Juan, 104
Popular Democratic Party, 27
population statistics, 2, 29, 68, 70, 78, 94, 109, 111,
     112–17, 124, 147, 150
Portillo, Lourdes, 99
Portinari, Candido, 71
Portugal, 70
Posada, José Guadalupe, *85*
poverty, 78, 109, 139
Premio Quinto Sol, 189
presidios, 10
Prida, Dolores, 197
Prinze, Freddie, 198
Proposition 187, 110
Protestantism, 94
Protocol of Querétaro, 22
public school system, 120
publishing, 188–89
pueblos, 10
Pueblos, 8, 10–11, 104–105
Puente, Tito, 54, 103, 153, 164
*Puerto Rican in New York and Other Sketches, A*, 54
Puerto Rican Obituary, 54
Puerto Ricans, 2, 32–33, 77, 140

Puerto Rican Studies, 125
Puerto Rican Traveling Theater, 197
Puerto Rican Young Lords (PRYL), 43, 47, 142
Puerto Rico, 2, 8, 12–13, 25–27, 53–55, 105, 107
Pulitzer, Joseph, 24
Pulitzer Prize, 110, 111, 155

## Q
Quechua, 131
*quinceañera*, *83*, 202
Quinn, Anthony, *198*, 199
Quintana Roo, 168
Quintanilla, Selena, 158, 160
Quirarte, Jacinto, 99
quotas, immigration, 31
Quran, 95

## R
rabbi, *95*
racial hierarchy, 12
Radio Unica, 200
radio, 133, 136, 191, 200–201
railroad industry, 34
*Rain of Scorpions and Other Writings*, 181
Ramírez, Manny, 173
Ramírez, Martín, 194
*ranchera*, 154–55
Random House, 111, 189
Ranjel, Rodrigo, 9
*rascuachismo*, 192
Raya, Marcos, 194
Rayo, 189
*rayuela*, 175
Reagan, Ronald, 66–67, 110
*Real Women Have Curves*, 199
Rechy, John, 83
Reclamation Act, 107
re-concentration, 24
*reco-reco*, 156
refugees, 60–61, 66–67
reggaetón, *136*, 137, 155, 164
Regla de Ocha, 92
*Reina Valera*, 89
religion, 3, 45, 74, 82, 87–95
Renaldo, Duncan, 198
Reno, Janet, 63
Repatriation, 35
Repertorio Español, 197
Republican Party, 149
*Resurrection Boulevard*, 198
*retablos*, 194
*Revista Chicano-Riqueña*, 187
*Revolt of the Cockroach People, The*, 184–85
Revolutionary War, 6, 105
Revueltas, Rosaura, 50
Ribera, José Rómulo, 188
Richardson, Bill, 110, 137, 143, *201*
Riis, Jacob, 55
Rincón, Bernice, 50
Rio Grande, *1*, 20, 36
Río Nueces, 20
riots, 40–41, 107–109
Ripoll, Carlos, 61
Rivas, Bimbo, 55, 182
River Plate region, 130
Rivera, Chita, *81*, 99, 199
Rivera, Diego, 194
Rivera, Geraldo, 109
Rivera, Tomás, 127, 181, 189
Robinson, Jackie, 172
rodeos, 175
Rodó, José Enrique, 187, *193*
Rodriguez, Jennifer, 111, 176, *177*
Rodriguez, Juan "Chi-Chi," 197
Rodriguez, Luis, 81
Rodriguez, Richard, 83, 184
*romancero*, 158
Romano, Octavio Ignacio, 189
Romero, Frank, 201
Romero, Julio Cesar, 170

Roosevelt Administration, 107
Roosevelt, Franklin D., 26
Roosevelt, Theodore, 25
roses, 91
Ross, Fred, 44, 51
Rough Riders, 25
Royal Chicano Air Force, *196*
Roybal, Edward Ross, 142, *143*
Roybal-Allard, Lucille, 142
Rubalcaba, Gonzalo, 165

## S
Saint Augustine mission, 6, 8, 105
Salazar, Rubén, 109, 197, 200–201
salsa, 137, 154, *162*, 163
*Salt of the Earth*, 50
Salt War, 16
Salvador, Brazil, *70*
San Antonio mission, 105
Sánchez, Alfonso, 49
San Diego de Alcalá mission, 105
Sandinista National Liberation Front, 67
Sandino, Augusto César, 67
San Francisco de los Tejas, 105
*San Francisco News*, 200
San Francisco Police Department, 51
Santa Ana, Antonio López de, 16, 21
Santa Barbara mission, *11*
Santa Fe, New Mexico, 105
Santana, Carlos, 103
Santería, 92–93, 192, *203*
*santeros*, 194
Santos, Daniel, 163
San Xavier del Bac, 105
Sarmiento, Domingo Faustino, 60
Schenley Wine, 51
Schifrin, Lalo, 155
Schomburg, Arthur, 127
Scott, Winfield, *15*, 21
Seguín, Erasmo, 106
Seguín, Juan Napomuceno, 142
Segura, Pancho, 174
Selena, 158, 160, 199
*Self-Portrait with the Other*, 184
*Serpientes y escaleras*, 175
Serra, Fray Junípero, 8
Serra, Junípero, *10*, 11, 105–106
Seven Cities of Cibola, 8
sexuality, 82–83
Shakira, 153
Shorris, Earl, 127
*Short Eyes*, 181, 197
*Shrunken Head of Pancho Villa, The*, 196
Sierra Maestra mountains, 58
*Simplemente María*, 198
single-parent families, 76–77, 119
Siqueiros, David Alfaro, 194
slam poetry, 182
slaves, 106
Sleepy Lagoon Case, 35, 40, 185
Smith, Marc, 182
Smithsonian Art Museum, 201
Smits, Jimmy, 198
soap operas, 168, 198
soccer, 167–71
Somoza, Anastasio Jr., 67
Somoza, Anastasio, 67
Somoza, Luis, 67
Sondheim, Stephen, 81
Sosa, Omar, 165
Sosa, Sammy, 103, 173
Soto, Gary, 182
Soviet Union, 59
Spain, 5
Spanglish, 36, 55, 57, 111, 129, 133–37, 193
Spanglishisms, 135
*Spanglish: The Making of a New American Language*, 135
Spanish-American War, 24–26, 54, 80, 94
Spanish Broadcasting System, 200
Spanish Empire, 1, 15, 24
Spanish Inquisition, 5, 88–89, 106

Spanish language, 36, 77, 95, 111, 120–23, 129–137, 188–89
Speedy González, 195
sports, 167–177
*Squatter and the Don, The,* 180
*Stand and Deliver,* 120, 199
Stavans, Han, 85
Steinem, Gloria, 50
*Straight as a Line,* 197
strike, 45, 48
Suárez, Mario, 181
Suárez, Ray, 200, *201*
Suárez, Virgil, 182
Subcomandante Marcos, 174
sugar cane, *33*
sweatshops, 36

**T**

*tabaqueros,* 54
Taco Bell, 136
tagging, *80*
Taíno, 12–13, 195
*Tales of the Alhambra,* 180
*tambora,* 156
tango, *165*
Tanton, John, 122
Taylor, Zachary, 21
technology, 120
tejano music, 155, 160
*tejanos,* 2, 16–19
Telemundo, 133, 171, 198
*telenovelas,* 198
television, 94, 111, 133, 136, 191, 198–99, 200–201
Teller Amendment, 26
tennis, 174
Tenochtitlán, 90, 104
Ten-Year War, 24
Texas Constitution, 16
Tex-Mex music, 160–61
theater, 196–97
Thomas, Piri, 55, 184
Thompson, Hunter S., 185
Thorns, William, 202
*Three Caballeros, 194,* 195
three Juanes, 93
*Tiburcio Vasquez,* 197
Tijerina, Reies López, 39, 48–49, 108, 142
timbales, 156
*Time,* 108
Title IX, 176
*Tlachili,* 168
Toltecs, 168
*Tomo todo,* 175
Tonatiuh-Quinto Sol (TQS), 189
Torres, Luis A., 188
Torres-Saillant, Silvio, 57, 127
Torricelli Bill, 110
Trambley, Estela Portillo, 181
Tratado de Mesilla, 22
*Travels of Father Kino and Other Jesuits to California and North America,* 179
Travis, William Barrett, 18Santa Ana, 18
Treaty of Guadalupe Hidalgo, 12, 15, 20–23, 42, 47, 49, 80, 106, 179–180
Treaty of Paris, 25–26, 107
Treviño, Lee, 174
*tropicalismo,* 192
Troy Haymakers, 106
*True Relation of the Vicissitudes that Attended the Governor Don Hernando de Soto and Some Nobles of Portugal in the Discovery of the Province of Florida now just Given by a Fidalgo of Elvas,* 9
Trujillo, Rafael L., *53,* 56, 107
*Tu Ciudad,* 132
Twain, Mark, 71
*Two Rode Together,* 19

**U**

UFW, 196
*Uncle Remus con Chile,* 203

unions, 44–45
United Farm Workers Union (UFW), 39, 42, 45, 51, 79, 109
United Nations, 110
Univisión, 111, 133, 171, 198
Unz, Ron, 121
Ureña, Camila Henríquez, 127
Ureña, Max Henríquez, 127
Ureña, Pedro Henríquez, 57, 70, 126
Uruguay, 68, 130
U.S. English, 122
U.S.S. *Maine,* 25, 107
*usted,* 130
Uxmal ruins, 168

**V**

Valdees, Zoe, 63
Valdés, Bebo, 165
Valdés, Chucho, 165
Valdez, Luis, 196–97, 199
Valdez, Luis, 85
Valens, Ritchie, 99, 196
*vaquero,* 105, *175*
Vargas, Gétulio, 71
Vasconcelos, José, 13
Vásquez, Richard, 181
Vásquez, Tiburcio, 158
Vega, Bernardo, 54, 184
Velasquez de Cuellar, Diego, 104
Veloso, Caetano, 163
*Ven Conmigo,* 161
Venezuela, 69
*Versos sencillos,* 24
Vieques, Puerto Rico, 55, 111
Vietnam War, 109, 201
Vigil, J. M., 188
vigilantes, *35,* 36
Vilar, Irene, 184
Villa, Pancho, 90
Villaraigosa, Antonio, 137, *142,* 143
Villarreal, José Antonio, 181
Vintage *Español,* 111, 189
Virgen de la Caridad del Cobre, 92–93
Virgil, Osvaldo "Ozzie," 173
Virgin of Guadalupe, 42, 74, *75,* 90–91, 192
virginity, 74–75, 82
visual arts, 194–95
Viva Kennedy campaign, 49
*Viva Zapata!,* 199
Volunteers in Service to America, 109
voting, 146–47
Voting Rights Act (VRA), 139, 146, *147*

**W**

*Waiting in the Wings,* 184
Walt Disney, 195
War on Poverty, 109
war on terror, 36
Washington Heights, 57, 135, 187, 193
Wayne, John, 19, 198
*We Came All the Way from Cuba So You Could Dress Like This?,* 83
welfare, 31
*West Side Story,* 55, 81, 108, 199
*Who Would Have Thought It?,* 180
Williams, William Carlos, 182
Wilson, Pete, 110
Wilson, Tom, 201
Wilson, Woodrow, 32
*With a Pistol in His Hand: A Border Ballad and its Hero,* 127, 202
women in sports
women, 50–51, 73, 76, 176–77
World Cup soccer, *167*
World Trade Center, 36
World War I, 31
World War II, 33–35, 40, 54, 56, 79, 107–108, 146, 204
wrestling, 174
Wupatki Pueblo Ruins, *11*

**X**

Xicanisma, 50

**Y**

Yahoo!, 111
Yáñez, René, 195
*…y no se lo tragó la tierrá /…and the Earth Did Not Devour Him,* 181, 189
Yoruba, 92
*Yo Soy Joaquín/I Am Joaquín,* 49
Young, Robert, 199
Yucatán Peninsula, 88, 168

**Z**

Zapata, Emiliano, 90, 185
Zapatista National Liberation Army, 110, 174
Zapotec, 131, 168
zoot suit, *41*
*Zoot Suit,* 85, 196, 199
Zoot Suit Riots, 35, *40,* 41, 108, 185
*Zorro,* 199
Zuni, 8

# Acknowledgments & Picture Credits

I wish to thank Donna Sanzone of Collins Publisher for the invitation to engage at an extensive Q&A on Latino history and culture. I've reflected on the material previously in these pages in *Imagining Columbus* (1993), *Art and Anger* (1996), *The Hispanic Condition* (2001) and *Spanglish: The Making of a New American Language* (2003). I was also editor-in-chief in the four-volume *Encyclopedia Latina* (Grolier/Scholastic, 2005). In my responses, I made substantial use of my earlier books and of the plethora of encyclopedia entries. I'm also grateful to Harold Augenbraum of the National Book Foundation for his support in the project and his friendship over the years, as well as Becky Vlamis of National Public Radio, Verónica Albin of Rice University, and Joan Rubin of the University of Rochester. Portions of chapters on literature and the media were discussed with Oscar Villalon of the *San Francisco Chronicle Book Review* and the ones on education are part of a conversation with José Prado of California State University, Los Angeles, and Enrique Murillo of California State University, San Bernardino. They are part of an interview featured in *Journal of Latinos and Education*. Finally, my deep gratitude to the incomparable Jennifer Acker, who worked on the manuscript and coordinated the illustrations. Once my student at Amherst College, we've have the opportunity to work together over the years and the experience has been immensely rewarding. Her effeciency and vision are superb.

The author and publisher also offer thanks to staff involved in the creation of this volume: Collins Reference editor Lisa Hacken; editorial assistant Stephanie Meyers; Hydra Publishing president Sean Moore; publishing director Karen Prince; editorial director Aaron Murray; art director Brian MacMullen; project editor Jennifer Acker; copy editor Carole Campbell; designers Erika Lubowicki, Ken Crossland, and Eunho Lee; editorial assistant Rachael Lanicci; picture researcher Ben Dewalt; proofreader Glenn Novak; indexer Jessie Shiers. Thanks to picture sources: University of Texas Austin Benson Collection; Pamela Gentile and the San Francisco Film Society; the League of United Latin American Citizens.

## PICTURE CREDITS

The following abbreviations are used: AP—AP Photos; IS—Istockphoto; LoC—Library of Congress; PR—Photoresearchers.com; SS—Shutterstock; SXC—Stock Exchange; Wi—Wikimedia

(t=top; b=bottom; l=left; r=right; c=center)

**IV**r SS/Denis Pepin **IV**cb SS/David M. Albrecht **V**t © Jonathan C. Conklin **V**b IS/Dana Baldwin

**Introduction**
**VI** SS/Timothy Lee Lantgen **1** LoC **2**tl LoC **2**br SS/Gina Goforth **3**tr SS/Mike Von Bergen **3**b SS/Miles Boyer

**Chapter 1: Colonization**
**4** LoC **5**background LoC **6** PR/Adam Jones **7**tl LoC **7**b PR/Sheila Terry **8** LoC **9**t LoC **9**c LoC **9**b AP **10**bl LoC **10**tr LoC **11**t SS/Jason Cheever **11**b SS/ Linda Armstrong **12**t LoC **13** LoC

**Chapter 2: Manifest Destiny**
**14** LoC **15** LoC **16** Loc **17**t LoC **17**b LoC **18**l LoC **18**r LoC **19**t LoC **19**b LoC **20**bl LoC **20**br LoC **21** SS/Mike Norton

**22** LoC **23** LoC **24**bl LoC **24**tr LoC **25**t LoC **25**b LoC **26** LoC **27**t LoC **27**b AP

**Chapter 3: Crossing Borders**
**28** AP/John Miller **30** LoC **31** LoC **32** LoC **33** LoC/Jack Delano **34**tl LoC **34**br AP/Elizabeth Dalziel **35** AP **36** LoC **37**bl AP/J. Pat Carter **37**tr AP/Roberta Reeder

**Chapter 4: The Chicano Movement**
**38** LoC **39** AP/Elisa Amendola **40** AP **41**l LoC **41**r LoC **42**tl LoC **42**br LoC **43** LoC/ The Young Lords Party **44**bl AP/Mark Elias **44**cr LoC **45** AP/Damian Dovarganes **46** Wi **47** SS/Timothy Lantgen **48**tl AP/Ginette Riquelme **48**br AP/Scott Dunn **49** ©Jesus Manuel Mena Garcia **50**tl LoC **50**br Wi **51** AP/Damian Dovarganes

**Chapter 5: The Caribbean**
**52** LoC **54** LoC **55** AP/Bebeto Matthews **56** Wi **57** AP/Mary Altaffer **58**bl AP **58**tr LoC **59**cl LoC **59**br AP **60**tl LoC **60**br LoC **61** LoC **62** USCG **63**bl AP/Alan Diaz **63**br AP/Jorge Rey

**Chapter 6: Out of Many, One**
**64** LoC **65** AP/Luis Romero **66** LoC **67** AP/Leslie Close **68** LoC **69**tr AP/Esteban Felix **69**bl Dept. of Defense **70**cl LoC **70**cr LoC **71** © Jonathan C. Conklin

**Chaper 7: Family**
**72** AP/Dean Hoffmeyer **73** LoC **74** LoC **75**tr SS/Gudelia Marmion **75**b LoC **76** LoC **77** LoC **78**tl LoC **78**br IO/FogStock, LLC **79** LoC **80**tr SS/Robert Deal **80**bl AP/ Damian Dovarganes **81**t LoC **81**b LoC **82** LoC **83**tl AP/Ryan Soderlin **83**br AP/Javier Galeano **84**l SS/Jacom Stephens **84**tr LoC/John Collier **84**br LoC/ John Collier **85**t Wi/Stephen Bridger **85**b Wi

**Chapter 8: Religion**
**86** AP/Joe Cavaretta **87** AP/George Osodi **88**tr SS/ Miguel Angel Pallardo del Rio **88**bl SS/Elisa Locci **90** Wi/Benjamin Wood **91**tr Wi/Benjamin Wood **91**b AP/Ric Francis **92** AP/ Javier Galeano **93**l AP/Domenico Sitnellis **93**r AP/Rick Bowmer **94** AP/John Klicker **95**l AP/Manu Fernandez **95**r AP/Jose Luis Magana

**Ready Reference**
Background LoC **96**bl AP **96**bc Wi/Benjamin Wood **97**tl Wi **97**bl ©Kim Zumwal **97**tr Courtesy of Ariel Dorfman **97**br AP/Santiago Llanquin **98**tl Courtesy of Wellesley College Class of 1960 Portrait Directory **98**tc Courtesy of Hostos Community College **98**bl AP **98**cr AP/Krista Niles **99**br ©Pamela Gentile/San Francisco Film Society **99**tl LoC **99**tr Courtesy of the University of Texas at San Antonio **99**cr AP/Jennifer Graylock **99**br LoC **100**tr AP **100**tr Courtesy of Linda Chavez **100**bc AP/Bob Galbraith **101**tl AP/Marta Lavandier **101**bl Wi **101**c AP/Mark Duncan **101**br Courtesy of Paquito D'Rivera **102**t Courtesy of NASA **102**bc Wi **103**tl Wi **103**tr Wi **103**cl Wi **103**cr AP/Camay Sungu **103**bl AP/Mike Albans **104**l Wi **104**r Wi **105** Wi **106** SXC/Chris Mitchell **107** LoC **108**tl LoC **108**cr LoC **108**bp AP **109** Wi **110**tl LoC **110**bl Courtesy of the U.S Department of Housing and Urban Development Office of Public Affairs **110**br Courtesy of RTNDA **111**t SS/ Sean Haley **112** SS/Frank Boellmann

**Chapter 9: Education**
**118** AP/Charlie Riedel **119** AP/Kevork Djansezian **120** Courtesy of the Center for Disease Control **121**tl AP/Charlie Riedel **121**br Courtesy of Linda Chavez **122** Courtesy of bioguide.congess.gov **123**tl AP/Al Goldis

**123**br AP/Kevin Karzin **124** AP **125** AP/David Perry **126** Courtesy of the Nettie Lee Benson Latin American Collection, University of Texas Libraries, The University of Texas at Austin **127** © University of Wisconsin Press/Jonathan Cohen

**Chapter 10 Spanglish**
**128** AP/Laura Smit **129** AP/Brian Tietz **130** Wi/Luis Garcia **131** SS/Peter Von Bucher **132**t SXC/Laszlo Harri Nemeth **132**b AP/Ric Francis **133** AP/Eduardo Verdugo **134** AP/Nick Ut **135** AP/Damian Dovarganes **136** AP/Henry Ray Abrams **137**tl AP/LM Otero **137**br AP/Joseph Dits

**Chapter 11: Politics**
**138** SXC/Alfonso Romero **140** SS/Mark Scott Spatny **141** AP/Damian Dovarganes **142** AP/ Kevork Djansezian **143**tl LoC **143**br Courtesy of RTNDA **144**bl LoC **144**tr AP/Danny Moloshock **145** Courtesy of the League of United Latin American Citizens (LULAC) **146** AP/Michael Dwyer **147**tr LBJ Library and Museum/ Yoichi Okamoto **147**bl SS/John Sartin **148** AP/John McConnico **149** AP/Phil Coale **150** SS/RealDealPhoto/Bobby Deal **151** SXC/Steve White

**Chapter 12: La Musica**
**152** SS/Trevor Allen **153** SS/Mariano Heluani **154** SS/Maria Weidner **155** SS/Jose Gil **156** Wi **157**tl SS/Falko Matte **157**tr SXC/Janderson Araujo **157**b SS/ 2EmgamiVividEast **158** LoC **159**l AP **159**r AP/ Rogers and Cowan **160**t AP/Joe Hermosa **160**b SS/RealDealPhoto/ Bobby Deal **161** AP/Paul Howell **162** SS/PhotoSmart **163** AP/Kim D. Johnson **164**l AP/Jean-Jaques Levy **164**r Wi **165**l SS/Yuri Arcurs **165**r SS/Yuri Arcurs

**Chapter 13: Sports**
**166** SS/Rui Alexandre Araujo **167** AP/Roberta Candia **169** Wi/Kåre Thor Olsen **170**tr SS/PhotoCreate **170**b SS/ WizData, Inc. **171** AP/Mark Duncan **172** AP **173** AP/Elise Amendola **174** IS **175** SS/Karina Maybely Orellana Rojas **176** AP/Elaine Thompson **177** AP/Elaine Thompson

**Chapter 14:Letras**
**178** AP/Guillermo Arias **179** LoC **180**tl LoC **180**bl LoC **181** AP/Dana Tynan **182**tr LoC **182**bl Photograph courtesy of Curbstone Press **183** © Lina Pallota **184** SS/Alan Freed **185** LoC **186**bl LoC **186**br AP/Marty Lederhandler **187** LoC **188** LoC **189** AP/David J. Philip **189** LoC

**Chapter 15: Art and Taste**
**190** SS/BarbaraJH **191** SS/Carolina **192** LoC **193**tl Wi **193**br Wi/Miguel Cabrera **194**tl LoC **194** © Bill Wrigley **195** SS/Simon Lee **196**tr LoC/Darien House **196**bl LoC/Royal Chicano Air Force **197** AP/Mark Crosse **198**tl LoC **198**br LoC **199** LoC **200** AP/Evan Vucci **201** AP/Luis M. Alvarez **202** SXC/Sarah Dawn Nichols **203**t SS/Calida **203**br Courtesy of University of Miami Libraries/Carlos Ortiz Cabrera

**América, America**
**204**tl SS/Svetlana Larina **204**cl SS/Alex Stepanov **205**br SS/Pilar Echevarria **206**cl SS/Graca Victoria **206**r SS/Elana Ray

**Cover** Front cover (clockwise from top): Georgia Morrissey; LoC; AP Photo/L.M. Otero. Back cover (top): AP Photo Back cover (bottom): Shutterstock/Elke Dennis